"The book is special because Isaacson captures t[...] among the female athletes. Not only were they teammates, they were pioneers of a sort. . . . A wonderful book that is both eye-opening history and a moving and deeply personal memoir." —*Booklist,* **starred review**

"An intimate, at times inspiring account." —*Kirkus Reviews*

"In *State*, Melissa Isaacson perfectly captures the birth of Title IX and a time when high school girls were starting to gain equality in sports and in the classroom, showing us how opportunities on the court can light a path for girls to become their authentic selves in all aspects of their lives."
—Billie Jean King, founder of the Billie Jean King Leadership Initiative

"Melissa Isaacson has written a beautiful book about a time and place that is almost unfathomable to us now: when girls' and women's sports were not yet popular, widespread, or vital to our culture. And yet the pages of *State* come alive with the riveting story of a team of high school basketball players whose dreams took them to the place all athletes hope to go: a championship that lives with them to this day. This is their inspiring story. This is Title IX come to life."
—Christine Brennan, *USA Today* columnist, CNN and ABC commentator, and author of *Best Seat in the House* and the bestseller *Inside Edge*

"Missy Isaacson takes us on a beautiful first-person journey we all should travel, showing us how a group of young women in the 70s changed the perception of women playing sports. And equally important, how they discovered the value of chasing a dream together. From fighting to play in the 'boys' gym' to bonding together to winning a state basketball title, this was a story I couldn't put down. I literally cheered out loud for these women as I read it."
—Julie Foudy, Olympic medalist, FIFA Women's World Cup champion, and founder of the Julie Foudy Sports Leadership Academy

"The best sports stories aren't actually sports stories—they're stories about life, highs, lows, bonds, exceptionalism, tragedy. That's what makes Melissa Isaacson's *State* such a tremendous piece of work. You think you're reading about a girls' basketball team, only to discover you've been lifted to new emotional heights. What a terrific read."
—Jeff Pearlman, author of *Sweetness: The Enigmatic Life of Walter Payton* and *Football for a Buck*

"*State* is storytelling at its finest. Melissa Isaacson will captivate readers with this long overdue memoir of heartache and triumph. Many will relate to the experiences Isaacson recaptures, and those who don't will gain a greater respect for trailblazers in women's sports. It is full of heart and history—a wonderful combination!"

—**Marjorie Herrera Lewis, author of *When the Men Were Gone***

"I loved reading *State* by Melissa Isaacson. Melissa covered the Bulls for the *Chicago Tribune* when I played in the NBA, and we had many discussions about our love of basketball. The topic of her high school state title–winning team came up now and then, and I knew she was proud of it. But not until now, after reading her fantastic book, did I realize HOW much basketball meant to her. This is a beautiful story of basketball and life."

—**Steve Kerr, head coach of the Golden State Warriors**

"I do not believe I overstate when I say this book belongs in, among all the other places, the Smithsonian, for its evocative, edifying tour of the female mind during the first crucial wave of cultural appreciation for the female athlete."

—**Chuck Culpepper, sports reporter for the *Washington Post*
and author of *Bloody Confused!***

"*State* delivers a lesson on masterful storytelling. It is part memoir, part oral history, seen through the prism of sports. She deftly develops her characters, and perhaps the best indicator of the power of her narrative is that even though you know the outcome, it is still gripping to read about the adventures and accomplishments of the 1979 Niles West championship team."

—**Andrea Kremer, Emmy-winning sports journalist and member
of the Pro Football Hall of Fame**

"A wonderful tale from a wonderful storyteller. Isaacson paints real people so richly, so authentically, you almost forget it's about basketball and realize it's about life, tragedy, yearning, and hope. I've known Missy for thirty-five years and I always knew she had a story like this in her. I'm so glad to finally see it in perfectly crafted prose."

—**Bob Wojnowski, sports columnist for the *Detroit News***

"Anyone picking up this book will be inspired and encouraged to also find their inner strength and, with the help of others, believe in themselves."

—**Jackie Joyner-Kersee, Olympic medalist and founder of the
Jackie Joyner-Kersee Foundation**

STATE

STATE

A TEAM, A TRIUMPH, A TRANSFORMATION

MELISSA ISAACSON

A Midway Book

AGATE

CHICAGO

ISBN 13: 978-1-57284-290-8
ISBN 10: 1-57284-290-3
Agate trade paperback printing: September 2020

Printed in the United States of America

The Library of Congress has cataloged the hard cover edition of this book as follows:

Library of Congress Cataloging-in-Publication Data

Names: Isaacson, Melissa, author.
Title: State : a team, a triumph, a transformation / Melissa Isaacson.
Description: First edition. | Chicago : Midway, An Agate Imprint, 2019.
Identifiers: LCCN 2019003382 (print) | LCCN 2019017257 (ebook) | ISBN 9781572848252 (ebook) | ISBN 1572848251 (ebook) | ISBN 9781572842663 (hardcover) | ISBN 1572842660 (hardcover)
Subjects: LCSH: Isaacson, Melissa. | Niles West High School (Skokie, Ill.)--Basketball--History--20th century. | Basketball for girls--Illinois--Skokie--History--20th century. | Sex discrimination in sports--Illinois--History--20th century. | United States. Education Amendments of 1972. Title IX | Women basketball players--Illinois--Biography.
Classification: LCC GV886 (ebook) | LCC GV886 .I73 2019 (print) | DDC 796.323/62097731--dc23
LC record available at https://lccn.loc.gov/2019003382

10 9 8 7 6 5 4 3 2 1   20 21 22 23 24 25

Midway Books is an imprint of Agate Publishing. Agate books are available in bulk at discount prices. Learn more at agatepublishing.com.

For Shirley and Peggy, the strongest women I know . . .
And for Arlene Mulder, who led the way

In loving memory of Courtney Brown, Deb Durso,
and Michael Altenhoff

CONTENTS

PROLOGUE

"You need to talk to him," the hospice nurse was saying. "You need to give him permission to die."

It wasn't the first time she had told me this over the last couple of days, but I wasn't exactly itching to do whatever it was she was suggesting.

"Sometimes, for reasons that are unclear, people in their last days hold on to life against all reason," she explained. "You need to tell him it's OK to go."

For 10 days my father had lingered, refusing all food or liquid, the very final stages for many Alzheimer's patients who simply forget how to chew, how to swallow, how to live any longer.

My mother sat not more than 10 feet away from him, trapped, amazingly, by the same hideous disease, thoroughly unaware she was soon to be widowed. Neither of them acknowledged each other anymore, but a couple of weeks earlier, my father had suddenly called out, "Where's Francine?"—perhaps a sign, the hospice people said, that in the deep recesses of his mind he was worried about leaving her.

And so he had to be told it was OK to die. And somehow, I was going to be the one to tell him.

The youngest of four children by seven years, I was the classic daddy's girl, hopelessly spoiled by his affection, the one you could find on most nights cuddled up on the couch with him, styling his hair or giving him a foot rub.

"How do we even know he can hear us?" I asked.

Like my mother, he had been on a steady decline with Alzheimer's for more than two decades. But for the last week or so, he had sat in a rented hospital recliner with his eyes half-open and his head buried in his chest, no obvious signs that anything at all was getting through.

"Even if it's not in his head but in his soul, he will hear you," the nurse promised. "We can leave the room if you want."

I glanced around, looking for a possible escape route, but all I saw was our den, as we called it growing up. There was the same couch—though twice reupholstered from the gaudy orange vinyl some hippie decorator thought was a good idea in 1970—where my father let me run wet combs through his hair in rousing games of beauty shop. It was now where we situated my mom, a place she had probably never sat for more than two minutes my entire childhood. The TV was turned to some random station she never would have watched, and on top of the coffee table sat a hospice pamphlet, a box of Kleenex, and some latex gloves in a heap she never would have allowed.

I had no plan, nor any useful experience to fall back on before speaking such seemingly important words to my father. I rambled a bit and repeated myself. But as I sat on the arm of the recliner, my head leaning against his head, he ever-so-slightly turned a warm cheek toward mine, and somehow, I knew that he did hear me.

"I'm going to miss you, Dad," I whispered in his ear. "I'm going to miss someone worrying about me the way you always have and loving me the way only you could. But I promise we'll be OK. I promise we'll never forget you. Every time I look into my children's blue eyes, I will be reminded of you.

"We love you, Dad. And it's OK. You did your job. You did a fantastic job. You can rest now. I promise we'll take care of Mom for you."

I got up shakily and looked over at my mother, suddenly realizing I had barely spoken to her over the past year. Sure, we visited, and I would hold her hand and tell her I loved her. Then I'd say goodbye.

Hello. I love you. Goodbye. Ever since she had stopped speaking, I had as well.

And so I talked to her, too. "I told Dad," I said, holding her hand. "I don't know if he heard me. You know he was never a great listener. But I told him we'll all be OK."

Alzheimer's patients in the late stages seldom look people in the eye. My mother's gaze had been at an off-angle for years. But as I spoke the next words, she looked directly at me, so much so that it stunned me for a second before I continued.

"I'm supposed to go to this 25th reunion at Niles West for our state championship team tonight," I told her. "Can you believe it? I'm going to see Connie. And maybe even Peggy. You remember Peggy, Mom. And Barb and Tina and Holly, and Judy Becker and Karen Wikstrom. Remember, Mom? Remember how great it was? And Mr. Earl will be there, too."

I looked closely to see if there was any kind of a flicker at the mention of our coach, Gene Earl. I thought maybe I saw one. "Yeah, well, I think it's probably time to move on, don't you?" I laughed softly, hoping I could keep her attention. But she went away as quickly as she had returned.

What the hell I was even thinking, running off to my old high school after an afternoon as wrenching as this one, I did not know. But after that night, I no longer wondered.

I had finished high school on the highest of highs after our team had captured the state basketball title, but personally, I was through. I was ready to move on, still somewhat bitter about my decreased playing time under a new coach and wanting very much to embrace college life, find a boyfriend, and leave behind my tomboy ways. And since then, frankly, I hadn't been all that interested in—as my mom used to call it—taking a walk down nostalgia lane.

And then Connie called.

Connie Erickson was the star of our team, and though she was one of my closest friends in high school, we had drifted apart. Over the last 25 years, we had only occasionally spoken, but she phoned from her home in North Carolina that week to ask if I was going to the reunion.

"If you're going, I'm getting a plane ticket right now and coming in," she said.

She told me she had read a column of mine online, the one I had written about us for the *Chicago Tribune*, and she needed to reconnect with us. She needed to come home.

When I walked into the Niles West gym that night, I immediately locked eyes with parents so familiar to me during my teenage years that they may as well have been my own. They looked immediately beyond me, searching expectantly for my parents. I explained as delicately as I could why they weren't there and was met with a shower of hugs and expressions of sadness and told that they would be my parents that night.

We were honored at halftime of the Niles West girls' game, a big screen set up in front of one basket, where a highlight reel of our accomplishments was shown. And later, we ended up at the home of Barb Atsaves, a junior starter on the championship team. She played a video of the final game as husbands, children, parents, and significant others gathered to watch. I had wandered out of the family room, still absorbing the events of the day, when I heard a loud cheer go up and calls for me to come back in.

For a good 20 seconds or so, the camera scanned the crowd before settling on my parents. They were cheering madly, my mom's bad arm thrust oddly but triumphantly above her head, both my parents so genuinely happy that I was both shocked by the sight of them that way and immediately transported back to that time.

The room grew a little quieter as I stared at the TV. And as we walked to our cars in the frigid Chicago cold a few hours later, Connie and I tried to grasp the enormity of what we had experienced, both that night and 25 years earlier.

"You have to tell our story," she said finally, her arms wrapped tightly around her for warmth.

I nodded.

In 1979, Niles West High School won the third-ever Illinois girls' state basketball championship. We beat future Olympic gold medalist Jackie Joyner's East St. Louis team with a merciless full-court press and a punishing transition game.

But that's not what Connie was talking about.

In my *Tribune* column, I had written about some of the things we hadn't known at the time. Like how our first coach, Arlene Mulder, would secretly huddle in the corner of the faculty lounge with the school's legendary boys' basketball coach, Billy Schnurr, and how he would teach her how to teach us. I had learned that our principal, Nicholas Mannos, like most high school principals back then, very stern and a little scary, was just as secretly our best friend, for years fighting the battle for girls to attain the same rights as boys in sports.

But, as it turned out, it was even more than that.

Six days after the reunion, my father finally stopped fighting. Coach Earl, who I had not seen in at least 15 years, attended the funeral. So did several of my former teammates, and the ones who didn't attend called or wrote, as did their parents. Over the course of the next several months, I reconnected with them and with others who played with us over the years. I searched for

Peggy, the only member of the team we couldn't seem to locate and the one with whom I had ultimately bonded the most. And I invited Becky Schnell to lunch.

"Becky, you have to tell me," I said as I began the reporting for this book. "Was I mean to you?"

She laughed. A freshman when I was a senior the year we won the title, Becky had supplanted me in the lineup, and I wasn't thrilled. Adding to my frustration was the knowledge that Becky lived in the Niles East district, not West's, and as far as I could figure, only played for our team because her father, a junior high physical education teacher in the area, must have pulled strings. It annoyed me at the time, and I wondered if Becky ever caught on.

"No, Missy. You were never mean to me," she said. "Don't you remember how much fun we had? Don't you remember how much we laughed?"

I was relieved, but I couldn't leave it there.

"But Becky, what was the deal with your going to Niles West?" I said.

There was a long pause. "You didn't know?" she replied.

"No," I said. "What?"

She leaned across the table, and I met her in the middle.

"Miss," she told me, "basketball saved me."

And there was our story and my start to this book. Some of it I knew, some I would find out, and some still comes to me in waves.

Over the next several months, I would pore over news clippings and whatever video and cassette tapes I could get my hands on; comb through our yearbooks; and talk to Niles West teachers, students, coaches, and administrators as well as our opponents. I would badger my teammates for their recollections, and without hesitation, they complied, handing over treasured scrapbooks held together by useless strips of Scotch tape, the very act of turning each page putting them at risk of crumbling completely. But that was just the beginning.

For the next decade, I worked and reworked the manuscript, picking it up for months and putting it down for years, struggling with doing justice to our story before ultimately falling in love with it all over again.

This story is about one group of girls sitting innocently at a monumental place in our nation's history. But it is not a history lesson, nor a treatise on Title IX, as significant and responsible as that piece of legislation was for our being there in the first place. Rather, it is about the sheer joy of getting our first uniforms, packing the same school gym where we were once not allowed to practice, and gaining access to life lessons previously only available to boys.

It is about Arlene Mulder, who taught us how to believe; Billy Schnurr, who taught us how to fight; and our last coach, Gene Earl, who took a crash course in the world of girls and would never be quite the same again.

It is about a hunger so insatiable, setbacks so painful, and a triumph so sweet that they altered the courses of our lives.

In the process, basketball removed us from troubled homes and sad circumstances and transformed us. It instilled confidence and gave us our very identities. We were no longer tomboys or outcasts or even normal girls with unusual interests. Suddenly and forever more, we were athletes, driven by one common goal, united for one solitary purpose.

To say that basketball changed us wouldn't be fully accurate. In truth, I would find out, it saved us all.

CHAPTER 1

Our Coach

SOMETIMES, WHEN WORK RAN UNTIL DARK and fatigue simply won out, she would spend the night in our locker room rather than drive the 17 miles home. We never knew that, of course. Just like we didn't know a lot of things.

Maybe we should have guessed that about our coach, Arlene Mulder, who evidently developed her work ethic as an infant, no doubt putting all the other babies to shame. The youngest of Anna and Joseph Borges's four children, the future Mrs. Mulder was born at harvest time in the fall of 1944 and routinely plopped atop a six-foot-long heavy canvas sack, the strap secured around her mother's waist and over one shoulder, and dragged up and down the rows of white-speckled crops as Anna picked cotton on the family's 40-acre farm in Tulare, California.

Arlene described her mother as a housewife who raised the kids, picked the cotton, and milked the cows when she wasn't driving the grade-school bus. She called her father a "bona fide cowboy" who roped steers and competed in rodeos.

As a child, our coach wore jeans and climbed trees and supposed that made her a tomboy, but no one called her that. Mostly, she was like every other farm girl whose daily chores included feeding the chickens, collecting their eggs, and mowing the grass. It's just what was expected. And Arlene usually did what was expected.

By the early 1950s, Tulare was recognized as the home of Bob Mathias, the two-time gold medal–winning Olympic decathlete. His father, Charles, was the Borges family doctor, and Arlene babysat for Mathias's brother's kids. And if it wasn't the Mathias influence that inspired her to run track, it did not hurt that Tulare was also the site of the 1952 Olympic decathlon trials.

As a teenager, Arlene set an Amateur Athletic Union (AAU) record in the 50-yard shuttle hurdle four-girl relay and had the scarred knees to show for it. She also played six-girl basketball and summer softball in a women's league, games that always attracted large crowds of boys, which she eventually figured out had not as much to do with the women's abilities as with their propensity to bounce up and down as they ran.

When it came time to think about college, Anna and Joseph discouraged Arlene from becoming the first in their family to attend, reasoning she would "just get married and have babies anyway." Joseph went so far as to offer his daughter a Corvette as incentive to stay home. But determined to major in education, she fearlessly set off for San Francisco State, a teachers college 230 miles north of the family farm, in the fall of 1963.

It was there that she took up field hockey, considered becoming a nun, and fell in love with Al Mulder, none of which had much to do with the others except that it was during field hockey practice her freshman year when she first spotted Al playing soccer on an adjacent field. And while contemplating the sisterhood had her thinking of moving to a convent in Chicago, her courtship with Al moved her even more.

After the two married and completed graduate school, Al's

job eventually landed them in the Chicago suburb of Arlington Heights in 1970 and in the same apartment complex as Judi Sloan and Tish Meyers, two physical education teachers from Niles West High School in nearby Skokie who instantly befriended Mrs. Mulder. Two years later, when a job teaching girls' PE opened up at the school, Mrs. Mulder, now 27 and a mother of two little girls, Michelle and Alison, applied and was hired.

It was 1972. And like most Americans outside the state of Indiana, Arlene Mulder was not overly familiar with the work of Birch Bayh. But she would find out soon enough about Title IX, a bill that was cosponsored by the 42-year-old US senator from Indiana, along with fellow Democrat and Oregon congresswoman Edith Green, and signed into law by President Richard Nixon on June 23. Title IX prohibited sex discrimination in any educational program or activity receiving any type of federal financial aid. Bayh wanted to grant the same rights and protections to girls and women that were guaranteed to ethnic minorities in the 1964 Civil Rights Act. What he had in mind was both academic and athletic equality.

For Niles West, it was a painfully slow process to turn Title IX into something tangible. In 1907, Illinois had become the first state to ban interscholastic competition for girls. And for the next 60 years, high school sports were the boys' domain. Even by the early '70s, after Title IX passed, members of the Illinois High School Association (IHSA) were still preaching the old line that sports like basketball weren't ladylike, and only seemingly genteel, noncontact activities like tennis, badminton, and golf had interscholastic competition for girls. If a girl had physical coordination, she would often be steered toward cheerleading. And the concept of athleticism was a fairly vague notion, used only in reference to girls who could keep up with the neighborhood boys, if it was used at all.

High school girls in Illinois who were interested in working up a sweat had to be content with twice-a-week intramurals and "play days," in which they might have a two-day softball tournament with other schools that passed for a season. They also had something called "postal tournaments," which Mrs. Mulder and the other woman PE teachers grudgingly acknowledged as progress. These were girls' sporting events—in swimming, bowling, and "basket-shooting"—run via the US Postal Service. In a sport like swimming, a morning announcement would be made over the PA system informing all girls interested in being timed in various events to show up at the pool after school. Those times would then be written on postcards and sent to the IHSA, and if the participants were lucky, they'd find out the results, or who "won," a month or two later.

This kind of cut down on the thrill of competition, but it was a start. Girls could be athletic, maybe even athletes, but definitely not yet jocks, that term commonly associated with boys who were obsessed with sports, sometimes to the exclusion of all else, and a label suggesting a certain toughness to which other kids aspired. Still, girls were starting to develop a mentality entirely different from what they were brought up to possess, and after the passage of Title IX, tennis and badminton were clearly not enough.

"The time is ripe for more," Leanne Heeren, coordinator of the Niles West girls' PE department, told the school's principal, Nicholas Mannos, that first fall of Mrs. Mulder's Niles West career, writing proposals for him to take to the IHSA to include other sports like volleyball, swimming, and softball.

They rejected every one.

"I can't reason with those crew cuts," Mannos, an IHSA executive board member, grumbled to family and colleagues after fruitless weekend trips downstate, each dismissal making him more determined than ever to get through to them.

The original proposals purposely left out basketball, a strategy Mannos adopted after being told in no uncertain terms by the downstaters that girls would not be allowed to take up valuable gym space in the winter months and, God forbid, on Friday nights, a sacred time for boys' basketball. And furthermore, basketball was too rough for girls anyway. "I keep telling them, 'Boys, the times are catching up with you. Get on the train here,'" Mannos told Heeren and other Niles West administrators.

Like the other woman teachers, Mrs. Mulder had already identified the girls in her classes who had athletic skills, girls like Char Defrancesco. "This kid is unbelievable," she told her friends in the PE department. "It's a shame she doesn't have an opportunity to use her natural gifts."

But by the fall of '74, things were looking up. Mrs. Mulder started a girls' bowling team and was named girls' tennis coach when her friend Tish Meyers went on maternity leave. And that winter, the school's athletic director, Harold "Bud" Trapp, named Mulder the girls' basketball coach for the inaugural 10-game season, not long after the IHSA finally voted to allow girls to compete in interscholastic play. Mrs. Mulder was happy to take the job, beating out the only other applicant, locker-room matron Lucille Swift. There was only one problem—Arlene Mulder didn't know how to coach basketball. Although she had played those six-girl games as a kid, coaching the five-man version and understanding strategy were quite a different story.

Trapp suggested that she seek help from Billy Schnurr, the Niles West boys' basketball coach. Though Trapp never actually asked Schnurr if he would mind, Schnurr saw an eager, interested subject in Mulder, and soon they were hunched over cups of coffee in a secluded corner of the teachers' lounge, covering paper napkins with x's and o's and quietly arranging their free periods together so that he could tutor her in the game.

At Niles West, Billy Schnurr had developed a reputation as one of the most respected basketball coaches in the state, but where it concerned Arlene Mulder, he thought it best they keep their arrangement to themselves. Mrs. Mulder shrugged and soaked it up, always one step ahead of her players as she passed on what she learned from Schnurr—the motion offense and full-court defensive press, principles he learned from following coaches like UCLA's John Wooden and Indiana's Bob Knight—sometimes moments after he taught them to her.

But she added some philosophies of her own, and as she repeated to her players over and over, it was not about winning. Rather, the message from Mrs. Mulder was to set goals, work hard, and play selflessly, remembering that the team came first. She talked to her players about being *hungry* to practice, to improve, to perform. Oh yes, and to always represent themselves well as both ladies and athletes.

Mulder was determined to teach her girls that they could be aggressive and athletic as well as gracious and feminine. And so she had her rules, like the one that required her players to bounce the ball to the referees rather than throw a chest pass. "Sometimes you might be a little upset," she explained, "and you will be less likely to throw it in their face."

She also hated the water bottles used by nearly every boys' team at the time, the ones with the long plastic nozzles that squirted water into your mouth and onto most of your face. To the girls, the water bottles were very cool and a sure sign that you had finally arrived. To Mrs. Mulder, they were not ladylike and so her players used Dixie cups.

This kind of etiquette was as ingrained in Mrs. Mulder as her religion. Certain thoughts she couldn't shake and didn't try. And she would never forget one of her students, a girl named Nancy who was a senior in the fall of 1972, Mrs. Mulder's first year of teaching.

Tall, athletic, and beautiful, Nancy had been running around the track in gym class one afternoon, trying to two-step between hurdles when she slammed her shin against the bar and split it wide open. Mrs. Mulder sent someone running to get the nurse as she fashioned a tourniquet out of the nearest sock to stanch the bleeding.

And her first cogent thought as she tried to calm the girl?

How terrible that this beautiful girl will be scarred forever. Girls should not be put in danger.

CHAPTER 2

"Well, I guess I'll go try sports"

It was Bari Abrams's fault.

"OK, what are we wearing tomorrow?" I asked her the night before the first day of school. The first day of *high school.* Assuming there had been a committee meeting of some sort among the Lincolnwood girls and that Bari was a reliable source, a loyal friend, and the obvious point person for something so critical, I took her at her word.

And so, the next morning, it was with only the expected level of nausea and anxiety that I stepped off the bus and walked through the doors of Niles West wearing sky-blue polyester bell bottoms with a polyester seascape-print blouse tucked in. And almost immediately, I spotted Bari and the other girls in their Gloria Vanderbilt designer jeans.

"They called me this morning," Bari pleaded as my stomach rolled once again.

And yet, all that considered, the Lincolnwood girls did not make the biggest impression on me that day. It was Connie Erickson.

Connie was one of those kids everyone noticed. It wasn't that she was necessarily the most beautiful or wore the best clothes or even had a flamboyant personality. Granted, she was a blonde-haired, blue-eyed kind of adorable that was an inescapable fact. But it was more this self-assured, positive energy that seemed to radiate from her, almost shockingly so given that she, too, was a 14-year-old just starting her first year of high school that fall of 1975.

But then, Connie was not your ordinary freshman. No less than 8 of 11 Erickson children had passed through the halls of Niles West before her—all five of her sisters either cheerleaders, homecoming queens, or, in the case of Jeanne and Marilee, all of the above—paving a soft and comfortable path for Connie, not unlike brand-new shag carpeting.

It wasn't just that all the most popular upperclassmen knew Connie when she got to high school. Niles West knew Connie before she got there. And she knew Niles West. The Ericksons lived down the street from the school in Morton Grove, and Connie attended the football and basketball games, pep rallies and bonfires, variety shows and graduations from the time she was a toddler. The Niles West gym was as familiar to her as her family's living room, the coaches like uncles, and the athletes like dozens more big brothers and sisters.

And so it should not have been shocking at all that there was Connie that first day of high school, sitting on—not at—a table in the cafeteria amid football players and cheerleaders, laughing and joking with these people as if it were the most natural thing in the world, while 98 percent of the other freshmen either hovered in nervous clumps by the pop machine, had their noses pressed up against their combination locks, or, like me, shuttled frenetically up and down the halls agonizing over the decision to wear polyester bell bottoms rather than Gloria Vanderbilt designer jeans.

If all that wasn't nerve-wracking enough, there were clubs to join and tryouts to attend, and first on the agenda, for Connie anyway, were cheerleading tryouts.

In her heart, Connie knew she was no more cheerleading material than her twin brother, Chris. But she also knew she was an Erickson girl and so, almost subconsciously, she found herself making her way to the gym after school.

"You're going to make cheerleader," whispered Kenny Beider, a gorgeous senior, football player, and friend of Connie's older brother Mark, as she passed him in the hall. "All your sisters did," he added. Connie tried not to blush.

The assumption was there. Connie was supposed to follow in her sisters' footsteps. But footsteps seldom follow a direct path, and in this case, due to the simple math of family birth order, Connie had spent most of her time as a kid with her brothers Mark, Chris, and Dave. Because of the slight gap between them and the older Erickson siblings, the four youngest were dubbed the "little kids" by the family, and if Connie was going to hang with the little kids, she had to play football and baseball and basketball—and she had to keep up.

Of course, this did not occur to her as she joined the other cheerleading hopefuls while they stretched, gossiped, and otherwise prepared for tryouts. For three days, they were told by the freshman coach, they would practice the same routine, then perform before the judges.

It took Connie approximately four seconds to figure out she was not a cheerleader.

As girls leaped and twirled all around her, Connie jumped and stomped before telling no one in particular, "Well, I guess I'll go try sports."

It wasn't that she necessarily considered herself an athlete, much less a jock. She simply had no point of reference for that identity, no feeling of real belonging. The closest most of us had come to being athletes was being labeled "tomboys" for most of our childhoods. And that never had a positive connotation. You weren't a boy. And you surely were not a girl in the way girls were supposed to be. The word *tom* referred to a male animal, like a cat or a turkey—not exactly flattering or something to aspire to.

As a kid, Connie had been fairly satisfied serving as water girl for her brothers' Pop Warner football teams. She was even more thrilled when the coach actually gave her a jersey to wear on the sidelines. But what she really wanted was to be on the field, on a real team, playing with the boys.

Me too. While the other girls were making important future prom plans and discussing the dual meaning of rounding the bases, I was staring through the holes of the chain-link fence at the boys' Little League games, obsessed with one thought only— that I wanted to be out there too, wearing those cool caps with the block *L* for Lincolnwood on them and sitting in a real dugout just like the Cubs and White Sox, except that the Cubs and Sox had, well, an actual dugout and our boys had a splintery wooden bench.

I stared at their rubber cleats and was so consumed with jealousy that it was all I could do to even stand there for very long, so sure was I that I could compete. And so I would trudge back home, forced to be content chasing after my older brothers or playing catch in the backyard with my younger neighbor Anthony, who, fortunately for him, did not rub it in that I was a girl as I burned fastballs at him.

By the fall of 1975, we were all running out of patience. For girls like me and Connie, high school came with the promise of being on a real, competitive team. Basketball tryouts were not until February, but I had no intention of waiting six months to begin my high school athletic career. So what if I had never played volleyball, had no tennis skills, and was more of a bobber than a swimmer? Those were the fall sports. And that was where it had to begin.

Connie went straight from the cheerleading disaster to volleyball tryouts. I tried out too, figuring I had a reasonable chance of making the team. I mean, how tough could it be? *Bumping and spiking?* Physically, I could certainly manage both. But I was rattled by the volleyball coach, Miss Kay, who walked by just as I tried to serve, the ball dribbling off the heel of my hand and onto the floor as she paused to make a notation on her clipboard. More like a big scratch.

Serving was not kind to me that fall. I tried out for the tennis team with no real knowledge of or ability in that sport either, other than a handful of lessons when I was 10, but I still thought I had a pretty good shot. That is, until I served. After the third ball rocketed over the fence and out onto the soccer field on Day 1 of tryouts, I decided that I probably wouldn't show up for Day 2.

As Connie happily bumped and spiked away, better than most of the upperclassmen, I moved on to swimming, persuading Bari to try out with me. It's not that I necessarily liked swimming or, again, had any real ability. I was thinking, given my skill at doing flips on my parents' bed, that maybe I would try out for diving. More than anything, I was compelled to make a team. Any team.

As freshmen, we had yet to take swimming in gym class. Perhaps if we had, it would have deterred us, for as we walked into the locker room and Miss Swift handed each of us a stretched-out, faded, purplish thing we could only assume was a bathing suit, we began to rethink the whole swim team thing. We were then instructed that we had to shower, and Bari and I traded frantic looks.

At Lincoln Hall, our junior high school, the girls never took showers in the gym locker room. To our recollection, no girl actually ever undressed in the gym locker room. We either ran into the nearest toilet stall to do it, or we devised a routine in which we would remove sleeves and legs of clothing while putting on our gym suits, all without any actual skin ever being exposed. And now this woman was staring at us and demanding that we get naked. I figured this must be how it felt when you went to prison, but somehow Bari and I got into our suits and made it out onto the deck, where we were immediately dizzied by the stench of chemicals strong enough to sanitize every pool in the greater Chicagoland area. On the bus ride home, I watched Bari's hair frizz, growing bigger at every passing stop until we wordlessly concluded there was absolutely no way we were going back for the second day of tryouts.

Meanwhile, Connie made the varsity volleyball team and fell in with older kids like Shirley Cohen, a sophomore. I already knew Shirley. When I was 12 and Shirley 13, Lincolnwood started a girls' softball league, which had roughly one kid per team who knew how to both throw and catch, not coincidently the same girl who would also hit a home run literally every time she was up to bat. The rest of the girls pretty much lived in fear of a ball ever coming near them.

I was the kid hitting the home runs. So was Shirley, who hit her home runs much harder and much farther and was playing for a coach—the novel idea was that only moms were allowed to coach in those first years of the league—who deduced early on that Shirley was her secret weapon. Forget the fact that when Shirley came to bat, the third baseman started crying and even the men along the outfield foul lines moved back and took their hands out of their pockets. No, the mom coaching Shirley's team had the brilliant inspiration one day that if she batted Shirley, say, fourth in the lineup and then again in the eighth spot, maybe no one would notice.

Shirley did what she was told. But the coach of my team, no dummy herself, quickly noticed her third baseman whimpering sooner than usual and pointed out this discrepancy both to the umpire and to Shirley's coach. Those who had never before seen two mothers going jaw-to-jaw on a baseball field were treated to a once-in-a-lifetime experience.

But no question, Shirley, who had become Niles West's first female four-sport varsity athlete the previous year, was special, and she admired Connie from the start. If the volleyball coach told the team to jog around the gym, Connie would sprint. When they practiced spiking, Connie tried to jump higher and spike harder each time. And more importantly to Shirley, Connie was a winner. The two had a fierce competitiveness and mercilessly teased each other if one of them choked in a big moment in practice or in a pickup game. But there was never laughter when the choke came during a real game in a crucial situation.

Shirley rarely choked. And neither did Connie. And so they bonded.

I also took note of freshmen like Karen Wikstrom and Judy Becker, and sophomore Diana Hintz, all volleyball players I knew were going to try out for basketball and who all surely saw the winter of 1975 pass more quickly than I did.

As I trudged through November and December and into the nation's bicentennial, counting the days until basketball tryouts, it was with little notice given to the outside world. Kids were sneaking off to midnight showings of *The Rocky Horror Picture Show*, and the Bee Gees suddenly had this new sound with "Jive Talkin."

While most kids around school favored the Eagles, Wings, Fleetwood Mac, Billy Joel, David Bowie, and Peter Frampton, I leaned more toward "Mandy" by Barry Manilow and "Sister Golden Hair" by America, but I kept this mostly to myself. I wore a mood ring, which never changed from black, and I disdained Pet Rocks and all those who owned one.

In the fall, a new show called *Saturday Night Live* premiered, giving the kid with no other plans on Saturday night a respectable excuse to stay home without feeling like too much of a loser. And in my house, there was always *The Mary Tyler Moore Show*, my mother's and my favorite, though again this was not something I shouted from the rooftops.

While the rest of the world, or at least our country, was busy worrying about the national debt, which had just risen to $595 billion, and talking about a figure skater named Dorothy Hamill as the Winter Olympics got underway, I was far more concerned about Bill Veeck buying the White Sox.

As basketball tryouts drew closer, I attended a few of the boys' basketball games, but I wanted to be out there and could hardly sit still, realizing this was the moment I had been waiting for since Miss Tatz's kindergarten class, when Eddie Rice did a headstand to much fanfare during show-and-tell while I was unable to prove that I could do one too.

It wasn't that I didn't know how to do a headstand. My brothers had taught me when I was two, and it was among my favorite pastimes at home. But girls were not allowed to wear pants to school in the Chicago suburbs until 1970—still four years away at that point—and try as I might, I could not figure out a way to perform a headstand without the entire kindergarten class seeing my underpants. I tried to do it real fast, thinking I could somehow beat gravity. But in the end, Eddie Rice was the hero and I, along with all the other girls, was somehow inferior.

I could not have known for sure, but somehow, I had the feeling Arlene Mulder would change all that.

CHAPTER 3

Grovers and Wooders and Billy Schnurr

CONNIE THOUGHT I WAS RICH.

This never occurred to me as I went to Ned Singer's sporting goods store in downtown Skokie and picked out two pairs of boys' gym shorts—one red and one navy, both with white piping—two six-packs of tube socks with red, blue, and green stripes, and a pair of boys' red canvas Converse gym shoes. I had yet to make a team, but I had big plans, so with little else to do for the few weeks until basketball tryouts, shopping seemed to be a logical first step.

"Those shorts are too wide," my mother announced a little too loudly, and offered the same evaluation when I tried on the shoes. There was no such thing as girls' basketball shoes at Ned Singer's, but I was perfectly happy getting the boys' basketball shoe of choice. The Chuck Taylors were practically wide enough to fit both of my feet next to each other. Fortunately, the tube socks, at full extension, could reach the tops of my thighs, and I wore two of them on each foot, so there was plenty of extra material to fill out the sides of the shoes, ensuring that they would stay on as I ran.

While I was picking out my new gear for basketball, Connie did the same for volleyball, rifling through her brothers' and sisters' hand-me-down shorts and cutoffs, and her old junior high gym shoes and socks, though she also collected discarded pop bottles for deposit and started a shoe fund.

I may have been spoiled. And my father owned his own business and wore a suit and tie to the office. We also had a cleaning woman, and my mother didn't work. But rich? No way. We lived in a four-bedroom bi-level on St. Louis Avenue, not exactly the other side of the tracks but definitely in one of the more modest neighborhoods on the east side of Lincolnwood. The far west side of Lincolnwood was known for its newest section, dubbed "The Towers," where the actual rich people lived in newly constructed homes of white brick and big double doors, Cadillacs in the garages and spectacular Christmas decorations up and down the streets.

It was where we went on Christmas Eve to look at the big houses and glorious lights after ordering in Chinese and going to the movies like all the other Jewish people we knew.

But all of us in Lincolnwood were rich as far as Connie and the other Grovers were concerned. That's what we called the Morton Grove kids. We were Wooders, a term of either endearment or resentment, depending on the occasion.

In 1975, Niles West—located in Skokie and sandwiched between the North Side of Chicago and the fast-growing and more affluent North Shore suburbs—had an enrollment of approximately 2,000 students, freshman to senior. The student body primarily comprised kids from Lincolnwood, a predominantly white-collar suburb with a large Jewish population, and kids from Morton Grove, a largely blue-collar suburb of a mostly gentile persuasion.

In the 1975–76 Niles West yearbook, there was not one black student, and the Asian and Latino faces were few.

Like most high schools since the dawn of time, Niles West was divided and subdivided into groups and subgroups—Grovers and Wooders, yes, but also jocks and drama jocks, burnouts and band geeks, cheerleaders and the others who made up the majority of the student body but whose very meaningful high school careers went largely unnoticed by those of us obsessed with our own extracurricular activities.

To me, the disparities in our high school cliques were far more significant and conspicuous than any economic differences. Oh sure, the wealthier girls dressed a little better, maybe, and some of the Lincolnwood kids had new cars, Trans Ams drawing the most envy. But the majority of girls at Niles West could manage at least one pair of designer jeans, and the boys all wore faded Levi's and T-shirts, so what difference did it make?

On the most fundamental level, we were all self-conscious teenagers united by our varying degrees of oily skin and differentiated by our allegiances to either Bonne Bell Ten-O-Six, Noxzema, or both, the common goal being to dry out your skin to the point of near-peeling with Ten-O-Six, followed by the cleansing and slightly rehydrating properties of Noxzema. What you were left with was essentially the same two or three zits you had before—if you were lucky—but at least they were exceptionally clean and fresh-smelling.

The objective for most of us was not to stand out but simply to blend in.

What we did not know was what went on beyond the superficial teenage angst, behind the closed doors of our friends' and classmates' homes. But maybe it was safer that way. Our parents were "Mr." and "Mrs." to our friends, and as friendly as we ever became with each other's families, we knew them only so well. Divorces were still shocking and most often delayed "until the kids were out of school." And the rest was simply not our business. What's more, you did not really want to know what went on in other people's homes any more than you wanted to be noticed yourself.

By the time I was 11, my house was sad and mostly empty, the dimly lit den a reminder of how lonely I felt after my sister, Susie, got married and my brothers, Barry and Richard, left for college. My dad was 40 when I was born, and it was as if I could feel my parents getting older, the mood more tense, my mom in more pain.

When she was 19, my mother took a train from Chicago to California to spend the summer with her sister and her family in San Jose. And it was there, while on a double date with two naval officers and hiking in the nearby Diablo Range foothills, that she lost her footing and, according to newspaper reports, rolled down an embankment before falling 20 feet straight down. Lying broken and semiconscious for an hour and a half before medics could get to her, my mother sustained internal injuries; lacerated her eye; broke her back, pelvis, right hip, and right shoulder; and crushed her right elbow.

She would never talk in any detail about the accident but carried with her an understandable fear of heights (the opening scene of *The Sound of Music* sent her running from the room) and the recollection that when her mother finally made it from Chicago to California to see her in the hospital, she stood at the door of the room and wrung her hands, proclaiming, "Oy, who's going to marry you now?"

After nearly a year's stay in the hospital, my mother left, miraculously upright but with a fragile and disfigured right arm, which underwent more than a dozen operations over the next 30 years.

From my earliest memories, my father always stationed himself protectively on my mother's right side in public in order to shield her from contact. But she still cooked and baked, sewed and needlepointed, walked miles in the absence of a driver's license, and rarely complained to us about an arm a good six inches shorter than the other in its slightly bent position.

Still, we all knew she rarely slept and was in chronic pain, and my dad doled out prescription painkillers to her judiciously, hiding the little pink and gray capsules in a shoebox inside the ductwork of our laundry room. It was often a source of conflict, and to her youngest kid, the medication didn't seem to work.

My dad was struggling as well.

During the winter of my eighth-grade year, he was snow-blowing the driveway when we heard the scream. He had reached in to dislodge a stick without unplugging the machine and ended up losing parts of three fingers on his right hand.

Just as bad, however, was the damage it seemed to do to his psyche.

My father was always meticulous about his nails, clipping and filing them and even getting the occasional manicure, as some businessmen who spent their days shaking hands did. But after a man at his barbershop recoiled at the sight of his missing and misshapen fingers a few months after the accident, my dad hid his hand in his pocket, worried he would get the same reaction from everyone he met.

As upset as he was over that and the loss of function in his hand, however, he was seemingly more despondent and embarrassed that the injury was essentially self-inflicted, that because he was familiar with heavy machinery from his scrap-iron business, it should never have happened. And he sat on the couch in the months afterward, TV turned off, cursing himself for allowing it. "Stupid," he would say, staring at his hand. "So stupid."

What I knew for sure was that most nights after dinner, my parents went off to opposite corners of the house, my dad retreating to the darkened den to watch one television while my mother holed up in their bedroom watching her own 12-inch set as I traded places between the two or stayed in my room.

I told myself everyone's parents argued as mine did, sometimes bitter fights that seemed to arise from nothing in particular, their yelling seeping under my bedroom door while I turned up the volume on the little orange TV set I got for my 12th birthday.

"You never know what goes on in other people's houses," my mom would often say, having me believe that no matter what was going on in ours, there was always something potentially much worse happening next door or across the street.

Their frustration was something I did not fully understand, but as I began high school, we were all looking for something, I think. For me, it was an outlet for my physical energy, a place where I truly belonged. For my mother and father, maybe it was just a spark they needed, something to latch on to that would unite them again.

What I do know is that in those next few years, the lights in our house came back on.

It would be hard to describe Connie's house as a three-bedroom or a four-bedroom primarily because at any given time, her father was knocking down another wall and reconfiguring it to somehow get a little extra space for his family of 13.

Connie's dad, Bob, worked for Illinois Bell, and her mom, Shirley, did part-time office work for a medical supplies company. But it was rare that Bob Erickson ever held down less than two jobs at one time. Once, in a family trivia contest, one of the questions was: "Name the four jobs Dad had in 1961."

While it may have occurred to Connie that she only wore hand-me-downs and that other girls had Sweet 16 parties while her sisters did not, she was not necessarily bothered by this. When she was little, she would lie in one of the basement bunk beds she shared with the older Erickson girls, listening as they discussed their boyfriends. And every summer, her whole family would go down to Lake of the Ozarks in Missouri, where they stayed in a little cabin, two girls to a bed, boys on the floor. Connie felt like a millionaire because they had all this and a small boat.

She would watch her big brother Tim, a star football player at Niles West, all tan and muscular and bare-chested, wake up early, run down the hill from where their cabin sat, and dive into the lake, and it was that hard-working, wholesome, athletic image to which she aspired.

When Connie was 11, however, that perfect picture would be forever altered. It was the summer of 1972 and her sister Marilee, the embodiment of everything Erickson—gregarious, fun, beautiful, a great athlete who started a powder-puff football league in addition to being a cheerleader and homecoming queen—had just graduated from Niles West. Marilee was headed to Southern Illinois University, the first Erickson girl to go to college, and it was a time of great celebration.

It was her 18th birthday, and she was on her way to her older sister Sharon's house in nearby Glenview. Marilee was driving a convertible, an old junker as Connie called it, that often stalled. She was at a stoplight and the family's theory is that she probably gave the engine a little gas to keep it from dying when she accidentally gunned it into the intersection.

She collided with another car and the impact ejected Marilee from her car and onto the side of the road.

Connie answered the phone when the police called. "Get your father right away," the officer instructed her. "There has been a serious accident."

Bob Erickson was out back, constructing still another addition to the house, hammering away, when Connie ran out to get him. Her older brother Randy stayed home and babysat the younger kids while their parents rushed to the hospital. After watching the kids continue to play and yell and generally fool around, Randy finally yelled at them to stop.

"This is really serious you guys," he told them.

Hospital rules prohibited the youngest Erickson kids from visiting their sister, but Connie's mom talked the nurses into it. Connie and her twin brother, Chris, stood by the bed, trying to convince themselves that it really was Marilee lying there. The only parts they recognized were her toes. Everything else was too swollen.

Her parents had decided they would not remove Marilee from life support but were told that leaving her on a respirator would mean a life of little quality. And so it was something of a blessing when the hospital called to say she had begun breathing on her own. It was now in God's hands, the family knew.

Marilee died that night.

It seemed the entire staff and student body of Niles West attended Marilee's funeral, hundreds and hundreds of adults and teenagers filing through the funeral home and, later, in and out of Connie's living room. It was the first time Connie ever saw her father cry, and silently she vowed that somehow she would fill her sister's shoes.

On the day of basketball tryouts, Connie worked her way to the gym, navigating the same gauntlet we all did.

Niles West royalty came in the form of varsity football players and other highly regarded senior boys who leaned against a wall of windows in the ironically named student lounge—more of a widened hallway separating the gyms, cafeteria, and auditorium from the rest of the school—and formed a virtual reviewing stand before which the school's population was forced to pass. The cheerleaders, prettiest of girls, and legacies like Connie would get winks, nods, and occasional hugs while the rest of us would hope simply to walk by unnoticed.

The west side of the school held an allure all its own, and we were magnetically drawn there. There were girls like Connie and Shirley and me, and Karen and Judy, a mix of girls from different sports, some of whom were not even sure which sports they would play. For me, the gym was the only place where I felt totally comfortable. With every insecure, traumatic step through the halls of the massive high school, in which I was simultaneously convinced that everyone was staring at me and that I was completely invisible, I became obsessed with the idea of being on a high school sports team, and so I lingered around the gym, hoping no one would notice how much time I spent there.

Fortunately for me, Mr. Skuban's homeroom happened to meet in the Contest Gym, more commonly referred to as the Boys' Gym, and our section of bleachers offered the perfect vantage point each morning to look up at the scoreboard, the names of the varsity boys' basketball players spelled out in dazzling white letters and staring down at us like a Broadway marquee.

It was not the only facet of boys' athletics that fascinated us, though. The varsity boys' locker room was, to the girls anyway, an urban legend.

"I heard it has chairs for every player instead of benches," Patti Hilkin whispered to me one day during homeroom.

"And don't forget the pop machine," another girl chimed in, our imaginations racing with images of a full-blown nightclub behind those doors.

The girls' gym, with its bifold door dividing it into two sections, and the South Balcony Gym, a tiny, airless compartment up one flight of stairs and most often used as a dance studio, as a meeting place, or perhaps for girls' free-throw practice if they didn't shoot with too high of an arc, were inferior to be sure. But they were all palaces to us. We watched as the woman PE teachers streamed in and out of their tiny shared office, scared to make eye contact with the tall, athletic-looking gymnastics coach, Mrs. Sloan; in awe of the blonde, petite track coach, Mrs. Armour; and intimidated by the very sight of Mrs. Mulder, who carried a certain intensity that appeared capable of both scaring you in gym class by day and perhaps winning Wimbledon by night.

Arlene Mulder was 31 years old in the winter of '76. She drove a cool car, wore a suede jacket, looked better in shorts than most of the other gym teachers, and exuded utter authority and confidence even as she wondered what in the hell she was doing.

Except Arlene Mulder would never say "hell."

As she stood before 70 of us JV and varsity girls' basketball hopefuls—up from 58 the year before—Mrs. Mulder was all at once steely eyed and warden-like, yet still feminine with the ever-present scent of Estée Lauder, and motherly, though certainly not like any mother we knew.

Tryouts were in the Boys' Gym, and the sensation of my gym shoes squeaking on the heavily lacquered court was thrilling in itself. "OK girls, if your last name begins with the letter *A* through *I*, I want you over here by the orange cones," Mrs. Mulder barked, startling me out of my lacquer-and-squeak-induced stupor. I didn't hear what she said after that or where the *J* through whatevers were going or what they were doing because I was busy sprinting directly to my corner, pleased that I was in Shirley's group and still a little shocked that I was actually there at all.

I looked around to see if anyone was shorter than my barely 5-foot-2 and didn't see any obvious candidates among the guards like Connie, who stood 5-5. Among the forwards, Shirley was 5-8 and Karen, 5-7. I didn't know the upperclassmen, but I saw girls who looked like they could play center at 5-10, maybe 5-11, all of whom seemed gigantic to me.

We each wore a number written in Magic Marker on a sheet of paper taped to our backs like contestants in a dance-off, and we rotated through stations manned by student volunteers and PE teachers with clipboards: 30-second shooting, dribbling around cones, agility drills, vertical jump, free-throw shooting.

Mr. Schnurr, the boys' varsity coach, stood off to the side with Mrs. Mulder, charting everyone's performance, while we moved anxiously from station to station, unaware that in addition to noting our free-throw percentages and vertical jumps, they were also studying things like our attitude, coachability, and hunger, even though most of us had never before heard that word applied to anything but eating.

I couldn't help but notice Billy Schnurr. He was a star around Niles West, and I was as thrilled to see him as I would have been if Bulls coach Dick Motta were standing there. But beyond being starstruck, I was in my element. This was a sport I loved and that I was good at. I may have been short and skinny, but I could dribble and run fast, and sneaking glances around the gym, I deduced I was at least faster than most.

Not faster than Connie, however. Connie was special, that much I could tell. She was wildly unpolished but athletic in a way I had never seen in a girl before, and it made me want to stop and stare. In sixth grade, my friend Gina told me that I walked like a boy (we were in a fight at the time). I think it had more to do with the way I held my arms than the way I walked, but whatever the case, it was one more thing to add to the list of things to be self-conscious about, and I made it a point after that to study how other girls walked so I could do it in a more feminine way. Connie walked like an athlete, a girl athlete, and this I had never seen before. There was a certain confident swagger, like the most talented boys carried, but also a grace and bounce to her step that suggested a greatness I could not quite decipher.

Inside, she was as scared as I was. Unlike the senior boys who were friends with her brother Mark and treated her like a kid sister, the senior girls in the gym did not seem to know Connie from the next freshman. Or if they did, they didn't show it. And as Connie looked around, she was in awe. Not only were the older girls like Maureen Mostacci, Pat Conklin, and Sue Schroeder really good, but Connie couldn't quite believe they allowed tryouts to be held in the Boys' Gym. Trying to ignore her nerves as she sized up a turnout she estimated to be in the hundreds, maybe thousands, she told herself to simply not do anything stupid while the older girls began to notice her talent and instinctive strut, quickly deducing that she was different.

Eventually, we broke up into short games of three-on-three and then were told to come back the next day for more of the same. Over coffee, Schnurr and Mulder conferred.

"Remember, Arlene," Schnurr told her, "you're not just picking the team based on what they can do in tryouts or who you think are the best athletes. You can't expect one player to do everything." He grabbed her clipboard and slid it across the table. "You have to look at their body frames, who can rebound for you and play forward, who can handle the ball, and who can play guard," he said. "You have to predict their learning curves."

She listened and learned. Arlene Mulder adored Billy Schnurr. And Schnurr was nothing if not a teacher. In rural Wilmot, Wisconsin, where he grew up the oldest of four children, his father was the high school principal, taught agriculture, and eventually took over the football, basketball, and baseball teams when it became clear that all the able-bodied (read: competent) men and coaches were off fighting in World War II. Trouble was, Marlin Schnurr knew very little about coaching, especially football. So he went out in the fall of 1943, bought the only four football books he could find, then looked at Billy and said, "All right, we have to figure out what we're going to do."

As a junior, Billy played quarterback and defensive back as well as acted as assistant coach. As a senior, it was his team all the way—they lost only one game and gave up just seven points all season. By his senior year at the University of Wisconsin, four years later, he decided to put his education on hold to coach the baseball team at Madison West High School.

Always thinking ahead, Schnurr wanted Mulder to plan for a future that was far from certain. At the time, there was still no state tournament in girls' basketball in Illinois, but Dr. Mannos continued to fight his downstate counterparts who still felt basketball was a boys' sport, and he was making progress with a longer schedule that season, from 10 games to 12.

I would have been happy with almost anything.

The morning after the second day of tryouts, I made my way to the gym to see if the team roster was posted yet on the bulletin board outside the girls' PE office. Mrs. Mulder had specifically told us she would not put up the list until noon, but as long as Mr.

Skuban's homeroom was in the gym anyway, I thought it wouldn't hurt to shoot a subtle glance in that direction.

Nothing.

The rest of the morning was excruciating. And the next chance I had to check, there was nothing cool or subtle about me as I sprinted from algebra toward the gym and stuck my face right up to the bulletin board.

And there it was.

Right under the heading NILES WEST GIRLS' BASKETBALL JUNIOR VARSITY was my name. I caught my breath and scanned the varsity list, seeing Shirley's name, of course, and then some freshmen—Connie Erickson, Karen Wikstrom, Tina Grass— which gave me a slight twinge of jealousy but more awe than anything. Who was I kidding? This was the high school varsity team we were talking about. If I continued to work hard, my name would be there someday, too.

I wondered what to do next, when we would get to practice, when our games would begin, what the coaches would tell us.

When we would get our uniforms.

It was always the promise of a uniform that called to me. Even Brownies, with their dumb dresses, somehow seemed enticing with the beanie and cool change purse on the belt. When I was a seventh grader at Lincoln Hall, the girls' basketball team wore pinnies with masking-tape numbers on them. They felt like part-jumper, part-apron, but they were something. By high school, my longing for a real uniform had hardly diminished. I did not really care what kind it was. Even the T-shirts we wore for Lincolnwood softball—which had an oversized logo of a girl with a 1950s-style curly bob and caps with a girly script *L*—were fine. But a real high school uniform, tops and bottoms, with satin lettering? The thought was more than I could bear.

Our uniforms were distributed the next day, handed to us in mesh drawstring bags, all of which smelled like a mixture of old socks and a metal gym locker scrubbed with a Brillo Pad. And we were no less thrilled than if we had just received a jersey with USA written across the chest.

Our jerseys did not have anything written across the chest. They were triple-ply, grade A, 100 percent industrial-strength polyester. If you stretched one out and poured a bucket of water over it, not a drop would seep through, which explained how the smell was so well-preserved. And when you rubbed it between your fingers, it had the distinct feel of sandpaper and seemed in danger of igniting at any moment.

The shirts were dark red with a pinched band of white elastic around the sleeves and a small solitary white number on the front and back. My first choice was No. 4, my junior high number and the number of my hero, Chicago Bulls guard Jerry Sloan, but a senior already had it. So I picked No. 10 and consoled myself that Bulls forward Bob Love was no slouch and that two digits filled out the jersey better anyway. Our shorts were also dark red with two white stripes down the sides, which was cool, and we were given white nylon knee socks, which we were to wear over our own, also with three red stripes.

There was no NILES WEST or INDIANS, or anything satin, and we found out that the JV team would have to share the handful of warm-ups because there weren't enough to go around. But we were lucky. Some of the schools we played that year had to share their uniforms among all of their girls' teams. At that moment, we were oblivious to the fact that the boys' teams had home and away uniforms with plenty of satin and their own warm-ups.

We tried to act as if our uniforms were no big deal as we slung the crusty mesh bags over our shoulders. But I was scarcely in the door that night when I pulled out each piece, my mother diplomatically avoiding any mention of the smell.

While modeling them for our families, it was apparent that even after stretching the white elastic bands around the sleeves to their limits, there would soon be permanent indentations on our arms. And the shorts, regardless of their size or our varying body types, would become part of our own skin.

Of course, none of us saw any real problem with this.

We were special. Important. Official representatives of our school. Our town. We were part of a team, not so far removed from the college and NBA teams we saw on TV. If we couldn't be them one day, we could look like them.

In reality, prison uniforms were more flattering and undoubtedly more comfortable. But these were ours now, and we took instant pride in them. We had an identity. We were athletes.

CHAPTER 4

Inappropriate Cheering and the Half-Court Shot

IN GRADE SCHOOL, I was always a little bored during recess. Rather than appreciate the fresh air, exercise, and fun that recess was intended to provide us, I usually viewed my options and was disappointed. Recess was always a ready and painful example of the gender divide. The vast majority of boys would go directly to the field or blacktop and play baseball, basketball, football, or some game with teams and competition. Usually all it took was a ball of some kind. And on the patch of concrete outside the front doors of the school, there were the girls trading stickers, playing jacks, or in the early '70s, playing with a toy called Footsie.

Footsie was one of those ingenious inventions, like the Pet Rock, that made people all over the country ask themselves, "Why couldn't I have thought of that and become a million-aire?" It consisted of a plastic yellow ring that went around your ankle. Attached to the ring was a plastic string and at the end of the string, a red, plastic bell. The object was to move your foot around in circles and jump over the red thing with your other foot. It took all the skill of haircombing, and though I owned one, as did every self-respecting elementary school–aged girl at the time, I thought Footsie was the stupidest thing I had ever seen, and it bored me beyond belief.

This could be the reason why, when finally given the opportunity, all the girls who aspired to play competitive sports loved doing so in any format available. And it probably explained why, though our first game, against Highland Park at home, was still two weeks away, the idea of having two full weeks of practice leading up to it was just as thrilling.

Mrs. Mulder ran into practice on the first day as if she were in a race, whistle blazing as she grasped her note cards, pausing only to blow strands of her dark, wavy hair off her forehead as the varsity and JV teams gathered together briefly in the girls' gym. The seniors on the varsity team looked like grown women. Maureen Mostacci was tall and quiet with long, dark hair, amazing red suede Converse shoes none of us had ever seen before, and a graceful quality about her on the court. She was also nice to the younger players, which made her somewhat rare among the upperclassmen.

Pat Conklin, the dark-blonde-ponytailed point guard, gave all the short kids hope with her aggressive style and fearless shooting. And Sue Schroeder, a forward, was platinum blonde and pretty and possessed a figure the likes of which most of us could only dream of having. Maggie Heinz, we heard, was an unbelievable softball pitcher and, like Pat and Sue, mostly sneered at the freshmen.

Karen Wikstrom was physically frightened of all of them. A freshman, Karen began having doubts as to her place on the varsity team about 10 minutes into the first practice, when Sue Schroeder boxed her out from under the basket and nearly bounced her out of the gym. Karen had never before experienced girls being so physical, and most of us had never before seen it.

One thing became quickly apparent about most of the senior

girls: they were confident. That was easy to tell just from listening to their boasts and from watching Pat hoist shots in practice from everywhere but the bleachers. But somehow the hustle wasn't quite there, nor the team attitude that Mrs. Mulder was preaching.

"Pat!" Mrs. Mulder would shout. "Shirley was wide open under the basket. Wide open. Look for your teammates."

It was subtle at first, but it did not take long for the real leaders on the varsity team to emerge, and one was a sophomore and the other a freshman. Shirley and Connie echoed Mrs. Mulder's pass-first directives and team-first mind-set, their confidence, superior skill, fierce competitiveness, and humility allowing them to get away with it.

Our JV coach, Nancy Majewski, was in her first year on the job, and we often found ourselves looking over to see what varsity was doing beyond the bifold door that split the girls' gym in two, straining to hear what Mrs. Mulder was saying.

One day early on, Mr. Schnurr brought in some of his players, who were already more than halfway through a very successful season, to show the girls' JV and varsity teams the fundamentals of a full-court pressure defense, a strategy predicated on defending the length of the court after scoring a basket, and something that required lots of practice.

Because Mr. Schnurr was in charge, the demonstration took place in the Boys' Gym, a forbidden place for the girls' teams. And even as future Olympic gold medal–winning gymnast and Niles West senior Bart Conner performed extraordinary routines on the balcony above the gym, our attention never wavered from Mr. Schnurr and the boys on court. To us, Mr. Schnurr was every bit the celebrity Bart was, and so were his players. And as Connie was called up to participate in the demonstration, she wanted only for all of us not to embarrass ourselves.

Mr. Schnurr grabbed Connie around the shoulders and walked her up the sideline, showing her how to trap the man with the ball, his boys playing the parts of ball handler and co-trapper with Connie. Next, he put the ball in play, and we all watched, thrilled when Connie did exactly as she was told, racing over to the trap and cutting off the ball handler, but with a speed and fluidness that had Mr. Schnurr shooting Mrs. Mulder raised eyebrows and a subtle smile.

Mr. Schnurr held our attention like no teacher ever could. It was as if a magician were suddenly tipping his hat and showing us how to perform his tricks. So this is what the boys were doing out there and this was how they did it. Slowly, entry to this wonderful and exclusive club became ours, and the world of basketball was opening up to us in a way we had never been exposed to before. Terms like *traps* and *backdoor cuts*, *strong side* and *weak side*, now made sense. Mr. Schnurr stressed that the full-court press was the weapon we would use to demoralize our opponents on defense and that on offense, the ball was "like a treasure chest filled with gold" and that we could not, under any circumstances, give it away.

One afternoon, we worked on a type of full-court press called the diamond-and-one, or 1-2-1-1, an aggressive and sophisticated defense that was high-risk, high-reward. If the opponent broke the press, it would likely lead to an easy basket. But if the defensive team worked in sync, if everyone knew their roles and committed fully to them, it would lead to turnovers and easy scores in bunches. It took smarts and athleticism. And because it required so much effort, it not only exhausted the opposition but also improved team chemistry because it required fresh legs, which necessitated rotating more players in from the bench. It was perfect for us. Perfect for Mrs. Mulder, who encouraged her players every practice to think, act, and play like a team.

Performed correctly, it could break games open, and the very fact that Mr. Schnurr was sharing this with us, that he entrusted us with this knowledge and had faith in our ability to pull it off, made it imperative that we not let him down—even if he had to raise his voice to make his point.

"Shirley, move!" Mr. Schnurr implored at one point. "Cut off the sideline, cut *off* the sideline."

The move required quickness, perhaps the only skill Shirley was lacking. And she teared up in sheer frustration. Mr. Schnurr looked over sheepishly at Mrs. Mulder, grimacing at his miscalculation. Sure he had gone too far, he reminded himself that we were girls and that he might want to back off. What he did not know, because he did not yet know Shirley well enough, was that she was not upset by his yelling but by the fact he had to yell at all.

Shirley gave me a ride home and on the way, she berated herself, infuriated she had not gotten to her spot in the press in time, hadn't jumped on the trap with Connie and pressured the boy with the ball. She hadn't cut off the sideline, which was a sure way for the offense to break the press. We were improving, but Shirley was afraid if she didn't perform precisely as Mr. Schnurr wanted her to, if we all didn't, he might stop coming around.

"Shirl, it's fine," I said. "You were great."

"Miss, I was not great," she moaned. "I need to be better. We all need to be better."

Like Connie, Shirley was always clearly gifted. She had powerful hands and a solidness that gave her awesome power as a hitter in softball and as a rebounder in basketball. Yet, she also possessed an agility and touch that made her a natural tennis player and blessed her with one of the softest jump shots we had ever seen.

She was also blessed with a D cup, the subject of endless wonder to the rest of us, though an albatross to Shirley and her 5-foot-8 frame, which never seemed to move quickly enough for her.

Shirley always seemed much older than the rest of us, smarter in that worldly way that did not necessarily reflect any more experience with boys or a genius much beyond pretty normal honor roll stuff, but there was just an air of common sense to her that the rest of us did not always demonstrate.

Raised in a conservative Jewish home, Shirley was the third of four children born to Elie, known as "Al," a native of Egypt, and Mimi, who was born in Lebanon. In the house, Shirley's parents spoke a combination of Arabic, French, and English, all of which made a visit to the Cohens both an enlightening and somewhat dizzying experience. Shirley's first language was laughter, a low giggle that began somewhere deep inside her soul and made you feel much funnier than you actually were. Shirley had a great sense of humor, but she was never silly, particularly when it came to basketball.

Inherently, we all knew these sessions with Mr. Schnurr and the boys were something special, that we were special, and that this scene was probably not being played out in any other girls' basketball practices around the state, and we hungered for more.

Practice was almost always an education and an introduction to pain that we had never before experienced. Among other things, we began running "suicides," the dreaded staple of every boys' basketball practice in history and now of our domain as well. It was a drill in which you sprinted from the baseline to the closest free-throw line, then ran back to the baseline; to the center court line and back to the baseline; to the far free-throw line and back; and finally to the far baseline and back, touching each line with your hand.

They were called suicides for obvious reasons, but I loved them. Maybe it was because at barely 5-2, I didn't have to bend down very far to touch each line. Or maybe it was just because I was annoying as hell and always had been when it came to showing off my quickness.

As a little kid at Jewish Community Center day camp, I would constantly challenge other kids to race me. In hindsight, I'm pretty sure they viewed me in the same way you might look at the kid in school who asks the teacher if there is any homework.

But my challenges extended to pretty much anyone in my line of vision, including my father, who I only knew as having gray hair and an ever-present stash of Tums in his breast pocket. Nevertheless, I would often urge him to race me from the parking lot to the front doors of the bank on our weekly Saturday morning errands run.

Carrying with him approximately $30 of excess change in each pants pocket, along with a fairly sizable belly, he would run with painful-sounding pants accompanying each step, the rattling coins providing the background soundtrack as I would make it to the bank with roughly enough time to eat lunch, read the paper, and possibly learn a foreign language before he got there.

So eager was I to establish my speed that I even fell for the oldest gag in the big brother handbook: agreeing to do almost anything for my brothers—run upstairs to the kitchen to get them Cokes, run down the street to Dairy Queen to get them Mr. Mistys—if they said they would time me. "What was my time?" I'd ask breathlessly, sweat trickling down my forehead and Mr. Misty juice running down my arm.

One of them would then look very officially at his watch and reply, "It was your best yet—6:32.05." And off I would go, happy as can be and not the least bit aware that they had made up the time.

To be challenged at basketball practice was fun, and I established myself as the best suicides participant on the JV team, something I'm sure no one else but I took note of or would lay claim to. There was very little scrimmaging in either the JV or varsity practices, just drills and more drills—dribbling around cones while switching hands, defensive slides, full-court two-on-ones. Our thighs burned, and most of us relished every minute of it.

Or at least Connie and I did. Though she was on varsity and I was on JV, enough of our drills overlapped that we quickly detected in each other more than just a love of basketball but an obsession with competing and an almost unnatural attraction to virtually anything close to it. If the teams were doing wall sits, we'd eye each other, wordlessly trying to last longer even as everyone else moved on to the next drill. And when it came to anything involving quickness, I'd use Connie as my gauge, as I knew she was the quickest in the gym.

The day before our season began, our parents received a letter in the mail from Mrs. Mulder congratulating them on our accomplishment of making the team and warning them:

> Our practices are long and strenuous and our games will be filled with the pressures of both excitement and disappointment, but the girls have enthusiasm.
>
> I need your understanding and support for all the girls at home and at our games. Girls' sports are new and we are certainly no supershow. It means so much to the girls to know you are backing them.

Few did. For some parents, it was no doubt a lack of interest. For most fathers, getting off from work early to attend games that began right after school was not an option. And so, for that first game, there was a modest sprinkling of moms, assorted friends, and a couple of teachers.

I was so excited I had barely been able to sit still that day in class. My mom was coming, driven by my sister-in-law Alysa, and it wasn't hard to scan the temporary bleachers set up in the girls' gym and find them. Despite our scratchy red uniforms, I was in my comfort zone, harassing my opponents on defense and scoring mostly on layups off steals and on free throws off drives down the lane that I had no business attempting. If I made any impression, it was on hustle more than anything, frantically sprinting and jumping as if this were the one chance in my high school career to prove myself.

The moms who came to our games quickly struck up friendships, huddled together in the bleachers while trying to decipher what they were watching. Often, they cheered at inappropriate times, like when one of us was called for a foul or traveling. When it became especially embarrassing, the offending mother's daughter would have to glance up in the stands with a look that said, "Not now, not now," and the moms would look sheepish and giggle and resume cheering for the wrong things.

In other ways, we were forced to play catch-up.

The previous year, in the girls' first season, the Maine South coach threatened to protest the varsity game won by Niles West because they claimed it was not played on a regulation-size court. And since that's where Niles West practiced, they claimed we had an unfair advantage. Of course, there was really no one to protest to except for the head of the Niles West girls' PE department, Leanne Heeren, who could only shrug and apologize. Our girls' court wasn't regulation; Maine South was right. It had simply not occurred to Miss Heeren or any of the woman coaches that they could even ask to play in the Boys' Gym.

Whether we were, in fact, ready for it was a matter of some debate as we had still not quite mastered certain nuances of the game.

For Connie, it was free throws. Before and after practice, she worked feverishly on her shooting, particularly on her form. Determined to learn a jump shot like the boys used rather than the set shot most girls settled for, she struggled—jumping and heaving, jumping and heaving. She had wonderful ballhandling skills, could zip a no-look pass with such aplomb that she routinely faked out her own teammates, and had the anticipation on defense of an accomplished pickpocket. But her shooting frustrated her, and that extended to the free-throw line. Looking desperately at Mrs. Mulder after each missed foul shot, Connie would routinely clank them off the rim and more than occasionally miss the basket and the rim completely.

I might have been sympathetic if I didn't have my own troubles. I was especially enamored of that point in the game, with time running out at the end of a quarter, when one player, usually a guard it seemed to me, would hoist up a half-court shot at the buzzer.

For weeks, I bided my time, waiting and hoping for this scenario to occur when the ball was in my hands. When it finally did, I let a shot fly from about 45 feet and wondered why a member of the opposing team grabbed the rebound and headed back upcourt while my teammates stared at me in utter disbelief. Apparently, instead of three seconds left on the clock, there were 13, a miscue I blamed on my eyesight and even went so far as to get contacts the next week to prove my point.

Despite that blunder, Mrs. Mulder must have seen a glimmer of potential, hustle, or sheer hyper quality to my effort because toward the middle of the season, I was asked to practice with varsity and sit on the bench for their games.

For the first time, I started to see up close how she operated, and I was transfixed being that close to someone with such an intensity about her. She demanded our attention with a piercing stare alone, and like the teacher she was, her classroom was all business, no fooling around, no wasting time. Every second was accounted for, every water break carefully planned, and with quick glances at her index cards, every instruction was stated clearly and repeated to make sure we understood. Even the staccato blow of her whistle was efficient. She was all about organization, about being completely focused on the objective at hand. Accomplishing more than one task at a time was something she did every day as a full-time teacher, wife, and mother. But when it came to games, her coaching skills were coming along a little more slowly.

During one game, she benched our center, Nancy Hohs, after early foul trouble. But it wasn't until her husband, Al, sent a folded-up note down to the bench asking, "When are you going to put Nancy back in?" that Mrs. Mulder remembered she had taken her out. But she was getting better and so were we, our improvement showing with each practice session and each game. We wanted to learn as much as we wanted to win.

We watched the boys' games like the fans we were, and when Billy Schnurr's team beat Gordon Tech in the '76 boys' sectional final at Niles West to reach the elusive Sweet 16—one victory shy of the state tournament—the coach was stoic in victory. Mrs. Mulder, however, was apparently not taking notes because Mr. Schnurr was standing quietly by the scorers' table after his team's victory when she came flying down from the stands and literally jumped into his arms.

The following week, the Niles West boys lost in the super-sectionals at Northwestern University's McGaw Hall, and for those of us from the girls' team who went to the game, we may as well have been watching the NBA playoffs. Even the concept that a high school sporting event was being played at a college arena was incomprehensible to us.

The end of our season came so quickly—varsity finished 9–3 and the JV, 6–6—it was painful turning in our uniforms. For me, the highlight was being asked by Mrs. Mulder to sit on the bench for the varsity games, but it only made it harder for the season to be over, and only the lure of my first high school softball season consoled me.

After basketball ended, Connie took a part-time job at Mister Donut, going to work at five in the morning and coming to school smelling like grease. She ate doughnuts until she was sick, made $2.30 an hour, and loved every minute of it. For one, she thought she was literally rolling in dough since minimum wage had just gone up from $2.10 the previous year. She also loved doughnuts, at least for the first month or so. And she and her friend Kitty, who also worked there, laughed their way through the grease.

When we got our yearbooks that spring, I worked up the courage to ask Mrs. Mulder to sign mine:

Missy—What a freshman year! You couldn't be happier! You're quite an athlete and have so much potential—the challenge now lies in how you use and develop that gift of coordination. With a lot of hard work—lots of jumping, etc.—you should have a lot to offer varsity basketball. Have a great summer! Look forward to seeing you next year.

Mrs. Mulder

I read it and reread it. Quite an athlete? So much potential? Develop that gift? It was the most inspiring thing anyone had ever written to me, and I could not wait to start working for next year. Shirley, as always, had to go visit her cousins in New Jersey that summer, an annual family tradition she both loved and was starting to resent for the time it took away from basketball. But Connie and I decided to attend a girls' basketball camp Mrs. Mulder had told us about on the campus of William Penn College in Oskaloosa, Iowa.

Our friendship had taken root in basketball and we were excited to go off on this adventure, maybe all the more so because we had never heard of a basketball camp for girls before, much less Oskaloosa, Iowa.

Connie said her friend Diane Defrancesco, an incoming freshman—Connie called her "DD"—was coming, and I talked Bari into going as well. She figured no one would care about her hair there, and besides, she wanted to lose a little weight. So did Connie, who estimated she put on about 10 extra pounds at Mister Donut.

It wasn't that girls did not perspire before the summer of 1976, but none of us had ever sweat like the week we spent under the tutelage of William Penn coach Bob Spencer and his staff. At lunch the first day, we spent the first few minutes staring at each other and ourselves with equal measures awe and disgust.

"Gross," Bari said, looking down at her yellow camp-issued T-shirt. "I don't even see a dry spot."

"Yeah," I responded. "How great is this?"

While Connie spent her off-hours nauseated over the strange hairs in the sinks of the communal bathroom, DD concentrated on finding the most original way to get herself almost thrown out of camp. Having apparently seen the movie *The Parent Trap* one too many times, she would pull the old take-the-lids-off-the-salt-shakers gag and pour cold water on the wrists of the nearest sleeping camper or teammate she could find.

While she was definitely keeping up with everyone on the court, it was also apparent DD liked to have fun. Connie and I doubted she could do both, and one night we had a mothers-daughter talk with her.

Us: "DD, you're going to get us all kicked out. Knock it off."

DD: "OK, OK, calm down. You're like my mother."

Each day was an education we had never before experienced. As hard as we thought we had worked under Mrs. Mulder, this was on an entirely new level. And it was in a hot gym in Oskaloosa, Iowa, where we truly learned what it meant to push ourselves beyond what we were sure were our physical limits. Sweat was a good thing, pain even better. We practiced for four hours in the morning and scrimmaged for four hours in the afternoon, and always there was running, suicides taking on a new meaning. Some of us even threw up, or at least came close, and didn't particularly care. If this was a cult, we were easily and quickly indoctrinated, with the possible exception of DD, who had clearly not signed on for this kind of punishment.

On the walls of the gym there were signs with such sayings as THERE IS NO "I" IN "TEAM" and A WINNER NEVER QUITS AND A QUITTER NEVER WINS, which we believed to be the work of Shakespeare, so brilliant were they in their simplicity and eloquence. We had never heard them before, so they were not clichés to us. What's more, they spoke to us, and we were set to live by them.

Back home, while I dribbled around my patio with my right arm tied behind my back in order to strengthen my nondominant hand, Connie worked her way up and down the sidewalk in front of her house, looking for any patch of gravel or uneven surface she could find after learning that this was the best way to improve your ballhandling. And she had worn away the paint on a patch of ceiling in her bedroom directly above her pillow from practicing her follow-through while lying in bed.

We had fully, inexorably, and happily found our purpose. From the tactile joy of our first real uniforms to our first peek into how the game of basketball was supposed to be played to the oppressive heat of an Iowa gym to the everyday, mundane pleasure of dribbling off our bedroom ceilings, there was no doubt. We had gone from athletes to jocks.

CHAPTER 5

"Son, son, get up!"

FOR THE RETURNING MEMBERS of the Niles West girls' basketball team, the fall was brimming with possibilities.

The rest of womankind, however, still had a way to go.

The Supreme Court had just ruled 6–3 in favor of General Electric that it was not gender discrimination for companies to provide insurance that covered some men-only disabilities but not disabilities resulting from pregnancy. The FBI issued a report calling wife battering the country's least-reported crime, prompting the women's movement to call for more public attention and more police effort in response. In more positive news, Barbara Walters became the first woman to coanchor a network evening news show for an unprecedented $1 million annual salary, though it should be noted that Harry Reasoner, her partner on *ABC World News Tonight*, made no secret of his hostility.

At the US Open, Chris Evert won the women's singles title, but it was Evert's role as men's champion Jimmy Connors's girlfriend that drew more attention to Evert than her gritty determination or blistering forehand. And the real news of the tournament was transgender Renée Richards, who was barred from competing in the women's draw after she refused to take a chromosome test.

It seemed we were all a little misunderstood.

For the 15th straight year of my life, I wore my hair short. And for probably the 12th straight year, I was often mistaken for a boy. Easing the pain somewhat was that this observation usually came from those over the age of 60 who also thought that any boy with hair below his ears was a girl.

Until one sweltering September morning early sophomore year, this had been a relatively private problem of mine. I had just finished playing tennis in Mrs. Mulder's PE class that morning and was standing in the cafeteria line when a wave of dizziness hit me. I was either going to throw up or pass out, I wasn't sure which. But I determined that either way, the cafeteria was not the place to do it. Rushing out of the lunch line and dashing through the heavily populated student lounge, I felt the strange sensation of the floor rising up and hitting me in the face.

So, this was what fainting felt like.

Almost immediately, I felt someone shaking me. I also heard the words that made me wish I had never regained consciousness. "Son, son, get up!" shouted Mr. Beeftink, one of the science teachers.

My reaction, at least in my own head, still facedown on the linoleum, was instantaneous. OK, I decided, transferring high schools might be a little extreme, so I will simply never walk through this particular hallway or go near the student lounge again for the next three years. I could do that. And anyway, maybe I was the only one who even heard Mr. Beeftink call me "son," which was considerably more embarrassing than the actual fainting.

I had just about convinced myself of this after blocking out the wheelchair ride to the nurse's office when a so-called good friend of mine, a junior whose sense of humor leaned toward Don Rickles, burst through the door to inform me that actually, "the entire school" had heard.

"And they're still laughing," she added, in case I wasn't traumatized enough.

How many days until basketball season?

The image problem was worse for some of us than others. People tended to view girl athletes as boyish, something many girls found frightening and some boys, frankly, found intimidating. For me, though painfully self-conscious, I was not inclined to change my ways. I liked boys, but unless I was playing catch or making jokes with them in the back of class, they pretty much terrified me, and I found basketball much more interesting than the prospect of attracting a boyfriend anyway.

Like seemingly everything else she did, Connie's social life came easily. She had dated an adorable blond-haired, blue-eyed boy named Bob Porcaro in seventh and eighth grades, and though they weren't officially boyfriend and girlfriend, they remained good friends, and anyone could tell Bob still liked her.

For Diane Defrancesco, the prospect of juggling basketball with the rest of her life her freshman year at Niles West was considerably more difficult. Her reputation as an athlete preceded her thanks to her older sister Charmaine, who had graduated two years earlier.

Char was a phenomenal athlete, very possibly the best female athlete Niles West had ever had up to that point, though it was hard to judge. During her freshman year at West, the only girls' sport was called aquasprites, a hybrid of swimming and water ballet. Char, a great swimmer, was not thrilled, but she went out for it anyway. Over the course of the next four years, every time the school would add a girls' sport, Char would try out and star in it—volleyball, swimming, badminton, tennis, softball, and finally basketball for the '75 inaugural team. After graduating from high school, Char received a $600 tuition waiver to play basketball for Northern Illinois University and once there, was recruited to play field hockey, where the first game she ever saw was also the first one she ever played in.

But as talented an athlete as Char was, DD was thought to be even better, more naturally gifted. The only girl to play Little League baseball in Skokie when she was 11, DD once picked up a softball in gym class and casually heaved it 250 feet without so much as a warm-up toss.

Although she barely avoided being expelled from basketball camp, DD wasn't a bad kid. She had a huge heart, was friendly and funny, and was never outright disrespectful to adults. We figured she was just a free spirit, the kind of kid who did things you wish you had the courage to do. DD only wished she had the stability that most of us apparently had.

Just as DD was starting high school, her mother was finally getting help for a drinking problem, and with both parents focused on her recovery, their youngest daughter was left to pretty much fend for herself. She had also begun experimenting with alcohol and pot and found she liked both. The only thing that could compete was sports. What she could not accept was the leap some kids made to equate sports with being boyish, especially when boyish meant something else altogether.

One day DD told us she had received a letter from another girl in school professing her love for her, and she was horrified. At 5-6, strong, and, like most of us, with a body viewed as built more for sports than for dresses, DD whispered to her friends, "I don't want people to think I'm some dykey girl." And from then on, she made a special effort at parties to flirt with the boys, before attracting the attention of Connie's twin brother, Chris.

The topic of woman athletes and homosexuality was one that came up every now and then, and there was little differentiation made between sexuality and femininity. The fact that if you looked or acted too much like a guy, you might very well either be mistaken for a lesbian or actually be one was something we all generally acknowledged.

Mrs. Mulder was sympathetic to our anxieties over our self-image. "You are always young ladies, and I never want you to give up your femininity," she told us as we blushed and whispered sarcastic comments to each other. "But on the court, you are also athletes."

Our coach was looking toward basketball season as much as we were. She had attended some coaching clinics over the summer, and her friendship with Mr. Schnurr was a solid one now. They were pals and co-conspirators in their plan to make us better basketball players.

The climate among much of the Niles West staff, however, was a tense one. There was serious talk of an impending strike over the perceived delay in the renewal of a new teachers' contract, and the staff was picking sides. But Arlene Mulder and Billy Schnurr didn't talk politics; they talked basketball. And tennis.

Both were avid players, and after discovering one morning that neither had a homeroom class to monitor that fall, they met on the tennis court and hit for the 10 minutes before each had to teach an outdoor gym class. This arrangement worked beautifully for three days until another teacher spotted them through a window and reported it to the principal, and they were told to stop. Now they were partners in crime as well.

Of course, there were more serious issues at hand. The teachers voted to strike, and it seemed all of Mrs. Mulder's friends and colleagues were ardent union supporters, taking to the picket line without hesitation. For Mrs. Mulder, however, there was a decision to make.

With the state tennis tournament about to begin and her talented sophomore Holly Bland one of the favorites to compete for the state singles title, Mrs. Mulder learned that Holly would have to forfeit her matches if she was not represented by her coach. Mrs. Mulder's decision was now clear. But in her first attempt to cross the picket line, she was horrified as many of the same people she thought were her closest friends harassed and taunted her with chants of "Scab!"

"Arlene, you're not going to go in there," said John Armour, a Niles West coach and the husband of Jean Armour, her good friend and fellow PE teacher and coach.

Mrs. Mulder hurried to her car, dissolving into tears. After driving home, she called Bud Trapp, our athletic director, and asked for his advice. "Arlene, come to school tomorrow morning at five and I'll give you a set of keys to the building," Trapp told her, appreciating her dilemma.

It was a decent enough plan. Before dawn each morning of the strike, Mrs. Mulder sneaked into the building before picketers arrived and avoided catching any serious abuse. But all around her, chaos reigned. In a bitterly contentious school board meeting, the teachers who remained on strike despite threats from the board—about half the staff—were fired. And the great majority of the student body, in a scene reminiscent of the '60s, marched outside, boycotting classes in a protest of our own.

Striking teachers taught their classes under trees in front of the school while Dr. Mannos took to a bullhorn, ordering students inside. It was all very exciting to a generation of kids who were too young to have had any real influence in the '60s, and we told ourselves that this was important and that we weren't just having fun cutting class.

Within a few days, however, it was a moot point as the teachers were rehired, students returned to classes, and the contract dispute was temporarily delayed.

Holly competed in the state tennis tournament, where she did not place but gained valuable experience. And Mrs. Mulder lost friendships she wondered if she would ever fully regain.

Basketball season started a month earlier than the previous year, with tryouts in mid-January. A new air of seriousness accompanied the early start. Everyone seemed to understand that there would be no room on the varsity team for those who weren't willing to make a real commitment.

Mr. Schnurr, like the rest of us, had his eye on the upcoming season. One afternoon, while substitute teaching a girls' PE class, he noticed sophomore Peggy Japely, a tall, gangly girl with obvious athletic ability, and asked if she was trying out for the basketball team after school. She looked at him as if he were a ghost, scarcely able to believe he was talking to her, much less discussing her basketball future.

Peggy was the girl in junior high whom no one really knew and no one really bothered to try to know. She had long, straggly hair that obscured beautiful blue eyes and was so painfully shy that most kids assumed she did not speak at all. She had tried out for the Parkview Junior High basketball team in eighth grade and hadn't made it. At Niles West our freshman year, she decided she wouldn't bother to try out at all. She occasionally found herself looking longingly toward the gym as each tryout rolled around but quickly put it out of her mind. She was a loser, she decided, and everyone knew it.

But now she was a 5-7 sophomore with the physical tools of a guard, the size of a forward, and the awkwardness of a teenager not yet used to her body. While she may have looked like a basketball player, she wasn't necessarily ready for Niles West tryouts or any more prepared for rejection.

"You're quick, you have good hands, and you have height," Mr. Schnurr told her.

"I don't know if I'm trying out," Peggy mumbled, her head buried in her chest.

Mr. Schnurr was undeterred.

"Which class do you have last today?" he asked. And when Peggy emerged from ninth-period history, there was the legendary Billy Schnurr, placing his hand firmly on her shoulder and walking her to the gym.

Peggy ended up making the JV team, and I feigned coolness at being one of 14 to make varsity along with our lone senior, Nancy Hohs; four juniors, Shirley, Diana Hintz, Bridget Berglund, and Toni Atsaves; five other sophomores, Connie, Judy, Karen, Nancy Eck, and Tina Grass; and three freshmen, DD, Tina Conti, and Toni's sister Barb.

At our first team meeting, there were no congratulations. No time was wasted on empty praise or a trite pep talk. Mrs. Mulder went through a few basic housekeeping details and then brought in Mr. Schnurr, who got right to the point: girls' basketball would have a state tournament this year.

Bureaucracy being what it was, we were seeing the results of a battle that had begun and ended before most of us had even started high school. Following extensive discussion in a meeting of the Illinois High School Association board of directors in November 1974, a motion made by Dr. Mannos was unanimously carried that the IHSA establish and sponsor state tournaments for girls in field hockey, golf, softball, and swimming in 1975–76, and in archery, badminton, gymnastics, and basketball in 1976–77.

Finally, Mr. Schnurr told us, we had a state tournament. And there was no reason, if we worked hard and were determined enough, why we couldn't be the team to win the title.

"Why not Niles West?" he asked calmly but directly. "Why not you girls?"

His words echoed in the tiny gym and we looked at each other dumbfounded. Win? Us? Just by virtue of hard work and determination? We could do that. We wanted to do that. If it's possible to hear another person's heart beating in her chest, then I was sure I could hear Connie's on one side of me and Shirley's on the other.

If we could have played for the state championship right then, we would have. Since we could not, we wordlessly agreed that we would win today's title for the most hardworking and determined team in Illinois. And we would do it tomorrow and the next day and the next.

Charging out of the airless little gym like we were about to play in the Super Bowl, it did not occur to us that we could very well have been one of the smallest, least athletic teams in the state. It was the advantage of ignorance. Mr. Schnurr was the best-known, most highly qualified basketball coach any of us knew, and if he told us we could do it, then so be it.

State champions.

Why not us?

CHAPTER 6

New Beginnings, New Rituals

WE THREW OURSELVES INTO THE 1977 SEASON. There were 12
days until the opening game against Fremd, a team from Palatine,
only about a half hour from Niles West. But they were not in our
conference—the Central Suburban League—and most of us had
never heard of them.

Mrs. Mulder knew about them, however. Fremd's girls' basketball program was older than ours, if only by a couple of years, was
better established, and already had a reputation as perhaps the best
team in the state, having gone 42–0 over the previous four seasons. And so, she decided, scheduling the second game against an
equally strong Libertyville team, she would see right away what she
had and how we stacked up against the best competition. Maybe
someday, she reasoned, this would pay off in state tournament play.

There was to be a new level of dedication on our part, and that
week, Mrs. Mulder sent a note home to our parents, congratulating them on our place on the girls' varsity team and urging their
support.

> You must be wondering what kind of a "crazy
> lady" is in charge here at the high school, because
> I know I have demanded long hours, extremely
> hard work, concentration, and dedication be-
> cause although we start with talent, we must then
> work to build a team.

She concluded by encouraging our parents to come to our
games and saying that she looked forward to meeting them personally.

> Perhaps then you will realize I'm not really mean
> and cruel for working your daughter so hard.
> We're all interested in reaching our goal of being
> the best and strongest team we can be.

This was not the first time we heard her talk about reaching for a goal. Striving for goals became a mantra Arlene Mulder
drilled into us daily. Before each game, she told us, she would be
giving us each an index card on which to write down our team
objectives and individual goals. As much as she learned about
the game of basketball from Mr. Schnurr, he had nothing on
her as a teacher and motivator. This came naturally. But she still
worried. "What if their parents think I'm pushing them into this
boys' world?" she asked her husband, Al. "Into this dark hole?"
The image of the girl with the bloody shin in her gym class never
really left her, even as she was blowing her whistle, demanding
intensity, and urging Bridget and Diana to "be mean" when they
were fighting for rebounds.

Intensity was Mrs. Mulder's favorite word, and it became
ours as well. We shouted it at each other during practice if one
of us was letting down in any way, and soon we incorporated it
with our coach's other favorite theme. Thus, PGI, or Play for your
Goals with Intensity, was born, and we decided we'd yell, "PGI!"

when we broke our huddle before games and at the end of time-outs. Instead of practicing our best autographs or fantasizing about prospective married names, we would doodle PGI in the margins of class notes. It might not have been that clever, but it was sort of a secret code. Our code.

What we knew early on was that something was already much different about this season. After camp at William Penn, we realized we could be pushed physically and, what's more, that we wanted to be. As for the overall commitment, every day was a new lesson. It was not as if we had not been pushed before, but this idea that we could achieve anything with the proper amount of discipline and determination was on a new level most of us had never experienced. While our parents might have expected greatness from us, Mrs. Mulder demanded it.

It was all new terrain. Before basketball, team unity had seemed to be the domain of boys and men, as unfamiliar to us as a pair of shoulder pads, and we had had little access to the lessons of teamwork, understanding roles, and sacrificing for the good of the group. We began to bond in a way the previous year's squad had not. We were becoming more than just better basketball players; we were becoming a team, and all the clichés we had learned in Iowa applied.

Mrs. Mulder would not have it any other way. The first time a reporter called her to write a story on us, she decided that she would never single out any one of her players. Similarly, there was no mention of how many points any of us scored, and all of us knew better than to ever get caught asking about or paying attention to such things, for she believed that detracted from what we were trying to accomplish together.

"I want you dressing nicely for game days, to look like ladies," she told us in our first meeting that season. That meant dressing better than any of us ever did for school normally. That also meant no jeans. Connie was a little nervous about that rule. Most of her clothes were hand-me-down jeans from her brothers, and the only Erickson girl still living at home besides her was her sister Laurie, who Connie feared would kill her if she tried to borrow any of her nicer outfits. But by begging from her parents and scrounging up enough from her own meager savings, Connie was able to buy a couple of new things for our game days.

Oddly, none of us was at all embarrassed by the fact that we were pretty much the only girls in school not wearing jeans. It was, in fact, a source of pride. We felt important. It set us apart. Who are those girls and why are they dressed up? It was sort of cool, though nowhere close to as cool as the brand-new varsity warm-up suits.

I was every bit as excited to finally wear the warm-ups as I was for the basketball season to start. They did not look like girls' warm-ups, which was a huge plus, and yet they were not made for boys either. The fronts of the jacket and pants were white and the backs were red, with red and white stripes down the sides, red collars, wristbands, and waistbands, and—over our hearts—a red script, ironed-on vinyl *NW* that I ran my fingers over. But undoubtedly the best parts of our new ensembles were our numbers—one on the lower right of the jacket and the other on the lower left pants leg.

Our numbers were a big deal, and they soon became as much a part of our identities as our names. But it was still new to us. The year before, another team had actually scouted Niles West games, a concept even Mrs. Mulder had barely heard of, and to counter this, she came up with the cunning plan that she would have us switch jerseys so that the team scouting us would not know who we were.

This might have worked, too, except that one of our best players, Maureen Mostacci, wanted no part of it because her No. 23 was chosen to honor her late mother, whose birthday was February 3. There was also the little matter of the official scorebook, which listed our names and numbers for each game. Unless we were going to dye our hair or wear false mustaches, Mrs. Mulder's plot was foiled.

I was so nervous about getting my new warm-up suit dirty that my father came home with a vinyl suit bag from the dry cleaner, and it seemed like such a great idea that he went back and got 13 more for the rest of the team. After games, the warm-ups were to be put right back in the bags until the next game. No washing them, and God forbid, no throwing them on the floor during the game. Our team managers, Terri and Marcy, would be in charge of scurrying about when one of us went into the game, folding the warm-ups and laying them nicely on the bleachers. Mrs. Mulder's rules.

Almost as thrilling as the warm-ups was a clause we almost missed in the new IHSA executive order, which required light and dark uniforms for the 1977 inaugural girls' basketball state tournament series. The disco look was sweeping the country, but the only fashion we cared about came in the form of red jerseys for away games and new white jerseys for home games, with NILES WEST in, yes, real satin lettering on the tops, though still with ribbed short sleeves that pinched our arms, which we wore with our same tight shorts. People were actually going to know which school we represented. Sort of just like the boys.

Connie and DD decided that with our new warm-ups, our regular old gym shoes looked shabby, and they had the idea of painting over the black stripes on their Adidas with red nail polish. Actually, at a glance, they did look neat, and we figured if we looked sharp, we'd play sharp—or at least look like we played sharp. Either way, it was official now. We were a team. And without having played a single game yet, we at least felt like one of the best in the state.

This was the first year the Niles West girls' teams practiced and played all our games in the Boys' Gym, and we still had to occasionally pinch ourselves that we were really there. The first several practices exhausted us even more than usual because the court had bigger dimensions, but it was, perhaps more than anything else, the sign that we had finally arrived. And if there was any doubt, we were reminded that first game of the season as we shuffled in before the JV game started.

I noticed right away and had to catch my breath. I pointed wordlessly, my mouth opening but nothing actually coming out. The others had seen it as well. Right there, in black and gleaming white, were our names on the scoreboard. Actually, it was our names and numbers in four-inch-high white block letters glued onto two-and-a-half-foot black strips of cardboard slotted into the scoreboard. For years we had grown accustomed to looking up during gym class or while attending the boys' games and seeing their names up there: Zyburt, Bruner, Fabian, Arns. It gave them a celebrity status no less than if they had been in *Sports Illustrated*. And now our names were up there, and we couldn't take our eyes off of them—21 ERICKSON, 10 ISAACSON. Walking off the court and into the locker room, we looked back blinking and refocusing, practically tripping over each other as we did.

In the locker room, we filled out our individual goal cards and practically missed warm-ups we took it so seriously, each of us composing lengthy lists and some of us even adding stick-figure illustrations, using the backs and fronts of our cards as if it were an essay test. I wrote "NO turnovers" at the top of mine, while Connie began her list with "MAKE my free throws," and for Shirley, "BOX OUT for rebounds."

The only thing left after that was the season. And a quick letdown.

We lost to Fremd 63–50 at home, and at Libertyville 47–46 to start the season 0–2. Mrs. Mulder insisted that she did not care about our win-loss record but only that we work hard, improve, and, of course, meet our goals. And we believed her.

We pretty much believed anything she told us. Even when Connie went down hard with a severely sprained ankle and was taken off the court by ambulance in the third quarter of our third game of the season against New Trier West, we didn't really think of the effect it had on our state championship aspirations because Mrs. Mulder had ingrained in us that we were all equal components of the total team effort. No one of us was any more important than another.

Another reason we were distracted from any potential panic over losing one of our best players was that even as she was writhing in pain, Connie was beside herself with embarrassment at the sight of the ambulance, a situation we fully exploited by making fun of her even as she was being carted off on a stretcher. When our student newspaper, the *West Word*, reported in its next edition that she was out for the season, we simply laughed at the misinformation. After all, this was the same paper that still used the ancient expression "cagers" in its headlines for basketball teams. It didn't know Connie like we did. And we didn't know pessimism like seemingly everyone else did.

With Connie sidelined by her sprained ankle, we defeated New Trier West and went on to annihilate Deerfield, Waukegan East, and Niles East before losing 44–41 to Glenbrook South. By the Maine West game on February 25, two weeks and one day after she got hurt, Connie was back on the court, helping us to a 70–41 victory. We would not lose again until the end of March, nine games later.

In general, our starting lineup was Connie and me at guard, Shirley and Diana at forward, and Nancy Hohs at center. But Mrs. Mulder was a big believer in utilizing her entire bench and occasionally rotated a newcomer who had worked especially hard in practice into the starting lineup.

In her effort to instill team play in one of our midseason games, Mrs. Mulder kept Connie on the bench until halfway through the second quarter, at which point she reinserted her, with our team trailing by 19 points. We ended up putting on our full-court press and winning, but the next day Dr. Mannos confronted Mrs. Mulder in the hall.

"Arlene, I don't understand your coaching style. You almost

gave me a heart attack," Mannos told her, shaking his head. "But I guess I can't complain because you keep winning."

Among Mrs. Mulder's requirements was that we attend all the JV games. It was fun sitting in the stands all dressed up, getting psyched up for our game, which started after theirs. Then, in the third quarter, we'd all get up and file into the locker room to change into our uniforms. We felt important, as the JV players and their parents would sneak glances at us as if everyone, not just us, was looking forward to the main event.

But we learned how important this team ritual—and rules in general—was to Mrs. Mulder one day when Toni and Barb Atsaves arrived well after the JV game had started because they were attending their piano recital. The Atsaves girls had told the coach that their mother would not permit them to miss the recital, and they also told her they would not be late for our varsity game. But Mrs. Mulder stood firm. This was their main commitment, she told them, and a piano recital was not an adequate excuse.

We all figured Mrs. Mulder would relent. The Atsaves sisters were terrific students, both cheerleaders, extremely well-mannered, and good team players. While Toni, a junior, was an above-average athlete, it was clear that Barb was going to be something special when she made varsity as a freshman—and she did not disappoint in practice.

But when they walked into the gym, late as they had warned, Mrs. Mulder did not care about their grades or their manners. She told both of them they would be benched for the game.

The rest of us were astonished. Since Mrs. Mulder believed in playing her whole bench, this left us two players down. But more surprising, these were the Atsaves girls, who had probably never gotten in trouble in their whole lives. Toni appeared quietly furious while Barb looked as if she might cry, convinced her basketball career, like the mythical permanent record we all had had hanging over our heads since kindergarten, had been unalterably tainted. But none of us consoled them much beyond a pat on the back. For the first time, it wasn't us versus authority. We had conformed to Mrs. Mulder's army and we followed her every command. If she thought Toni and Barb should be benched, then we did, too.

"They have to make a decision," Connie and I whispered like the newly indoctrinated members of a cult that we were. "They need to get more serious about basketball. They can't have it both ways." Toni and Barb were also trying to balance cheerleading with basketball, and though Connie and I both knew and liked some of the cheerleaders, we clearly considered our pursuit to be eminently more serious and more important. The Atsaves girls had better realize this and climb aboard.

One way or another, we were coming together just as Mrs. Mulder had planned.

As the season progressed, we developed other rules and rituals as important as the games themselves. Mrs. Mulder had us eating and brushing our teeth with our nondominant hands and even sleeping with a basketball because she had read it could cut down on turnovers. She also insisted that we load up on carbs like pancakes and pasta on nights before games.

Connie and I constantly tried to outdo one another with a new ballhandling drill—behind our backs or between our legs—that we had learned in camp or had seen the boys do. And someone commandeered an old record player so that we could listen to The Beach Boys, Queen, Styx, and, only because of my insistence, Barry Manilow singing "It's a Miracle" while we shot free throws before and after practice. We particularly loved "Be True to Your School" by The Beach Boys and all sang in unison to the lyrics, "Now what's the matter buddy, ain't you heard of my school?" We would then shout the next line: "It's number one in the state!"

The male coaches, including Mr. Schnurr, rolled their eyes as the music blared, probably another sign to some of them that girls were not as serious about sports as their boys. But to us, it was just another way to enhance team spirit and to infuse a little added excitement. And we wondered, as the boys trudged out of their practices, sweaty and exhausted, if their coaches weren't just a little envious of our energy and enthusiasm.

Everything was lyrical to us. We adopted Helen Reddy's "I Am Woman" as our unofficial anthem, playing it as we ran onto the court each game through a paper sign as we had seen done before football games. Of course, since there were never many people in the stands, only a handful of parents ever saw this elaborate routine, but it hardly mattered.

Hours before each game, we would line up at the wall of folded-up lacquered wooden bleachers, and as a team—mostly because it took the collective strength of all of us—we would pull them out. And each game we would optimistically pull out one or two more rows in the hope they would actually be necessary.

We also each drew a secret PGI partner from a hat, sort of like a secret Santa for each game, and decorated posters for our PGI partner's locker and brought her little gifts, like candy bars. Bridget's boyfriend, Scott, made Bridget PGI signs for her locker himself, which we snickered about, but it made us all privately jealous and proud we actually had a boy interested enough to buy into our rituals.

In our constant effort to make game days special, we also began the practice of secretly delivering a rose to Mrs. Mulder before each game, which I thought would be nice to accompany with a poem. Except that no one else really wanted to write the poems and I had nothing else to do all day but go to class, so I volunteered. The first one, delivered before the Libertyville game, was not my best, but Mrs. Mulder read it aloud to the team:

> A flower from Thursday
> And a flower for today,
> It's because we think you're special
> In your own funny way.

Soon, they became inspirational in theme:

> Spirit holds our team together,
> United we'll find success,
> But if that bond is ever broken,
> Our future is only a guess.

Other times, I was clearly desperate, and when Mrs. Mulder read this one, I got some unintentional laughs:

> Our most important game is the next one,
> In this case it's Maine East,
> We'll concentrate and make them run,
> Then we'll go to IHOP and feast.

In practice, meanwhile, Mrs. Mulder introduced us to some unconventional techniques. One day, she had us lie on our backs while she turned off all the lights in the South Balcony Gym.

"Relax," she instructed us. "Let every muscle sink into the floor. Start with your face, now your neck, your shoulders." She worked her way down to our toes, then had us visualize what we were supposed to do on the court. Since Connie was working on improving her free throws, she visualized herself with perfect form, total concentration, good follow-through, and the ball swishing through the net. Shirley needed to box out on rebounds, so she pictured herself clearing out space under the basket, going up strong with shoulders squared and holding on to the ball with her elbows out.

We all giggled a little at first. None of us had ever heard of positive visualization, much less tried it. DD usually ended up snoring rather than visualizing. But Mrs. Mulder was always up for something new. And as with everything else she introduced, we accepted it without question.

During her first season, in the middle of a game at Highland

Park that Niles West was losing, Mrs. Mulder had noticed her team was exhausted. She had never studied hypnosis before, didn't necessarily believe in it. But in a fit of desperation during one timeout, she told her players to close their eyes, that they were falling asleep, having a good rest, and when they woke up they'd be suddenly energized.

The players bit their lips to keep from breaking up and shot each other glances that said, "Who is this woman and who put her in charge?" But when they ended up winning, nobody laughed at Mrs. Mulder again.

CHAPTER 7

Shirley's Arm, Bridget's Face, and Mighty Hinsdale South

I NEVER REALLY QUESTIONED where my athletic ability came from. It was just mysteriously there. Mysterious until the one day I was goofing around with my brothers on our backyard rim when I was still in grade school, and my mom came out to throw away the garbage.

"Come on, Mom. Take a shot. Take a shot!" we yelled, hardly able to contain ourselves.

My mother had eventually regained some use of her right arm in the years since her accident—actually amazing function given the severity of her original injuries and the medical limitations at the time. But she had never shot a basketball that we knew of.

"Come on, Mom. Shoot," we giggled.

She looked at us with an expression of utter disdain that said if we were going to be that patronizing, we'd better be prepared to be very sorry for it. Then she demanded the ball, clutched it in her left hand, and released a hook shot so sweet that it weakened us at the knees and barely rippled the net as it went through.

The backyard erupted. And my mom, just as cool and smug as could be, turned on her heel and walked back into the house, her basketball career over. Perfect.

The point is, my mom was a great athlete. My brothers and I had to get it from somewhere, and we had deduced, after about the 12th time my dad broke his glasses playing catch with us, that it hadn't come from him. It had just never occurred to us that my mom could have possessed those genes.

She later pointed to a small scar on her knee and told me it came from a bully's shove during a neighborhood stickball game when she was a girl. For a chosen few during the early years of World War II, there was tennis, golf, and track and field, and for a very select group, the All-American Girls Professional Baseball League. But there were certainly no organized sports for girls like my mother.

I was already starting to take it for granted. But there were still some little, shall we say, nuances of the game we had not yet mastered. It seemed just as we started thinking we knew it all, something would happen to tell us we did not.

Hence, the ball-rolling incident.

I had seen it on TV, well at least once, and maybe in a varsity boys' game as well, and couldn't wait to try it myself. In an attempt to milk the clock at the end of a quarter in order to get off one last shot, the guard receiving the inbounds pass after the opposing team's basket—provided he was unguarded on his end of the court—would let the ball bounce downcourt untouched (knowing the clock does not start until it is touched inbounds) before scooping it up and starting the offense.

It seemed to me that the ball hardly bounced at all as the guard galloped next to it but rather sort of skimmed along the floor. At least that's how I had envisioned it. And I could not wait until I was in the featured role—that of the guard who let the ball bounce untouched. But wanting to hasten this brilliant play, I, as the person passing the ball inbounds, decided to roll the ball to Connie to get things started.

Surely I believed she would know what I was doing, as she was always up for innovation. Perhaps it was because I failed to warn her what I was about to do that my good intentions unraveled. Or more likely, it was because in my excitement, I rolled the basketball with the velocity of a bowling ball, which Connie, along with the eight other players on the court at the time, simply stared at in shock as it went whizzing by.

When it reached the other side of the court, it was promptly scooped up by an alert opposing player, who raced back upcourt and past a still-stunned Connie for an uncontested layup.

In a somewhat quieter fashion, Peggy Japely was also learning exactly how the game of basketball was played. Now that she had made the JV team, she was starting to gain some notice, though not always in ways she wanted. In her first game on JV, the first organized game of her life, Peggy was sitting on the bench when the coach motioned for her to enter the game and, like any obedient kid, she headed straight on court. Trouble was, she had failed to sign in at the scorers' table—this entailed saying something like "10 in for 21"—where an official would then signal her to come into the game as both the rules required and most kids fully understood by seventh grade. The game was still in play when Peggy bounded onto the court, some obvious confusion ensuing, the whistle blowing, and Miss Majewski motioning her back off with the admonition that she needed to sign in.

"Where do I sign?" she asked, to the howls of the other players.

By the end of the season, Peggy was practicing with varsity.

We defeated Maine South 54–51 on March 11 in our last regular-season game of the 1977 season to clinch the Central Suburban

League South title with a 13–4 record. That week, the first letter to the editor in the school paper began:

> Dear Editor,
>
> I would like to bring to the attention of the entire student body the apparent neglect of girls' sports teams here at Niles West. There have been pep rallies for the football team and fan buses to the boys' basketball games, but there is no attempt to get the students behind the girls' teams.

The lack of support was starting to bug us a little, too. At first, we watched with pride as we had to pull out new rows of bleachers to accommodate the growing number of fans. But going from five rows to eight was not good enough. After the boys' varsity team had gone to the Sweet 16 and finished with a 23–5 record the year before, they were now devoid of returning seniors and had finished 7–18, yet still had drawn better crowds than we had.

I thought about it a lot, so much so that for my seventh-period expository writing class, I turned in a paper entitled "Varsity: Girls vs. Boys," in which I detailed the ways in which I felt girls' teams were discriminated against.

I wrote about our lack of practice jerseys, leather basketballs (unlike the boys, we practiced with vinyl ones), and bags for the basketballs to be stored in (we gathered ours in an old shopping cart Mrs. Mulder found or stole), as well as the disparity in locker rooms, training equipment, and facilities. "Gym space for the boys' varsity is always available. However, where the girls are concerned, much 'bargaining' has to be done before any gym space is acquired," I wrote with indignation.

I detailed the differences in media coverage and attendance for girls' versus boys' games and the fact that referees were paid more for officiating boys' games than girls' "with no logical explanation." I concluded hopefully, but with some resignation, that this was just the way it was.

> I realize that boys' varsity basketball has been in existence much longer than the girls' and therefore not as much should be expected. The Niles West girls are even "lucky" in a sense because at other schools, the situation is worse.
>
> In years to come, girls may be a lot closer in comparison to the boys. As I said before, we have progressed a long way already. For example, before this year there was one set of warm-up suits for all the girls' teams. Last year, the contest gym was not available for any girls' basketball games. Now, the situation is changing.
>
> This year, the first annual girls' state basketball tournament will be held and next year, the schedule of games will be doubled. I don't expect that girls' athletics will ever be equal to the boys', which is sad because a lot of talent may pass unnoticed and, in a sense, be wasted.
>
> I am grateful, however, that there are any athletics for girls to participate as well as to compete in. I only hope that in years to come, a female won't find any setbacks in her quest to become an athlete.

I received a B-plus for that effort, which was probably a little generous on Mr. Klebba's part. While we were jealous of the boys and their privileges, I would not say we resented them.

To prepare us for the postseason, Mr. Schnurr continued to help us, even handpicking a team of boys who, though not on his team, were good athletes and, more importantly, nice guys who were more than willing to scrimmage against us.

Again, however, Mrs. Mulder worried what our parents would think. Playing with boys? And not just with boys but against them? For those of us who grew up with older brothers, an occasional elbow to the nose was within reason. But she was concerned and so was Mr. Schnurr, who picked boys who were on the small side but quick and agile and, unbeknownst to us, cautioned them not to block our shots or play too rough. Shirley and Connie and I loved it. We wanted Mr. Schnurr to pick apart our games, to make us better, tougher. And we loved mixing it up with the boys, though we spent much of our first practice sessions with them just walking through plays.

It was a heady week after securing our conference title, but we were not the biggest news at Niles West. Citing fatigue, Billy Schnurr quietly resigned as the boys' basketball coach after his 16th season ended, shocking the student body and staff. He would remain at the school as a PE instructor, he said, but at 49 he was worn out.

The fact that we were still receiving his words of wisdom, even as he made his announcement, made us feel privileged.

Our first postseason was just days away, but somehow we still did not quite grasp the responsibility that came with it. Or at least not when there was the possibility of a good laugh involved. One day after practice, we were talking in the parking lot when a sophomore on the JV team decided to suddenly peel out in her car. The only trouble was that at the time, Shirley was sitting on her hood. She fell off and immediately grabbed her elbow as we all yelled at the girl for being an idiot. Shortly after determining that Shirley was fine, we also decided that the girl had been just a little too flip in her reaction, driving off quickly when we started to give her a hard time.

And so a plan was quickly hatched.

The next day at practice, Shirley showed up wearing a fake cast on her arm as the rest of us feigned shock and devastation. Just as the sophomore's face began to drain of color, Shirley pulled off the cast, clapped her hands for the ball and dribbled off, leaving the rest of us to roll on the court with laughter.

This was all, of course, planned carefully so as to occur before Mrs. Mulder came into the gym for the start of practice. She was not in a particularly humorous mood on the brink of her first postseason game, and we assumed she would not find it funny that her star forward had been bounced off the hood of a car the day before.

But we weren't always so careful. After practice the day before our game, I picked up a wet towel and threw it at Shirley. She, of course, threw one back and soon it became an all-out water fight with most of the team involved. Before long, we were all sliding through puddles on the locker room floor, our towels now serving as effective towropes. It was all great fun until, as luck would have it, I whipped around a corner and slid directly into Mrs. Mulder, who had just walked in.

"I guess you don't take tomorrow's game seriously," she said, her nostrils flaring and lips pursing, giving new meaning to our secret nickname for her: Mean Arlene. "Maybe with that attitude, you shouldn't play," she said as I struggled to get to my feet, instead slipping back down on the smooth, wet concrete floor while my teammates stifled laughter behind Mrs. Mulder's back.

More damning words I could not have imagined, and I slunk home convinced my basketball career, and life as I knew it, was over. Too embarrassed to tell my mom or anyone else who hadn't been there, I barely ate dinner and was staring at my homework when the phone rang that night. Though she had never before called my house, I knew it was her.

"Are you ready to play tomorrow?" our coach's voice barked.

"Yes," I trembled. "I'm sorry. That was not smart."

"No, it wasn't," she said and hung up.

The first-ever Illinois girls' state regional tournaments were played March 14–17, with Niles West hosting one of them. We needed the home-court advantage. After getting past a much taller Luther North team in the first game, 52–43, we were trailing St. Scholastica—a tough all-girls Catholic school with a particularly physical star player in six-footer JoAnn Feiereisel—by nine points at the half of the regional final.

Feiereisel's father, Ron, had been an honorable mention all-American for Ray Meyer at DePaul in the early 1950s and had had a brief NBA career with the Minneapolis Lakers. His daughter was the tallest and most physical player we had ever faced, and our 5-10 center, Nancy Hohs, had her hands full.

As we filed into the locker room at halftime, more than one of us were thinking about our goals. On our index cards, there was the usual: make free throws, follow missed shots, no bad shots, get good rebounding position, play with intensity but with cool heads.

But Mrs. Mulder read a card from a new contributor.

> Coach Mulder and every team member,
>
> From now until nine o'clock, you must be totally possessed with just one thought—putting everything you can possibly muster into playing the fiercest, most intense basketball game of your young life. If you do that with good defense, strong rebounding, and no cheap scores for the opponent, you will win.
>
> Best of luck.
> B. Schnurr

As she read, we felt the hairs on our arms standing up. We remembered Mr. Schnurr's pep talk at the start of the season. Why not us? We did not want to let him down.

We ended up beating St. Scholastica by five, and afterward, we spontaneously went over to the scorers' table where Mr. Schnurr was the official scorekeeper, and one by one, each of us stepped up and gave him a hug. I sneaked in a kiss on the cheek as well.

He was a shy man, and you could tell he was a little shocked at first, but you didn't have to look too closely to see his eyes were twinkling.

Next, someone told us we should cut down the nets. Most of us had never heard of such a thing, but it was a celebratory ritual and sounded good to us. We weren't exactly sure how we were supposed to get up there, nor what to do exactly once we did, but someone grabbed a tape cutter and up we went—DD standing on Diana's shoulders, me on Connie with Shirley steadying one of my legs, and Barb standing on Nancy and holding on to the rim for dear life.

Connie tried to tell me how to snip the net so that each one of us would get a strand; I tried, but I was pretty sure I wasn't doing it right. My strand looked a little shorter than the rest. Mrs. Mulder looked up nervously, afraid that we would fall and break someone's collarbone and, knowing her, sure we were violating some school rule by cutting up their basketball nets. Finally, we just tore down each net and draped one around Nancy's neck and the other around Shirley's.

We stood by the scorers' table as our families and friends surged all around us, Connie grabbing at Nancy's arm, me grabbing at Connie, Shirley holding up her index finger, and little Alison Mulder standing before her mother and trying to take it all in. They were cheering us, both students who knew us and many who did not, and I knew in this instant that there could be nothing finer than winning a basketball game for your school.

If we were not already thoroughly intoxicated by competition and the many joys of team sports, we were now. If this was what it felt like to win, we wanted more. The four-team state sectionals were next. The next round was at Maine South, where we would face another parochial school in Timothy Christian.

After clinging to a 21–19 lead at halftime, we finally shook Timothy Christian in the fourth quarter with our press, outscoring them 22–4 in the final eight minutes. But with 31 seconds left and the outcome no longer in doubt, Bridget took an elbow in the eye and had to be taken to the hospital for stitches. We beat Timothy 51–30, but we were worried about Bridget. Up until then, she had not exactly established herself as one of the toughest players on our team. At the first sight of blood, she screamed for her mom.

At some point during the season, Shirley had broken her pinkie finger and never told a soul about it, including her mother, for fear she would be forced to stop playing. But Bridget was not Shirley. Despite her 5-9 frame, Bridget was slightly built and tended to play like a girl. To that end, her goal card for regionals read: "I didn't achieve my goal last time, so I still want to be mean and possess the ball, not deflect it."

At the hospital as she prepared to get stitches, Bridget was pretty much consumed by two thoughts—that she was permanently disfigured and that her teammates hated her. Since the doctor wouldn't let her see her face, she figured she was hideous, and looking at her reflection in the lid of the metal wastebasket did nothing to dissuade her.

"What?" the doctor said as Bridget moaned. "Is your face your fortune or something?"

Bridget was one of those girls we just didn't know very well. She had moved to Morton Grove during eighth grade after being raised on a farm downstate and had not one friend when she entered Niles West. She had not once considered going out for the basketball team until Mrs. Mulder came up to her in gym class and suggested she give it a try.

"But I don't think I'm any good," Bridget had said.

"It doesn't matter," Mulder had responded. "I want you to try."

Wanting desperately to gain acceptance and please everyone, Bridget would have consented to go out for the knife-throwing team at that point.

Three years later, during her first full season on varsity, she had what we all knew was a serious boyfriend in Scott, a fact that impressed most of us but only made Bridget feel left out. We didn't know that. Nor did we know that her parents had just separated, which left her resentful toward her mom, who soon started seeing another man, and more dependent on her dad.

Bob Berglund was a handsome guy for a father, or otherwise. He was 6-foot-4 with dark, wavy hair and long sideburns, and he wore blue jeans and looked like the Marlboro Man. And when he came to our games, it was always an event for Bridget. He'd bring enough Big Red gum for everyone in the gym and always offered to take the team out for dinner or ice cream afterward, which he did several times, even though Bridget knew he couldn't afford it.

On the many other occasions the team would go out for dinner after games, Bridget was often a no-show. We figured she didn't want to come with us. But for Bridget, it actually meant one of two things. She was either out with Scott, whom she didn't get to see all week since he went to another high school, or it was an opportunity for her to see her father, whom she missed terribly during her parents' separation.

Bridget adored her father. When she got her first pair of leather high-top Converse and was afraid they would get wet in the snow, her father carried her to their car. To us, she was a bit of a princess, and when she showed up for practice the day after she was elbowed, sporting a butterfly bandage and ready for the sectional final against Resurrection, we were shocked and more than a little impressed by her toughness.

To our surprise, the school announced that it would supply a bus to take fans to the game. Apparently, word had finally circulated that we were pretty good and our games entertaining and, oh yeah, that we were two wins away from becoming the first-ever Niles West basketball team to go downstate. In no small way, the boys we scrimmaged against in practice had become our most effective salesmen. Once they began helping us, they started coming to games and then more boys and, naturally, girls followed.

The Resurrection game was another defensive slugfest, but

their best player fouled out in the third quarter, and we slipped by with a 39–31 victory to advance to supersectionals and a showdown with Hinsdale South at Addison Trail High School. The winner would advance to the inaugural Illinois girls' state basketball championship.

Out of the 475 schools to enter the first-ever girls' state tournament, we were one of the top 16. Our supersectional game, to be played the following Tuesday, the traditional day for boys' basketball supersectionals in Illinois, was going to be on the radio, which both thrilled and scared us, despite the fact that nobody had actually heard of the radio station broadcasting the game.

We had, however, heard of Hinsdale South, a school in the southwest suburbs, and their freshman sensation Dawn Hallett. A 5-9 lefty who, everyone marveled, had only one year of organized basketball experience, Hallett had been nearly unstoppable in sectionals, with 27 points and 10 rebounds in the title game. Put her together with Hinsdale's 6-2 senior center, Debbie Lueken, and we were more than a little intimidated. On top of that, word of the game was spreading throughout our school, and the Addison Trail school officials were expecting a big crowd.

In the *Chicago Sun-Times* on the day of the game, famed prep sports writer Taylor Bell profiled Hinsdale South coach Lynne Slouber. The profile focused on the hardships of being a wife, mother, and coach and on Slouber's husband, Mark, handling the "babysitting" duties in caring for their six-year-old son while Lynne coached basketball for three months. "There's only one more week of basketball," Slouber was quoted as saying. "After that, Mark said I could buy a new dress and we'd go to Pheasant Run [a local resort] for a weekend."

In another Bell column, Slouber admitted to feeling the burden of competing in a state tournament. "It scares me," Slouber said. "Many women don't want the kind of pressure that the boys have. We lose a game and I hear someone say, 'Maybe someone ought to help Mrs. Slouber." All sports should be fun first and winning second. But that's not the way it is."

The night before our game, Marquette defeated North Carolina for the NCAA basketball title in an epic upset for the team from nearby Milwaukee and its popular coach, Al McGuire. It was inspiring, and we tried to feed off of it. We certainly could not imagine our own season ending. And yet, with a record of 13–3 to Hinsdale's 19–1, we wondered if we were not about to meet a team for the first time that was more skilled than we were.

Their uniforms struck us first. They were the flashiest we had ever seen, black with electric gold piping, the shorts looking suspiciously like the ones the boys wore rather than our plain, tight red ones. And when the Hinsdale South players ran onto the court, seemingly in perfect lockstep, they jump-stopped at each corner, then sharply reversed direction before jogging to the next corner. We were playing the Harlem Globetrotters. Great.

We sneaked glances at the stands, which seemed dominated by Hinsdale South fans. "Where we going? Where we going? State, state! State, state!" they chanted.

Our own crowd on the other side of the gym was bigger than we had enjoyed all season, which only made me more jittery. Shirley flexed the swollen finger on her shooting hand, trying not to wince.

What had we gotten ourselves into? Yeah, sure, "Why not Niles West?" I'll tell you why not us, I thought to myself. Because we're scared out of our shorts, that's why. Because this team with their professional uniforms and giant freshman is good, really good. Because we're not ready for all of this. I stared at Shirley and Connie, hoping their inner voices were braver than mine. But for the first time all season, I could sense our lack of confidence.

Nancy and Shirley exchanged glances as the 6-2 Lueken walked into the center circle for the opening tip, and Shirley saw fear in Nancy's eyes. And when the game began, the nerves manifested in our mass confusion. Connie and I were playing our usual 2-1-2 zone defense, while it looked like Shirley and Diana were in a man defense. Nancy was doing a little bit of both. We screamed at each other in an effort to correct ourselves but could barely be heard above the din. Passes that had been crisp and accurate all season now sailed wide and long and past the outstretched fingertips of our teammates. Before we knew it, it was halftime and we were trailing 29–19.

We could barely find Shirley in the jungle that was Hinsdale South's 2-3 defense, much less get her the ball. And Hallett was unbelievable. The kid just did not miss. She ended up hitting 70 percent of her field goal attempts for 24 points.

We whittled down an 11-point lead to five, helped by a pair of free throws by DD and a layup by Shirley off an inbounds play with five and a half minutes left in the game, but Hinsdale South called a timeout, and we never got closer. Shirley ended up with 18 points, but it wasn't enough. Our next-highest scorer was Diana with seven. Connie finished with six. And we lost 50–39.

Nancy, our only senior, buried her head in her hands on the bench afterward as one by one, friends and family walked over and whispered words of consolation in her ear. The rest of us fought off tears, realizing that we were simply beaten by a better team.

A reporter approached Shirley. "What are your future plans?" he asked.

"I think we're going to start practicing tomorrow," she replied.

Shirley couldn't imagine returning to school.

How could she face all those teachers she had begged to come to games, not to mention the boys who had scrimmaged with us and would now think we let them down? We choked, and that was unacceptable, and she was damn sure not going to let anyone see her cry, which she was bound to do if anyone tried to talk to her.

It was as good a time as any to go get the finger x-rayed, she figured. But after having the splint applied to what was indeed a fracture, she decided she might as well go to class. Every eye in the room focused on her as she slinked to her desk, trying desperately to blot each tear before anyone noticed.

It was not until after school, when she decided on the spot to forgo the spring's softball season after being a standout her first two years, that she began to feel better. Basketball would be her priority now. She would play tennis and volleyball the next fall and winter, but starting today, she would go back to the gym, splint or no splint. We needed to start practicing immediately if we were going to win state the next year. And no discussion was necessary to determine that was exactly what we intended to do.

Letters continued to appear in the *West Word* about our lack of fan support, buoying our spirits and solidifying our determination.

"The Niles West varsity basketball team (girls) lost last night to a good Hinsdale South team," one letter began. "I don't feel the girls got the attention they deserved in their super effort to try and win the state championship." It ended with the writer congratulating us on a fine season. "Maybe they didn't capture the state championship this year," it read, "but a state championship can't be too far off for this team!" It was signed, "Sincerely, Impressed Male, Class of '79," which impressed us as well.

Before anything, however, there were a few details to take care of. Hinsdale South had made us look silly with their cool pregame warm-up routine, and Connie and I decided it was up to the two of us to make up one for next season. It would be a ball-handling routine, and it would have to be great, the kind of stuff we had been fooling around with since camp at William Penn, dribbling through our legs and behind our backs. We started planning it the day after our loss.

Our next order of business was deciding that we were going to Illinois State University to watch Hinsdale South and the first-ever girls' state tournament that weekend. Shirley, Connie, and I piled into Mrs. Mulder's small car, while the rest of the team drove with the JV coach and trainer. Bridget told us her parents couldn't afford to send her, and she stayed home.

Mrs. Mulder's greatest concern was Shirley. It was Passover, and Shirley's parents had OK'd the trip, as had mine. But our coach knew that Shirley's family was more religious than mine, and she knew that Mrs. Cohen had told Shirley to make sure to observe the holiday.

Mrs. Mulder quietly worried as she turned onto the highway. She was not in the business of disappointing our parents, but this was all foreign territory to her. She didn't know how to make sure Shirley would observe the holiday.

As the only other Jew on the team, I stepped up.

"You know, Shirley," I said, as straight-faced as I could, "maybe we should go to a truck stop and see if they have gefilte fish. We can have a seder."

Shirley did not find it all that funny, nor did Mrs. Mulder, who became stricken by the thought that maybe we really did need to go on a gefilte fish hunt. "You can lead us, Shirley," Mrs. Mulder said. "It will be educational for all of us."

"Yeah, Shirley," I said. "You can lead us."

Shirley shot me a dirty look, and sure enough, Mrs. Mulder steered us into the back room of a roadside smorgasbord restaurant, explaining to the manager that we needed a private area for a special religious ceremony. We had to bite our lips to keep from laughing. But Mrs. Mulder was so sincere, never cracking so much as a smile, we managed to control ourselves. She even convinced the restaurant that we needed a little bit of wine in plastic cups. OK, so maybe this wouldn't be so bad.

Shirley and I lurched our way through a pseudo seder, though without matzoh, a shank bone, or bitter herbs of any kind, we were pretty much forced to sing a couple verses of "Dayenu" and call it a day. At least Mrs. Mulder was happy.

Once in Normal two hours later, we shuffled into the Horton Field House for the state tournament, equal parts excited to be there and depressed to be in street clothes. Even though we knew Hinsdale South was a good team, it still hurt to think of them here. They would be playing Fremd, also 20–1, in the first game, and we weren't sure whom to root for or whether or not we even cared. Wallowing in self-pity, we went to purchase the $1 programs. "Hey!" someone yelled. "Look, it's Bridget."

And there, sure enough, on the cover of the first girls' state basketball tournament program, inside an outline of the state of Illinois, was a photograph of our starting center guarding a girl from Libertyville.

Quickly overcoming our initial jealousy at not making the cover ourselves, we screamed and cheered, all while trying to appear cool, of course. Suddenly, we all felt a little more important as we took our seats, thinking we might even be recognized as Sweet 16 finalists and fanning ourselves with our programs so everyone could see.

We ended up rooting for Fremd, reasoning that their school was geographically closer to Niles West than Hinsdale South, and besides, the pain was still fresh from our supersectional defeat. Fremd won a thriller over Hinsdale South, 48–47, but that night fell to eventual state champion Sterling, 69–57. By then we had gotten over our disappointment, but we still hated every team there and vowed this would not happen to us again.

Once back home, I returned to softball, starting in center field for the varsity team for the second year while Connie surprised me only a bit with her decision to join Shirley in giving up softball and spending the spring and summer concentrating on basketball.

Ever the writer and the suck-up, I wrote a letter to Dr. Mannos, thanking him for the tickets he provided us for the state tournament. "Next year, you won't have to worry about where we sit," I wrote. "We'll have the best seats in the house (on the court)."

Days later, in Mr. Skuban's homeroom, I was handed an envelope with notepaper inside that had "Memo from N. J. Mannos" across the top. Very impressive, though I thought it best not to share our principal's letter with anyone else around me.

> Dear Missy,
>
> Thank you for your kind note. I was very pleased that you had the opportunity to attend the first state girls' basketball tournament. It was an exciting affair! I'm with you 100 percent—next year I am sure that you will have the best seats in the house—right on the basketball court!
>
> Keep up the excellent pride and esprit de corps that has been established in the girls' basketball program. Delighted that you had a good time at the tournament.

In April, we had our basketball banquet, the first time we had our own banquet separate from the usual sports awards dinner, and we insisted that Mr. Schnurr be a part of it. Many of the parents thanked Mrs. Mulder, which finally seemed to ease her fear that they all thought she had inflicted on us irreversible physical and psychological harm. And they gave her special praise for getting us to dress up occasionally, given that they were seldom able to do the same.

Then Toni Atsaves played the piano—a delicious irony we all privately noted—Mr. Schnurr gave a speech on perspective, and Mrs. Mulder read all of my poems from the season. But the best part of the night came at the end, when we were given real varsity letters, just like the boys. None of us knew they were coming, and we could not have been any happier had they handed us diamond rings.

When we got home that night, I got a couple of straight pins out of my mom's sewing basket and pinned my varsity letter to an old windbreaker I put on over my pajamas, imagining how it might look if girls actually had varsity letterman jackets. Then my mom and I sat at the kitchen table, talking about the season, about how nice it was of Mrs. Mulder to include my poems in the program, and how good Toni was at piano.

"I'm so proud of you, honey," my mom gushed.

Later, I sat propped up between my parents in their bed, coaxing more compliments out of them on the season, how well I played, and how fun it all was until both of them fell asleep on me. This year, I noticed, I was the one tucking my parents in and not the other way around. I also noticed I had to remind them about some of the season highlights, even my season-high 10-point game I thought they should have remembered. When my dad forgot things like this, I just ascribed it to his general absentmindedness. Our family always laughed that he was a few sentences behind in our dinner table discussions. My mom was the sharp one, but lately, she seemed kind of absentminded, too.

I was too tired to analyze it, so I focused on the fact that in these last few months, my parents were happier, more connected. Our games became an event my mom and dad genuinely looked forward to, and as I lay in bed that night, I felt good about doing that for them.

When the Niles West yearbooks came out that week, I shyly slipped mine onto Mrs. Mulder's desk and walked away. When I retrieved it a little later, I thumbed through it to read what she had written, but there was nothing. Not in the front or back where all my friends had signed, or in the sports section, where Connie had taken up a whole page, or under her picture, which is what she did last year and what Mr. Schnurr had done, signing, "Good Luck in basketball next season. B. Schnurr" under the picture of him in his cardigan sweater.

I figured she hadn't had time, and I was too embarrassed to give it back to her. It wasn't until days later, as I flipped through it a little more thoroughly, that I recognized the blue marker and the neat cursive on page 127, under the headline STUDENT APATHY INCREASES and above a picture of an empty classroom.

> Missy—Thanks to all of you this page does not apply to girls' basketball. Besides basketball, you're quite a girl—don't allow anyone to discourage you—keep your enthusiasm and that "little girl" quality—you can be 40 and still have it. Don't judge others too quickly and don't make decisions too quickly. Above all, be patient with me and all of my "meanness." I enjoy working with you and look forward to camp. Enjoy the summer, work at b-ball—grow in your jump—it may someday match the size of your heart! Fondly, Mrs. Mulder.
>
> P.S. Stay hungry.

I closed the book and opened it again slowly. This time, I noticed something I had not seen before. Mrs. Mulder had written on a page with several color photographs of a sunset, a snowy path through a forest, a boat cutting through fog, and a red rose in full bloom with water droplets on its petals.

In that familiar blue marker, she had drawn an arrow pointing to the rose. And next to the arrow she wrote: "A very special picture."

CHAPTER 8

Dark Secrets

BEING A 15-YEAR-OLD in the summer of 1977 meant I could work as an assistant counselor at Lincolnwood Recreation Day Camp, but I couldn't be paid. It meant I had friends who could drive, but no one had cars. It meant that it was going to be a long summer, and it meant that with Connie seemingly a million miles away in Morton Grove and Shirley in New Jersey visiting her relatives, there was no one to play basketball with every day as I had planned.

Apparently, Shirley was not much happier. In her latest letter, she described in painful detail how her family's car broke down on the way to New Jersey. But if that was supposed to cheer me up, it did not. Her next paragraph detailed the "mansion" she was staying in with four floors and 10 bedrooms and a backyard 10 times the size of hers. But she did say she was bored stiff and had no friends, so that made me feel a little better.

Shirley never talked too much about these trips east she made every summer, seemingly against her will. The mansion was her grandfather's house; her mother's father was an importer of children's clothing. The community in which she was ensconced was basically the entire Sephardic Jewish population of Brooklyn. They came to Deal, New Jersey, every summer, a tight-knit group that looked after one another and cared about each other, a group where the women cooked and shared recipes, got their nails done, and shopped for shoes while their husbands provided for all their basic needs and much more. Mostly, their income came from importing and exporting, and mostly, like Shirley's grandfather, it was in the garment business.

It was a world where the husbands made exotic buying trips to Hong Kong while their daughters had great figures and wore high heels to the pool and did not go to college for, surely, they would just get married anyway. And it was a place where Shirley's parents hoped Shirley and her older sister, Denise, eventually would find a suitable (read: rich) husband.

Shirley knew all about her parents' intentions, but while the other girls in New Jersey were busy applying makeup and talking about which shoes to buy, she worked as a cook's helper at a summer camp, played one-on-one whenever she could get up a game, and worried that the rest of us were working harder than she was.

"I swear I'm all excited for b-ball already," she wrote to me in August. "Maybe it's because I haven't played too much. I played a boy (15 yrs. old and good) and I beat him but it was close and I should have wiped him. But nevertheless, I AM HUNGRY."

We were hungry, too. Well, some of us, anyway. Connie and I were signed up for Niles West's two-week basketball camp, but we were a little concerned that Diana and Bridget were not. What we didn't know was that Diana was doing missionary work for the Mormon Church with her family that summer and that Bridget's parents told her they couldn't afford to send her to camp.

Mrs. Mulder, wanting to spend more time with her family, handed over the basketball camp reins to Mr. Schnurr and made periodic visits. Connie and I could have stayed there all day instead of the couple of hours we had each morning, savoring the time we had with Mr. Schnurr. Besides, any extra time in the gym was still considered a treat, and despite our best intentions, it was pretty much the only time we ever got to play together that summer.

I rode my bike the five miles from my house to Niles West, then went back to work at Proesel Park for my assistant counselor duties. After basketball camp ended, both of us went back to work full-time—me as a counselor and Connie, who had turned 16 in January, as a waitress at a restaurant in Morton Grove. With Connie not having a driver's license and with both of us working, we may as well have been on separate coasts.

And so we had to be content to give each other daily phone reports on our progress. Connie worked the playground and Morton Grove Community Center hard, while I shot on our backyard hoop and picked up games with male camp counselors whenever I could, which frankly did not do me a lot of good unless I could find miniature camp counselors. In between, I set up folding chairs in the backyard, as I had done since I was eight, and tried to work on dribbling with my nondominant hand. I was a good ball handler, could dribble through most any press, and was great at dribbling through my legs, which would work out wonderfully if that opportunity ever presented itself in a game and Mrs. Mulder would not promptly remove me from the team for trying it. But I was still weak going to my left side, and any defender who had any head at all could exploit that, as my brothers had been telling me for years.

Peggy had something to work toward as well, and suddenly the body to work with. After spending the last part of the season on the varsity roster for practice purposes, she was now 5-10 and among the tallest girls we had coming back next season. Her mom, noticing the newfound enthusiasm in her daughter and looking for something to keep her busy, took note of an advertisement for Badger-Sloan basketball camp in the church bulletin.

Ed Badger was the head coach of the Chicago Bulls, and

former Bulls great Jerry Sloan was doing part-time work as a scout and struggling to find a niche after his career was ended prematurely by a knee injury the season before. Their camp was in Angel Guardian Gym, where the Bulls practiced on the city's North Side, and it took Peggy, her mother, and Peg's friend Holly Andersen, an incoming Niles West freshman, three bus transfers to get there from Morton Grove.

Charming but run-down, Angel Guardian was once the site of one of the largest orphanages in Chicago. To Peggy, it may as well have been Chicago Stadium, and she trembled in Sloan's presence the first time they met. One of the most intense competitors in the history of the game and a future Hall of Fame coach, Sloan, unbeknownst to most, had grown up in a tiny southern Illinois town where he played on a grade-school team with three girls, and he now had a soft spot for female athletes. Sloan felt bad because the girls were the best players on their team but had to settle for becoming cheerleaders and pom-pom girls when they got to high school.

Peggy and her mother walked into the gym and found Sloan.

"All I have is $20 with me," Peg's mom told him while Peggy cowered by her side, "but I get paid next week. Is there any way I can pay you in installments?"

Sloan looked down at Peggy, eyes narrowed. "Do you want to play ball?" he asked. Peggy felt as though Sloan could see right through her. Since she had made JV last year, she knew her game was improving, but she also knew she needed to work harder if she wanted to make varsity next season.

"Very much," she stammered.

"Well then, forget the money," he said. "Get out there."

But Peggy's mom had another small problem. "I don't get off work until five," she told Sloan. "Can she sit in the gym for an hour until I pick her up?"

Peggy flushed. How much more could her mother embarrass her? "Don't worry," said Sloan, "I'll take her home."

That day, Peggy and Holly rode home in Sloan's Lincoln Town Car, and Peggy thought it was a limousine. By the end of the summer, she had met his wife, shot hoops with his kids in their driveway in suburban Northbrook, about 20 minutes from Peg's house, and for all intents and purposes, found herself another family.

I loved Jerry Sloan. So did my mom. We were Bulls fans, of course, as most Chicagoans were, and you could not help but admire Sloan's aggressive style of play. We also thought he was adorable. But mostly, Sloan was the guy no player wanted to have guard him, and no one dove for loose balls or took charges like Sloan did. That was the way he played, and it was the way he expected those whom he coached to play, whether they were men or teenage girls. I had been to Angel Guardian Gym to watch the Bulls and Sloan practice while he was still playing, but I had no idea he had a girls' camp or maybe I would have signed up, too. It was Peggy's secret. And Jerry was Peg's new hero.

But Peg had a few other secrets.

She lived on the second story of a four-family two-flat in Morton Grove with her mother and two brothers, Al and Michael. Her mom worked as a secretary and didn't own a car. That much I knew. A lot of other things, I did not. When Peg's freshman English teacher, Mr. DuBois, joked one day to the class, "You know you're old when you start reading the obituaries," Peggy grimaced.

She had been scanning the obits since she had learned to read at age six. Every day she looked for her father's name, praying that he had died.

If anyone ever asked, she would tell them her father was dead. She considered her stepfather, Ted Japely, to be her father anyway, so she figured she was only half-lying—Ted had died of leukemia when Peggy was six. Her biological father, Al King, had been diagnosed as schizophrenic. The day she was born, Peggy's mother, Mary, called him at a bar to tell him she was going into labor. He told her he didn't have time to go to any hospital.

One day when Peggy was seven or eight, her father dressed up as a priest and showed up at St. Monica's, the Catholic school Peggy and her brother Al attended in Chicago.

"It's Al King—it's Al King!" Peggy screamed to her brother. "He's here."

They didn't call him "Dad" but "Al King" because he was like a character to them. A monster. Peggy's brother Al asked the nuns if he and his sister could go inside and practice their handwriting, and once inside, Peggy told her teacher, "That's my father out there."

"Yes, that's right, that's Father King," the nun replied.

"No, no, that's Al King," Peggy said frantically. "Call my mother at work."

After that, Mary made sure that Peggy and her brother stayed at the convent after school every day until she could pick them up, which only enhanced their reputation as outsiders. Once, in second grade, Peggy was with some girls in the neighborhood when she saw her father sprinting past, four cops in full pursuit.

"Isn't that your dad?" the girls asked as she shrunk in embarrassment.

"No, I don't think so," said Peggy as the police tackled him to the ground and threw him into the paddy wagon.

He had been stalking the family ever since Mary took her kids and fled when Peggy was a toddler. For four or five years, until the family moved temporarily to Colorado, where Mary would meet Ted Japely, Al King would regularly track them down, often breaking in windows and beating in doors in the middle of the night. Once, in a drunken rage, he lined up the whole family against a wall, waved a gun in their faces, and told them he was Hitler, they were dirty kikes, and he was going to kill them all.

Often, they would manage to call the police, and eventually her mother filed a restraining order. But Al King's brother was a sergeant in the Chicago Police Department, and as fast as Mary had him hauled in, his brother would get him out. Not surprisingly, Peggy did not mention any of this to the kids at school.

As much as I wanted to work in all the basketball I could, summers were about counseling, umpiring, and playing softball. Lincolnwood had just started participating in a traveling softball league, and though I wasn't yet 16, I played with the 16- to 18-year-old team. So did Barb Atsaves, who was only 14 and turning out to be a great basketball and softball player.

In between, I decided to take a free CPR class at the Lincolnwood police station. Since I was the only kid, I got a lot of stares, and I took mental notes on all the others in my class for my weekly letters to Shirley. I told her about the cute paramedic who taught the class and about the woman who drooled on the CPR dummy right before I was supposed to put my mouth on it. I also told her about the course unexpectedly paying off shortly after I completed it when I found myself performing mouth-to-mouth resuscitation on my mother on our kitchen floor.

I think I took the class because I subconsciously knew my mom was not well. She had had numerous surgeries on her arm, but she had also had a few scares with low blood sugar and took medication to control a case of borderline diabetes. More than once, ambulances were dispatched to our house for one thing or another—a fainting spell or, in the case of that summer, after she had passed out and stopped breathing when her blood pressure inexplicably plummeted.

My father was surprisingly calm in emergency situations, but he did not know how to perform mouth-to-mouth and I did. As they wheeled my mother out, a blanket barely concealing her nightgown, kids I had never even seen before, on bikes and on foot, crowded around the ambulance for a peek as I yelled at them to stop rubbernecking and get the hell away.

I didn't share the episode with anyone but Shirley. And it

wasn't something even my family discussed much. It was just another unfortunate hospitalization that we hoped would end quickly.

My relationship with my mother was so close it was telepathic. And my brothers and sister used to say it was my mother's fault I cried at the briefest of separations—once when she was only in the next aisle at Shoppers World, a 30-second span that nearly sent me to therapy. But the truth was, I didn't want to leave my mom. We shared a love of Barbra Streisand and Dionne Warwick, as well as of Robert Redford, James Garner, Mary Tyler Moore, and Walter Payton. And above all, we shared a humorous outlook on most everything.

She understood me, and I her. Once, my sister, Susie, distraught that I was showing no proclivity for girl things, stole me away to the bathroom, dressed me up, and slathered me with makeup. I was five. "She looks like a hooker," my mother said when she saw me, my brothers collapsing with laughter as I ran back outside where I belonged.

Routinely, I would come home to find Shirley or other friends sitting at our kitchen table, talking and laughing with my mom. She wasn't trying to be our friend—she despised the very notion of the buddy mom. She was just naturally funny, warm, and loving, and kids found her easy to talk to.

She was a storyteller and even as her usual sharpness began to dull, she fell back on old standbys that held up through the years. As a little kid, her stories enthralled me, and whether I was snuggled next to her in bed or walking with her to the grocery store because she couldn't drive, I would listen and laugh and grip her good hand a little tighter as we crossed Devon Avenue on the way to the Jewel.

"Please, you have to promise," she would say to me, gesturing to one senior citizen or another bundled up on a street corner on a sweltering afternoon. "I know, I know," I would reply. "No sweaters in the middle of summer. Promise, I won't let you."

My mother would also tell me about how my father was "rich" growing up, an accusation to which he took great offense for some reason. In truth, anyone who didn't run from landlords trying to collect the rent was considered rich to my mom, and tales of her childhood were always part tragic, part hilarious. Like when she told me of renting one pair of roller skates with her best friend, Rhea, for seven cents an hour—four cents from her and three from Rhea "because she was *really* poor," my mom would say. "Her father was on relief."

Pretty much limited to one doll and one roller skate for entertainment when she was growing up, my mother told me of the day her father gave her a goldfish for a pet. They placed it on the windowsill in the kitchen until one afternoon, boiling in the hot sun, the fish "jumped out of the bowl, out the window, and committed suicide," my mom lamented.

"Committed suicide?" I asked, horrified.

"It was the Depression," she deadpanned.

My mother loved sports, but she did not come by her fan role naturally. One day, wanting to impress my brothers and their friends, she came into the room while they were watching a football game on television and casually mentioned that she had read a very interesting article at the beauty shop written by a woman who knew so much about football, it almost sounded as if she played.

"Her name is Fran Tarkenton," my mom said proudly.

Tarkenton, of course, was the star quarterback of the Minnesota Vikings. And a man.

My brothers and their friends howled with laughter, and my mom scurried out of the room after telling them it wasn't nice to make fun of a mother. But from then on, she made a point to be the most astute and devoted sports fan in the house, going from season to season with the Bulls and Bears and White Sox and, of course, the Niles West girls' basketball team.

My parents went to my softball games in the summer, but it

was the promise of winter, normally a dark, dreary time in Chicago and a sad time at home with reminders of snowblowers and a general dislike of the cold, that consumed them. Each basketball game was an event to anticipate, live, and relive. If life's demands kept my mother and father from attending every event of my siblings in earlier years, they were not about to miss any more at this stage of their lives. More than that, watching us play seemed to give them a second wind, a diversion from my mom's physical pain, my dad's melancholy, and the feeling that their increasing forgetfulness was becoming a problem.

CHAPTER 9

Shirley's Gremlin and Those Weird Lumps

Wow, Dean Turry had a hairy back.

He was a good-looking guy, Jerry Turry, Niles West's dean of the senior and sophomore classes. Even at 30-whatever-he-was, we could see that, and a good number of the cute junior and senior girls would flirt with him, thinking no one could tell. But he did have a slightly receding hairline and, in school, he wore clothes. So it was no small shock when a few of us wandered into the Boys' Gym one morning and saw him on the basketball court playing a full-court game with some other male coaches, guidance counselors, and teachers, his shirt off and his hairiness very apparent.

Any trauma at seeing our dean half-naked and hairy, however, was quickly overshadowed by another emotion: intense jealousy. Why can't we do that? And how can we do that? The answer, after considerable pleading, was that we could, just as long as we were out of the gym by the time the men showed up to start their game.

At 6:30 a.m.

No problem, we figured. If we got to school by five, we could get in some decent scrimmage time. We had worried about getting in enough practice. Granted, the school year had just started and basketball tryouts were still a couple months away. But the girls' season had been moved up again, this time to coincide with the boys' season, and our first game was December 14. In other words, time was a-wastin'.

The best part about the 1977–78 Niles West girls' basketball season was that after playing a 12-game regular-season schedule the last two years, we now had 21 games before regionals. And included in those games were two tournaments. It would be the first time a Niles West girls' basketball team had ever played in a regular-season tournament, which would, by every measure, tell us the kind of team we were as well as the kind of team we were capable of becoming.

After school, the gym was booked. Shirley, Connie, and some of the other girls had volleyball practice, and it was vital to us that, once again, we established ourselves as the imaginary titleholders of the hardest-working team in the state.

The next day, Shirley's Gremlin came rumbling up the street at 4:30 a.m., and my father almost had a heart attack. "You're going to wake up the entire neighborhood," he said, frantically shushing me as if I could somehow silence Shirley's nonexistent muffler from our kitchen. I shrugged, kissed him goodbye, and bounded for the car.

"Shirley, we have to do something!" I screamed. The noise from inside the car was just as intense as from the outside. "And why don't you have any heat in this car?"

It was fall in Chicago, which would qualify as winter in most places, and I could see my breath. Shirley assured me that from then on, she would cut off the engine and coast into my driveway. And as for the other problem, I might want to consider layering.

Shirley was the one who first suggested we begin working out in the middle of the night, and she never got an argument, her upbeat mood giving every scrimmage a festive feel. "Good morning, sunshine," Connie chirped at her while the rest of us shuffled into the gym, still rubbing our eyes and clearing our throats and generally gathering our wits about us.

The first few days, our early sessions consisted of two-on-twos and maybe three-on-threes, the attendance less than stellar. We put the word out—phrased more as a threat—that everyone had better show up. We wanted to play full-court. Soon, sophomores like Tina Conti and Lynn Carlsen and other girls who desperately wanted to make varsity started coming. Shirley, Connie, and I were regulars. So were Barb and Peggy, Judy and Karen, Bridget, Diana, and another senior, Jo Vollmann.

It was basketball for the sheer joy of it. And yet we were deadly serious about why we were there. This was preparation for the state championship, and no one had better have any doubt about that. Connie and I, the most enthusiastic about self-inflicted torture, decided that when we were kicked off the floor by the men at 6:30, we would run. Specifically, we would run up and down the circular staircase leading up to the gym balcony. It was about 20 steps up and then 20 steps down the other side, and around and around we went, counting as we completed each circuit like a regiment of Marine recruits. First, 10 trips sounded about right, then 20 and then 30 and then 40 until the freshmen and sophomores and those who didn't have the stomach or the mentality for it fell off.

Connie was manic, with the endurance of marathon runner Jim Fixx, and it would invariably be she who would urge us to do 10 more, then 10 more, singing out cheers as we ran. And then we would drag ourselves to the locker room and get ready for school, running to our first classes with still-flushed faces and damp hair, satisfied that for one more day, we were still the most dedicated team in Illinois.

Some days, Shirley and I would swing by and pick up Connie and Peggy on our way to school in the morning. On other days, Tina's father, who worked the night shift at the family's bread

company, would pick up the entire Lincolnwood contingent—
me, Shirley, and Barb—and take us to Niles West. Connie would
sometimes be able to get the family station wagon as long as she
returned it before school, and there were as many adventures
with that car as Shirley had with the Gremlin.

Connie made it for days on one headlight until a patrolman
stopped her one morning after she rolled through a stop sign.
"I'm sorry, officer," she told him. "I'm on my way to basketball
practice." So impressed and probably more than a little shocked
was he at the sight of a cute, blonde teenage girl going to play
basketball at four thirty in the morning that he let her off with a
warning and a smile.

So intent was Peggy on getting to our morning session when
Connie was unable to drive her one morning, that her mother
rode up Marmora Avenue in the snow with Peggy on the handle-
bars of her bike.

At some point it entered our minds that maybe we should
challenge the male teachers to play, thus extending our own practice period. But they immediately nixed that idea, and considering their game was a combination of basketball and the movie
Ben-Hur, it was clear we would be taking our lives into our hands.
Theirs was not a sport we recognized.

It was all at once a wonderful and yet still strangely confusing
time to be a girl growing up in our country. During that 1977–78
school year, 65,000 people marched in Washington, DC, in support of the Equal Rights Amendment. An Ohio court ruled that
girls could play on Little League baseball teams. The first female
general in the Marine Corps, Margaret A. Brewer, was appointed.
And at the University of Chicago, the first female president of a
coed university, Hanna H. Gray, was inaugurated. A lawsuit by
Sports Illustrated reporter Melissa Ludtke was also resolved by
US District Court Judge Constance Baker Motley, who ruled that
Major League Baseball teams could not keep a female sportswriter out of the clubhouse following a game.

At the same time, shows such as *Three's Company, Charlie's Angels,* and *Laverne & Shirley* ruled the airwaves, pretty much reinforcing the idea, for three nights a week anyway, that dumb, beautiful, or preferably both was what America still wanted a woman to be.

When Bridget noticed one day with pride how strong her legs had become and pointed this out to her mother, her mom responded in horror, "You look like a boy." And Shirley's mother, while outwardly supportive of her youngest daughter's athletic endeavors, also harbored concerns that all of that exercise was making Shirley bigger all over and was perhaps the reason she didn't have a boyfriend.

Besides basketball, I was focused on September 29, my upcoming 16th birthday and the party I was planning. I invited my teammates as well as a large group of other friends to a luncheon at a Japanese restaurant. I wore a blue velour pants suit, which was as girly as I cared to look, and cut into a giant cake in the shape of a basketball player wearing our red-and-white Niles West warm-ups, No. 10 of course. Among other gifts from my parents, I received a coveted leather basketball, and no one in the room had to guess what I wished for when I blew out the candles.

If I had known, I might have thrown in a wish for Shirley. She had recently applied to the University of Illinois, where she was planning on studying physical therapy. And on the advice of Mrs. Mulder, Mr. Schnurr, and others, she was also trying to elicit some interest from Illinois women's basketball coach Carla Thompson for a possible scholarship. Shirley had glowing letters of recommendation from the coaches, Dr. Mannos, and Dean Turry. And now, after a phone conversation with the Illinois coach, she had an appointment to meet her on campus that Sunday.

Shirley gathered newspaper clips and film of our games, and with her parents made the two-and-a-half-hour drive to Champaign. The Cohens arrived a half hour early for their noon appointment at the student union. They called Thompson's office when she was late in arriving, talked to a security guard who knew Thompson, and then tried the athletic department, all in vain. After several hours of waiting, they decided to turn around and drive back home.

Shirley, at her parents' behest, left message after message for the coach to call back. She never received a reply. Shirley barely talked about it. She was embarrassed by being stood up, but she was also conflicted. She was confident but acutely aware of her shortcomings as a basketball player—primarily a lack of quickness and height for a power forward. Maybe, she thought, this was God's way of telling her that she really wasn't good enough to play college basketball. And like some of us, she also wasn't sure that she really wanted to be a college athlete.

If we had managed in high school to sidestep the stigma that still existed for female athletes, it appeared to be that much harder for girls in college. Plus, Shirley's parents could afford to send her to college, and she had good reason to believe she would be accepted to Illinois with or without basketball.

Shirley's father fired off a letter to the Illinois women's athletic director asking for an explanation, if not an apology, for the coach's inexplicable behavior, but Shirley wouldn't let him mail it. And soon, she shook off the disappointment. But this was all the more reason, she told herself, why winning a state championship this season would be so necessary, so perfect.

We all found our own forms of motivation. One day that fall, Connie was finishing volleyball practice when Niles West's JV wrestling coach Bill Mitz, who had once dated one of Connie's older sisters, stopped to tell her he was working out at a community gym and had seen the star of Maine South's basketball team, Kathy Pabst, shooting by herself. By our junior year, Maine South had established itself as our biggest rival. Its best players, Sue Leonard and Liz Boesen, had graduated, but Pabst was their heir apparent. And that day, she became Connie's personal nemesis.

"It looked like she was working pretty hard out there," Mitz goaded.

Connie rolled her eyes. "Come on," she said. "Is she running stairs at 4:30 a.m. like we are?"

"All I'm saying," he said, "is that there will always be someone working harder than you are."

Connie scowled and decided right then and there that no one, not Kathy Pabst or any other girl in the state, would outwork her.

Whether Peggy was shooting after practice had ended or I was lingering at the foul line or Shirley was practicing her inside moves on someone, Connie would make sure she shot longer, practiced harder, and was the last player to leave the gym.

With any free time before volleyball practice, Connie and I would work on creating our new ballhandling routine. For me, I wanted us to look flashy, like Hinsdale South, to use it to get more psyched up before games. For Connie, it was more than that. It was a way to bond as a team, come together in warm-ups, and perform in sync, as one, with none of us standing out from anyone else. It showed both her humility and leadership, a maturity that, like Shirley's, was beyond that of most 16-year-olds.

She had also begun dating her friend Bob, another sign that Connie had it made, at least to me. Bob Porcaro was cute and sweet; had a fabulously dry sense of humor; played football but was hardly the dumb jock type; and was crazy about Connie. I thought they were the cutest couple I had ever seen in my life. They even had their own song, Connie once confided in me without sounding corny: Billy Joel's "Just the Way You Are." And maybe the best thing about Bob was that he was genuinely supportive of her interest in sports and an actual fan of ours. It was the only way Connie would allow herself a commitment outside of basketball. Not only did Bob come to our games last season but he also covered us for the school paper. No one questioned his objectivity.

In November, Mulder named 14 girls each to the new freshman basketball team and JV squad, and 11 to varsity. The only newcomer to varsity was Peggy. There were four seniors—Shirley, Diana, Bridget, and Jo Vollmann; five juniors—Connie, Karen, Judy, Peggy, and me—and two sophomores—Barb and DD.

Though as talented as always, DD still perplexed us. She seemed to be more distant than ever, especially when her on-again, off-again relationship with Connie's twin brother, Chris, was off again, and she had little interest in putting in any extra time on the court, though she was always good for a laugh when she was around.

It felt great to be out on the court as a team again, and my brand-new Converse gym shoes with the bold red star logo kept catching my eye as I ran drills. Leather Converse—bought from the boys' section of the store—were all the rage that year, and most of the girls on the team pined for high-tops. I thought they were hideous and because I did not have ankle problems, opted for the standard low-tops, which saved my parents 12 bucks.

Still, my mother and I never actually *told* my father that I was buying $40 gym shoes, and Connie quietly collected Coke bottles to combine with babysitting money for her high-tops. She might have come up with the money a little easier, but in a surprise move, Connie's mom had made her quit her waitressing job, telling her she had the rest of her life to work and that now she needed to work at basketball.

When we were younger, there was no such thing as a girl buying boys' basketball shoes. Girls wore deck shoes or pointy PF Flyers. My new Converse reminded me that when was 11, I got a pair of the smallest Tretorn tennis shoes they made after begging my parents to let me take 10 lessons for $20 at the new Touhy Tennis Club. I also begged for—and received—a pair of white boys' tennis shorts to go with my T-shirt. I loved Chris Evert, but she wore tennis dresses and cute scrunchies, and I couldn't relate, and there was no way I was running around in a dress on a tennis court when I could barely stand to wear one to temple for the High Holidays.

For most of us, the shoes were a huge deal, and we accepted without question that the same pair would most likely carry us through high school. Right after practice, I returned mine to their original box as if returning a baby to its crib. It wasn't just that the shoes looked great or were real leather or expensive, though all those things factored in. It was as if, with each new basketball accessory, like our warm-ups suits, we were that much closer to being real basketball players, to being taken seriously and taking our sport that much more seriously.

Though everyone who knew about our morning sessions could not help but be impressed by our dedication, that did not mean the male coaches were any more inclined to share gym space with us for practice after school. As basketball season approached and the boys' and girls' seasons were to run concurrently for the first time, Mrs. Mulder saw firsthand which male coaches were not quite as liberated as the others. To further complicate matters, this was the first season we had a girls' freshman basketball team, which meant even more sacrificing of gym space, and the not-so-quiet grumbling of the older male coaches eventually made its way into the PE office.

Mulder had fought this battle before and remembered the conversation she had with Judy Kay, the girls' volleyball and badminton coach, when Miss Kay stomped into the office one day during the fall season. "These guys are just ignoring me," Kay said. "I told them we're splitting the gym and that I want these two and a half hours, and they can have these two. And you know what they said? 'We'll take it under consideration.' *They* can take it under consideration."

"Judy," Mrs. Mulder told her, "you have to start small."

"Baloney," Kay huffed.

Mulder was not worried. She had paved the way for her

teams to get gym time by starting small a year earlier. She also knew whom to talk to.

"Billy, do you think I can get the gym once a week?" she asked Schnurr. "The team is at a disadvantage not playing on a regulation court."

"No problem, Arlene," Schnurr told her. "We can play later. We'll work with you."

Arlene Mulder never considered herself a feminist, though she had a fierce interest in seeing females get the same basic opportunities as males. She was simply a realist, and unlike her close friend, gymnastics coach Judi Sloan, who would also become angry when the male coaches openly discriminated against the women, Mrs. Mulder went more for the kill-'em-with-kindness approach. She also learned from Miss Heeren, whose strategy was to get the men to think it was their idea.

Mulder was no politician, but she did have her own opinions. And in meetings with area coaches in the early days of Title IX, she would stand up and urge them, "Let's not get so caught up with equality that we repeat the same mistakes the men have made," and the other women in the room would applaud in approval.

Sloan was happy for Mulder and the other women taking whatever approach worked. But Sloan had been fighting battles for longer than all of them and knew the frustration of having to fight for a seemingly simple matter, like getting a photograph of a top girl gymnast and the school's first female conference champ mounted on Niles West's Wall of Fame.

That was in '72, only five years earlier, and Sloan had her picture in the school paper during that battle and was depicted as the Bella Abzug of Niles West by male staff members. She also received hate mail over the incident. But she persevered. And when her gymnastics team had to take apart their own equipment and move it from the balcony down the bleachers and into the gym for their meets because the school wouldn't pay maintenance to do it, she gritted her teeth and did it. The men laughed at Sloan when she had her girls jogging in the pool and jumping on and off boxes because she had read about plyometrics as a means to increase foot speed and agility.

Mulder's advantage was that she had Schnurr as a respected ally, who could also be a conduit to the other male coaches if necessary. And she had Sloan as a trusted confidant to lean on. All we knew was that no one was kicking us out of the Boys' Gym, which had gradually become known only as the Contest Gym, a small sign of progress, but it was something.

Though our official practices had begun, we continued our unsupervised morning sessions. We also continued running our stair circuits, adding two-pound ankle weights to increase the pain, if not the actual benefits. And Mrs. Mulder added jumping rope to our regimen.

Connie and I finally had the ballhandling routine worked out. We decided that the team would take the court at a dead sprint, form a circle, and then perform the between-the-legs, around-the-back thing of beauty. But teaching the others, particularly the taller girls, was another matter entirely, and neither of us was a particularly patient type. "*Twice* through your legs, Bridget," I said between obviously clenched teeth, giving little thought to the fact that she had to bend about a foot lower than I did to perform the maneuver. But Bridget and the others were good sports, bought in, and worked diligently to master it in the spirit of the team. DD, of course, got it on the first try and then generally disrupted everyone else.

To the rest of us, this all still seemed like a gym class she was trying to avoid. Regularly DD would come to practice late, and when she didn't, she'd slide around the gym floor in her socks, taking crazy half-court shots until Mrs. Mulder showed up. It exasperated us, and Connie and Shirley would chide her, but she was so damn happy-go-lucky, it was as hard to stay mad at her as it was to get through to her.

In practice, Mr. Schnurr continued to help us, enlisting another group of boys who were mostly football players and wrestlers with good attitudes to scrimmage with us. Only this season there was a notable difference. "Look, guys, I don't want you to think of them as girls," Schnurr told the boys. "Obviously, keep it clean, but I want you to give them your best. That means block their shots—and no one gets a free path to the bucket."

Occasionally, there would be a bloody nose, and Bridget routinely got hammered under the basket, once getting sandwiched by two boys going for a rebound. She got up gingerly and in obvious pain but was struck by the same thing all of us were when one of us went down—get up quickly and shake it off or they're not going to let us keep playing with the boys.

Mrs. Mulder remained wary about these scrimmages, watching us literally bump heads with the boys and looking as if she were ready to step in at any moment. But with each incident, we would glance over at our coach, then at our injured teammate, silently and sometimes not so silently willing them to get up and keep playing.

One day, however, that just wasn't possible. Karen Wikstrom was defending one of the boys during our unsupervised morning session, and as he jumped to make a pass over her, he inadvertently elbowed her directly in the forehead. "You're fine, Karen," we all but screamed at her before she even hit the floor. "Get up! Get up!"

As always, we immediately looked around to make sure there weren't any teachers or coaches in the vicinity, then checked on Karen, who quickly struggled back to her feet. But after staggering into the locker room and to the first mirror she could find, she saw an egg-shaped lump growing on her forehead, promptly panicked, and began hyperventilating. At that point, we could hardly keep Mrs. Mulder away. She got wind of there being an injury, rushed into the locker room, saw a kid going into shock, and promptly called an ambulance.

Karen was a very good volleyball player who was still miscast as a power forward. She was a little too graceful to fight for rebounds as she was expected to do, and a little too nice to have the killer instinct Mr. Schnurr and Mrs. Mulder thought she should have. But, like Bridget, she surprised everyone by shaking off her injury and practicing the very next day.

It was funny, though. As concerned as Mrs. Mulder was about not getting us roughed up physically, there were certain things she did not feel uncomfortable expressing. She had no problem, for example, telling Judy that if she lost a little weight, she'd be quicker defensively. And Judy had no problem hearing it. Nor was Judy's mom at all hesitant to follow through with the coach's advice and help her daughter maintain a better diet at home.

Weight just wasn't a touchy subject when it came to basketball. We'd hop on and off the scale in the locker room with no one giving it much thought. Height was actually more important. I insisted I was 5-3, even though I barely cleared 5-2, and that I be listed as such in the game programs. Bridget was every bit of 5-11 but would rather be listed at 5-9.

Peggy was 5-10 and loved it.

Since Peggy was new to varsity, I didn't know her that well yet. But I knew I liked her, mostly because she thought I was the funniest kid she had ever met in her life. We shared a fairly strange affection for older male actors—I was in love with Robert Redford and Peg was obsessed with Clint Eastwood. We also discovered in each other a dual appreciation for gossip—both giving and getting it.

We quickly came up with a common philosophy. We didn't care if others talked behind our backs as long as we didn't know about it. Thus, we reasoned, no one should care if we gossiped behind theirs. One day I showed Peggy a Peanuts cartoon I had cut out that had Charlie Brown telling Lucy a secret in one frame and Lucy promising, "I swear, cross my heart and hope to die, I will not tell." The next frame had Lucy announcing the embarrassing revelation over the school PA system. Peggy laughed so hard she fell down the bleachers.

Soon, we had our own weird lingo. Instead of laughing, we'd simply yell, "Auuuuugggghhh!" as if the joke were too funny to waste a simple laugh on. And any particularly good piece of gossip or pointed zinger from one of us would be met with the other screaming, "Shut up!" If something was too nasty, even to us, "Not to be mean, but . . . " would basically absolve us of any responsibility. And the response to anything we found stupid, unpleasant, or otherwise unfortunate was always, "That's great." Basically, everyone thought we were nuts. We thought we were hysterical.

Peg, who welcomed her first full season on varsity with a new short haircut, was more interested in boys than I was, but neither of us knew how to use whatever femininity we possessed any more than we knew how to speak Mandarin. At school, the running gag for girls with flat chests was that we had charter membership in the IBTC—the itty-bitty-titty committee. It was not something we were proud of, but neither were we embarrassed. It was just the way it was. Peg possessed a few more curves than I did, but at 5-10 she weighed a slight but sturdy 145 pounds and looked more boyish than vampish. But then both of us longed much more for the perfect jump shot than we did for a C cup.

We also longed to have our uniforms fit us properly, which was an impossible proposition on most days, worse on some than others. Our mothers often wondered what took us so long to emerge from the locker room before each game, our pregame preparation lasting anywhere from 20 minutes to an hour and a half, with conventional primping taking up only about 10 percent of it.

Sure, there was hair brushing and, in the case of Bridget, makeup applying, but for most of us, two things kept us trapped in the locker room and both involved our, uh, equipment. In order to not merely play basketball comfortably but to walk upright and move our arms, we had to make certain adjustments. No matter how short or how skinny you happened to be or what uniform size you were able to pilfer, wearing those Niles West uniforms was like trying to fit into your little sister's clothes after your mother accidentally shrunk them. This was heavy-duty polyester, guaranteed not to shrink, fade, or breathe. You could not pass a knife through it, but not because we didn't try.

And so there we were, as if competing in a giant red taffy pull before each game, two teammates yanking on each tourniquet-like ribbed sleeve, our own hands down our shorts trying to stretch the waistband while simultaneously doing deep knee bends. Then we would go to work on the bustline, even if we didn't happen to have one. Those who did have one at least had the advantage of having the material provide some added support since the advent of the sports bra was still years away.

The shorts always presented their own problems, magnified several times over at certain times of the month, which for any given game affected at least one of us. During our first game of the 1977–78 season, it was me. There were no such things as ultra-thin maxi pads or super-plus tampons. There were tampons and there were sanitary pads, which were roughly the width and thickness of your average hand towel and which did not fit inconspicuously in our purses much less in our teeny-tiny uniform shorts. And so there we were, trying to make it work so that (A) we were afforded the amount of protection required for a basketball game and (B) we did not look like we had male genitalia.

"It looks like I'm wearing a diaper," I told anyone who would listen as I tried to navigate two side-by-side pads into place.

"No," whispered Peggy, "it looks like you have a penis."

"That's great, much better," I said, giving her a dirty look. We were about to go up against New Trier West, and my biggest concern was whether someone might think I was really born a boy and just trying to pass myself off as a girl.

Connie, meanwhile, was busy looking for sugar pills. Always on alert for anything that would give us an advantage, be it something the boys' teams might be doing or something that was remotely cool in any way, Connie had already begun wearing kneepads, wristbands, and ankle tape, and now came into the locker room with an economy-size container of dextrose pills.

We acted as if they were amphetamines, "greenies" like I had recently read about in Jim Bouton's book *Ball Four*, which revealed, among other things, the hidden drug abuse among Major League Baseball players. In truth, these dextrose tablets were giant horse pills that, when chewed, closely resembled a piece of chalk, both in texture and taste, though that part could certainly have been explained by the fact that they had probably exceeded their expiration date by a decade or more. They were supposed to give us energy, or so Connie had heard. She had found them in a back cabinet of the tiny training room, remembered her brothers taking similar tablets in football—actually salt tablets, but whatever—and decided it had to give us an advantage.

We crowded around her and without any hesitation popped these stale hunks of chalk into our mouths and then, almost in unison, choked at the bitter taste and crumbly texture.

Now we were ready for anything.

Once again, we delivered a rose and a poem to Mrs. Mulder before the game. And once again, I was the designated poet. We could only hope I had improved from last season.

> Here we are in '77, ready to play our game,
> We'll meet our goals, stay intense, and keep our
> respected name,
> The only way to achieve this, we know, is to
> always concentrate,
> Now all that's ahead is putting it together, only
> we can determine our fate.

We led New Trier West 19–8 at the end of the first quarter, shut them out with our smothering full-court press in the second quarter to surge ahead 27–8 at the half, and cruised to a 60–28 victory.

Our next game was eight days away, but it was against Forest View, a team that we knew little about, except that they were tall. Mrs. Mulder had just started having our games filmed, and together, the day after the New Trier West game, we huddled in a cramped, low-ceilinged, glorified storage closet in the corner of the hallway outside the gym and watched the flickering images of a dusty projector.

The film quality was not great. I squinted at the black-and-white picture on the screen, trying to make out which team was us—and what sport we were playing.

"Do you see how Karen is moving to box out No. 14?" said Mrs. Mulder, pointing to two unidentifiable blurs on the screen. We all nodded diligently. It was cool to be sitting there, all huddled together. "Now Karen is in the perfect position to grab the rebound."

We had to continue to work on fundamentals, our coach told us, on boxing out and rebounding, or we would lose for sure. She knew we were a good team and she knew that we were aware of that as well, and she was concerned we would become overconfident. And so, every opponent was another behemoth, and we were sure to get crushed if we didn't play our very best. We got the message she was sending, but we were also aware of the psychological game she was playing.

We knew her too well. Or at least it must have seemed that way to Mrs. Mulder when she opened the card and started to read the poem before the Forest View game, and had to catch her breath for a moment.

> The survival of the seed we've planted depends
>   on our desire,
> It relies on our will to learn and push and jump
>   just that much higher,
> The seed's development has now just begun,
>   though an uphill fight it may seem,

That's our goal, that's what we want, it will take
patience to fulfill our dream.

That week, she had found out she was pregnant with her
third child but had not told anyone outside of her closest friends
on the staff. The seed's development has now just begun? If only
they knew, she thought.

CHAPTER 10

Addition by Subtraction

FOR ALL OF THE WORK ETHIC, goal setting, and general humility drummed into us by our coach, the opportunity to show off our development as a team and, let's be clear, strut our stuff was in no way beneath us.

Among the staples of boys' basketball, the regular-season tournaments, especially the ones held over the holidays, were among the coolest. Though there was no more significance to a regular-season tournament win than any other, playing and, more specifically, winning a tournament in which you'd have to play three games in two days demonstrated a certain toughness and dominance and elevated the games to a greater importance than they actually had.

In other words, sign us up.

The second annual Evanston High School Invitational was scheduled for December 28–29, and it was considered among the most prestigious in the state. Our first opponent was defending tournament champion Buffalo Grove, one of the perennial top teams. Also at Evanston, in addition to the host team, were Fremd, Forest View, Maine South, Resurrection, and St. Scholastica.

It was exciting for us to be playing games while school was not in session, and because it was the start of a long holiday weekend, most of our parents, including mine, could come to all the games. After our opening game Wednesday night, a 57–44 victory over Buffalo Grove in which we outscored the Bisons 18–8 in the fourth quarter, we stuck around late to watch the Forest View–Fremd game, which Fremd won, then spent the entire next day at Evanston High School.

We remembered Fremd, of course. It was the school Mrs. Mulder had scheduled the year before as our season opener, a barometer, she reasoned, for where our program stood compared with the best teams in the state. Fremd was one of those teams and had pasted us that day at home, going on to finish third in the first-ever Illinois girls' state tournament. In Thursday's 1 p.m. game in the second round of the Evanston Invitational, we avenged that defeat with a sound 59–43 victory over a team with much the same personnel as the year before.

The day was a blast. We trounced Fremd, showered, dressed, went out for lunch, then came back to the school, got into clean uniforms, and then, to kill time before the game that night, played cards, read the paper, and took naps on the scummy, disgusting floor of the boys' locker room, which had been cleared out for us. So this was what being an athlete was all about.

"St. Scholastica won," Connie informed us. "And they look pretty good."

While some of us were killing time debating the relative cuteness of the oldest brother on *Eight Is Enough*, Connie and Shirley had been keeping a close eye on St. Scholastica's game against Evanston, and they were keeping us focused.

It wasn't that difficult. Knowing that many of the other teams and their fans were sticking around to watch our game that night fed our egos like nothing before. We were the special ones who got to hang out all day in the locker room because we were playing in the championship game. We were being watched. We were special. We were also ready.

We told ourselves that every good team in the state was paying attention, and we were excited to show that we had officially arrived. Per Connie and my persistent harping, we sprinted onto the court for our pregame warm-up like it was the state championship, performing our ballhandling routine crisply and without any flubs. And it carried over to the game as everything seemed to click—our defense, strong as ever with Connie, Barb, DD, and me flicking away passes in our press and converting them into easy layups, and our offense, led by Shirley, firing on all cylinders.

St. Scholastica's JoAnn Feiereisel, who had given us all we could handle in the regional finals the previous spring, scored 29 points before fouling out. But Shirley played the game of her life, leading us in scoring with 19 points, while Connie and Diana also finished in double figures to spur us to a 62–58 victory.

In the *Chicago Tribune* the next day, we were shocked to discover a huge photo spread devoted to our Evanston triumph. In addition to a couple of action shots, one photo had us on each other's shoulders cutting down the nets. There were also two photos of Bridget, including one of her dad twirling her in a giant celebratory hug at midcourt.

We were 5–0 and suddenly a team that even Mrs. Mulder could not make into underdogs any longer. In the *Suburban Trib*, Susan Sternberg, the only woman sportswriter I had ever heard of, led her article with this:

> Arlene Mulder would like to be a contestant on *I've Got a Secret*.
>
> However, it wouldn't take a John Q. Daly or a Garry Moore to figure out that the Niles West girls' basketball coach wouldn't have a chance to stump the show's panel—if it were made up of her

north suburban coaching peers. But you just can't blame Mulder for wanting to try.

Mulder wishes this season was like last year when her Indians played their 'mystery team' role to the hilt—winning the Central Suburban League South Division title and advancing to the super-sectionals before losing to Hinsdale South. The Indians were able to sneak up on a lot of teams last year.

Mrs. Mulder joked in the article that maybe it would have been smarter to lose at the Evanston Invitational. But now the secret was out. We were still small, as Sternberg pointed out, and we still didn't boast great shooters or a finely tuned offense. But we put up one of the most furious defenses around, we had depth as Mrs. Mulder still used our entire roster, and we were experienced. And clearly, whether our coach liked it or not, there was no turning back now.

Our first game back after winter vacation and our Evanston triumph was our conference opener against Waukegan East on January 11, and our momentum carried us as we blew past Waukegan at home, 75–38. We were on our way, and that week this letter appeared in the *West Word*.

Dear Editor,

There is a team here at Niles West that has been highly overlooked. This team is the girls' varsity basketball team. The most unfortunate part about this is that they are most overlooked by their own student body. Already this year the girls have gone 6–0, capturing the first-place trophy in the prestigious Evanston Invitational Tournament (their first tourney ever, we might add).

During this tourney, the cagerettes managed to knock off Fremd (third in state last year and this year, basically the same team). Even Channel 2 News had to sit up and take notice of this powerhouse team.

Every team the girls have played thus far has greatly outnumbered Niles West in fan support. This is one of the first times in history that Niles West has been shown up in the spirit department. Of course, we can't expect the bleachers to be filled as they are at the boys' games (god knows why!) but there are barely enough fans to fill a mini-bus.

How about it Niles West? Are you ready to let a potential state championship team slip through your fingers? Come out and back the Indian girls. You'll probably be pleasantly surprised.

Names withheld upon request

Shirley and I figured the "cagerettes" mention was an especially clever touch, given that we would sooner wear ball gowns to school than call ourselves that. Anyone who knew me, however, could see right through the sarcastic shot at the boys' team, which was in the midst of a horrendous season, and know we wrote it.

We were still performing our game-day duty of lining up and pulling out the bleachers ourselves before each of our games, and it annoyed us that we were still stopping at about five or six rows. But we were making small strides. On our own, we each found teachers who either already knew about our success thus far or were at least interested—Mrs. Gordon and Mr. Klebba from the English department; Mr. Brennan, who taught Spanish; Mr. Karbusicky, who taught history; and Mr. Kettleborough, the driver's ed teacher. Guidance counselors Mr. Sortal, Mr. Hoosline, and Dr. Cocking, who were participants in the men's morning scrimmages and refereed high school boys' games, were also supporters of ours.

Shirley was taking auto mechanics as an elective—I could only guess that maybe she thought she could learn how to make the Gremlin a little quieter—and struck up a great rapport with her cute young teacher, Mr. Anderson. He liked Shirley because she was the only girl in his class and because it was hard not to like Shirley. And he joined forces with her to get fans out to support us, even offering extra credit to any of his students who attended a girls' basketball game. After that, we could look up and there on the top row of bleachers was a healthy representation of fifth-period autos, mostly slumped over and disinterested and before long, sneaking out to the parking lot for a smoke, but actual fans just the same.

In the midst of our campaign to rally support, it was announced that McDonald's would be filming a new commercial in our gym and needed extras to shoot a crowd scene. Hundreds of kids showed up, including us, but we watched in disgust as the same people we could not drag into the place to root us on in a real game cheered maniacally on cue for the director, all for the price of a gift certificate for a free hamburger.

"That's great. Maybe we need to give out hamburgers at our games," I shouted into Peggy's ear.

"Losers," she said, surveying the comical scene.

Mr. Schnurr continued to be a huge influence on our team. He helped Bridget refine her free-throw shooting technique, expanded our defensive repertoire to a half-dozen different sets, and worked with the forwards and center to improve their rebounding and shooting. He patiently urged Peggy to make the release point of her shot higher above her head, rather than under her chin, which she had done out of necessity when she began playing a year earlier because, like most of us, she didn't possess the arm strength to shoot like the boys.

He was no longer officially coaching but found that we still needed and wanted him around, and Mrs. Mulder continued to lean on him heavily for advice and guidance. Lunches and coffee breaks were reserved for daily sessions, and lately, Schnurr had been preaching how important it was to be composed and confident on the sidelines while demanding total intensity of the team.

"You're like a doctor in an emergency room, Arlene," he told her. "Even while all around you is chaos, you have to convey total calm."

She hung on his every word. She was getting a lifetime's worth of advice from someone who wasn't known to open up to just anyone. Schnurr had been at Niles West since it first opened as a four-year high school in 1961, the same year most of our junior class was born, arriving in Skokie from the small Wisconsin towns of Whitewater and Stoughton, where he'd coached football, basketball, baseball, and golf.

When the opportunity presented itself to go to Niles East in 1956 while construction on West was being completed, Schnurr passed up two other jobs in Wisconsin because the Chicago suburbs seemed a more prosperous place to raise a growing family. It was also a more expensive place to live on one teacher's salary, even with the $350 coaching stipend he received for coaching freshman football and the two $275 stipends he was paid for being the assistant basketball and assistant baseball coach.

But then, Billy Schnurr never coached or taught for the money. And he didn't come by coaching the conventional way.

During his sophomore year at the University of Wisconsin, while coaching high school baseball, the selective service was reinstituted and Billy, like many of his classmates, enrolled in ROTC. That way, he reasoned, he would be able to stay in school and not be drafted immediately, though upon graduation, he would be commissioned as a second lieutenant and eligible to be called to active duty for five years.

It was during his second semester in graduate school that he was called to duty and, in April 1952, sent to Korea. He had been there only two months when the war made a mark that would remain with him forever. While he was on a mandatory five-day R & R, the Chinese launched a surprise attack on T-Bone Hill, among the most bitter ground fighting in the war, and two of Billy's fellow officers were killed while another was seriously wounded. A squad leader and four other men in his platoon died as well. And in his heart, Billy knew he had escaped almost certain death.

A little more than nine months after he arrived in Korea, he was sent home, carrying the relief and guilt with him. Within the next three years, he married, his wife had twin boys, and he was coaching at Niles East. Over the next six years, a daughter and another son were born, and he became the head basketball coach at Niles West, where he would remain for the next 16 seasons.

When he retired the previous year, Billy Schnurr was the only varsity boys' basketball coach the school had ever known. His teams' record over that 16-season span was 222–154, which hardly did him justice until you considered that in six of the eight years from 1969 through 1976, Niles West won at least 19 games. Under Schnurr, West also won four conference titles and three regional championships, and made two trips to the Sweet 16, both ending in close defeats.

Never blessed with great size or the talent of so many of their foes, Schnurr's teams beat schools they often had no business competing against. And when he stepped down, he was hailed as one of the great tacticians in Illinois high school basketball.

Yet, despite his accomplishments and the regard with which he was held, he was starting to look enviously at Arlene Mulder and the way she coached. Sitting in the corner of the faculty lounge, scraps of paper and napkins with diagrammed plays sitting in a tidy pile in front of them, Schnurr and Mulder talked until their conversation, as it sometimes did, turned to us, her players. It was where everything started and stopped with her coaching, and as he listened to her speak about our various personalities and the life lessons she wanted to instill in us, he began thinking about what he could have learned from her in terms of motivation, about teaching sports in a way that had nothing to do with winning basketball games.

Mulder rested her hand on her stomach. They had developed both a mutual respect for and trust in one another, and Billy Schnurr was one of the few colleagues she had told about her pregnancy.

She had begun wearing baggy velour warm-ups pulled down low, which we all took note of, as we took note of virtually everything our coach wore and every new hairstyle she attempted. But she was largely devoid of morning sickness and as active as ever, and not one of us theorized she might be pregnant. We just figured her fashion taste was slipping.

After our conference-opening win over Waukegan East, next up on our schedule was Evanston, and we handled them easily, 63–44. We were getting a little cocky, and Mrs. Mulder was worried. Glenbrook North was up next, and she knew they were not pushovers.

It was an away game, the gym, as usual, more heavily populated than our own, and it was obvious at the start that we had taken them too lightly. Slowly, they chipped away at our lead and overtook us in the second half. We were so confident that we could reel off points whenever we chose to increase our defensive pressure that we hardly worried. Until, that is, we looked up at the scoreboard and saw that we trailed by 10 with just under two minutes remaining.

Then we panicked.

Not Shirley, though. "Hey listen!" she screamed at us in the huddle. "I just read about this college team that scored 10 points in the final minute of the game to win."

Mulder stayed quiet, letting Shirley take over. Despite the

fact that our coach was a control freak about what we wore, what we ate, and how we behaved, if someone had something meaningful to say, she stepped back and let us talk.

"We have *two* minutes," Shirley continued. "There's no problem. Now, come on."

We looked at each other and nodded.

"Intensity!" Connie shouted. "We can do this."

Mulder merely told us to execute. We ran a motion offense based on the one Bobby Knight taught at Indiana, and we had few set plays. Ours was based on constant movement, on setting screens for one another, and on finding the open man. We knew what we had to do; we had just neglected to do it. With Shirley's pep talk still buzzing in our ears, we scored on two consecutive possessions, then turned two steals off our press into two more scores and a free throw. With six seconds remaining, Diana grabbed the rebound off a missed Glenbrook North free throw and called a timeout. We were trailing by one.

On the inbounds play that Mrs. Mulder had diagrammed, Judy took more than the five seconds allowed to find an open man, but fortunately for us, the official gave us an extra second. It was just enough time for Judy to find Shirley, who posted up her defender before scoring on a turnaround bank shot to put us ahead by one, 59–58, as time expired.

We looked at each other in amazement for a split second before letting loose in celebration. It was an incredible comeback, but Connie quickly settled down a whooping Judy and a jumping Bridget and quieted us with a look we knew well, not unlike the way a mother might glare at her kids for being too wild in the grocery store. We had been to the state supersectionals, for crying out loud. We should have beaten Glenbrook North, even as close as we had come to losing. And cheering in wild celebration was not the attitude we wanted to convey.

Still, that was the game, Mrs. Mulder figured. She knew a letdown was coming—and it came. And now she had our renewed attention. We were beatable. It was exactly what she had wanted to happen. And it hardly even mattered that Shirley had made up the entire story of the college team she used to motivate us in the huddle. Our minds were clear now. Each obstacle was another step toward the goal in front of us. We knew what we had to do the remainder of the season. But we also knew there was something else we had to do first.

Several of us were warming up before our next practice when Connie paused and took a look around. We knew what, or rather whom, she was looking for.

"Has anyone seen DD?" she asked.

Peggy glanced up from tying her shoe. "She's not in the locker room," she said. "I just came from there."

Connie, Shirley, and I exchanged looks. DD had been a minor distraction for weeks and on this morning, it looked like she was a no-show.

"You know I like her," said Connie, who sometimes treated DD like a little sister, "but this has got to stop."

"We almost lost that last game," I added. "We can't risk any more mistakes."

Shirley sighed. "Let's go," she said, and a bunch of us followed her into the PE office.

"We need to talk," Shirley told Mrs. Mulder.

"What's up?" Mulder said, peeking out the office door into the gym. "Where's Diane?" She rarely called her DD.

We stared at each other.

"It's not working," Connie said.

"We can't do this anymore," I piped in.

"We have to do something," said Shirley.

Mrs. Mulder wouldn't have known a joint if she smelled one, and it didn't seem worth it to explain why DD's eyes were often glazed over during practice or why she was one step behind most days. But somehow our coach still knew.

"I'll take it from here," she said.

The decision was obvious, and by the end of practice it was final, though not one our coach had come to easily, nor one we took lightly. Being a member of the Niles West basketball team was sacred to us, and the very thought of any of us being kicked off the team made us almost physically ill. Plus, we liked DD.

Connie should have been the most conflicted. Just weeks earlier, the two of them were sitting in the stands at a boys' game when DD said she was going out to the parking lot to smoke. Connie knew she wasn't talking about cigarettes and tried to talk her out of it. It was a losing battle. And it angered her that DD would take her responsibility to the team so lightly.

Mrs. Mulder had talked to DD, as we all had. She had also cut back on DD's minutes, which hurt us at times. DD and Barb, along with Connie, had the quickest hands on our defense, and at 5-6, DD was one of the tallest of all the guards we faced and could be a strong presence inside, which we always needed. But for all of her gifts on the basketball court, DD's presence had become counterproductive to our mission.

Mrs. Mulder walked with leaden feet to DD's front door that afternoon, not sure exactly what reaction she would get. It was, she knew for sure, the single hardest thing she had ever had to do in her years of coaching.

She knocked at the door and Mr. Defrancesco answered. He was an especially dear man who had been the team's scorekeeper since girls' basketball had come to Niles West. He invited her inside. "DD," he called, "your coach is here!"

Mrs. Mulder chose her words carefully. She would never say she "kicked" DD off the team. Not to the Defrancescos, nor to anyone else. "It's so unfortunate," she said to the family, "because there's so much talent in this girl. But it's unfair to the other members of the team, and unfair to the school, and I have to ask you to turn in your uniform."

There was no argument from the Defrancescos or from DD, only a strange sense of relief. Emotionally, she was reeling between the hardships of living with an alcoholic parent, the intense feelings of her up-and-down relationship with Chris Erickson, and the social pressures we were all experiencing. *Good*, she thought defiantly, still remembering the love letter she'd received from another girl the year before. *Now I don't have to worry about looking like some dykey girl.*

Deep down, however, she wondered if one day she would regret it. Mr. D. remained our scorekeeper. And we simply moved on.

By now, playing against the boys was no longer a novelty but an integral part of our practice sessions and one that was paying off in ways we could actually start to detect.

It was gradual at first. We'd score on a well-executed offensive possession against the boys and congratulate ourselves. Then we'd score again, only this time we made a point not to make a big deal out of it because this is what we were supposed to do. We were a team with regular practices and set plays and coaches making sure we did it right. They were a group of boys who were good athletes, but they were not a team. They tried harder, but we kept improving.

And so it went until one particular day, when Connie fed Shirley perfectly for an open shot underneath as time expired on our half-court scrimmage, giving us an easy victory. The boys' faces were red and sweaty, and they were more than a little annoyed. I think we all heard the *Rocky* theme song in our heads. But this time, Connie didn't have to calm us down. There was no celebration.

The following week, we annihilated Maine West 76–26 and readied ourselves for our first meeting of the season against our rival, Maine South. The game was at Maine South and the Hawks were ready.

Why we would pick this night of all nights to act like teenagers is anyone's guess, but we did. Well, Bridget did anyway.

We were all in the locker room before the game when Bridget spotted a Maine South Hawk mascot costume on top of one of the lockers.

"Hey, Holly," Bridget said, "put this on."

Holly Andersen was a 5-11 freshman center on the JV team, but she had been practicing with us on Saturdays. Holly was in the same class as and friends with Bridget's younger sister Michelle, so Bridget knew enough about Holly to know she was gullible and decided to have some fun.

"Come on, Holly," Bridget urged. "It'll be so funny."

It didn't take much urging. Holly accepted a dare like it was a Baby Ruth bar. She put on the Hawk head and raced out into the gym before pregame warm-ups, slapping hands with whomever crossed her path. She figured she was safe since the giant head obscured her own. She forgot one small detail.

Holly's mom had found her shoes on sale that year. So, while the rest of us wore red, white, or some combination of both, Holly was perhaps the only kid in the school—and perhaps the state—who wore green gym shoes. Mrs. Mulder hardly had to be Detective Columbo to identify her, and she unraveled the mystery in about two seconds.

There's no telling if it made Maine South want to beat us even more than it usually did, but we were tight at the outset, as off-kilter a start to a game as we had had in two years. And the Hawks—towering over us with their triple-post offense featuring three starters at 5-10, 5-11, and 5-11—were conversely as hot as they had ever been. They seized the opportunity, not missing a shot for most of the first quarter, and ran out to a 17–0 lead before we knew what had hit us.

We called a timeout and looked at each other with ashen faces. Bridget couldn't make eye contact with anyone. But like reaching for a favorite old stuffed animal, we turned to our full-court press for reassurance, and it was there as always as we reeled off eight straight points following the timeout to pull to 19–8 at the end of the first quarter.

The game was fast-paced the rest of the way as we regained our equilibrium. Trailing 38–27, we were calm at the beginning of the third quarter, methodically chipping away at Maine South's lead and using our speed to offset their overwhelming size advantage. Connie was all over the court forcing steals with Barb, and she and Diana all but took over the offense, scoring 16 and 14 points, respectively, in the second half to lead us to a 68–64 victory. Connie finished with 24 points and Diana with 20 as our record improved to 10–0.

Fate was smiling on us, we decided, press or no press.

Well, fate and our pregame rituals, which had suddenly become superstitions and were the topic of discussion after the game. The way we opened our lockers and folded our socks and ate our pregame meals all took on immense importance. And after the Maine South win, someone pointed out that Bridget was wearing the same hideous underwear she wore when we won the Glenbrook North game in dramatic style.

Our center, whose taste in lingerie leaned toward the lacy bikini variety, was now stuck wearing her ugliest, least feminine pair, which came up not far below her armpits and made her feel as if she were about 60. Pleading that she only wore them when she was running low, she no longer had a choice. We could not take any chances.

CHAPTER 11

Having It All

OUR FAN BASE WAS GROWING.

It wasn't overwhelming or sudden, but one day we looked around the gym and noticed there were people no one really knew, just townspeople, neighbors of all of ours who came because they were curious and came back because they liked what they saw.

Among those strange faces was that of a skinny, blonde eighth grader named Becky Schnell, who had been attending our games with her father, a gym teacher and coach at Old Orchard Junior High School in Skokie. Coming to our basketball games was a refuge for Becky from life at home with an alcoholic mother.

Becky remembered well the day six years earlier when Title IX passed. She remembered because her father was well aware of the limitations placed on girls, and without a son, he had high hopes for Becky. "You're going to be able to play high school basketball now," he excitedly told Becky and her older sister, Pam. Becky was only a third grader at the time, but she was already showing unmistakable signs of athletic prowess.

And the first time she glimpsed our new red-and-white warm-ups, she was in love.

She watched Connie and me especially closely because we were guards like she was, studying exactly what we did and how we moved and marveling at Connie's overall ability. She had attended our supersectional against Hinsdale South the year before with her dad and had cried when we lost.

As an excruciatingly shy 13-year-old at tiny St. Paul Lutheran School, Becky never told anyone about a homelife that was quickly becoming intolerable because she thought she was the only kid going through such a mess. Just like DD. Just like Peggy. While her mom was able to hold a job and keep it together during the week, Becky grew to fear Saturdays and Sundays. And she knew by nine in the morning if it was going to be a good day—or not, as was more often the case.

I've got to get out of the house, she thought.

Alone by then with her sister a five-hour drive away at college, Becky called Pam when things were especially bad. "Here we go again," was all she needed to say. "I don't think I can handle this."

It was her husband's fault, in her mother's mind, that her daughters weren't feminine enough, that they didn't have boyfriends, and that they didn't get invited to dances. "I never got to raise daughters," she said to her family when the liquor was talking and she wasn't telling her girls they would never amount to anything.

What seemed to bother Becky's mother most was the age-old frustration of failing to keep up with the neighbors. Or anyone who seemingly had more than they did, people who could go on regular vacations and buy whatever they wanted. And she made no secret of her opinion that her husband and his teacher's salary were to blame for this as well.

"People don't really have all the stuff you think they do," her daughters and husband would tell her. But she scowled and simply got angrier.

Peggy could have related to the feeling of isolation.

Though life had settled down for Peggy in high school and she was quickly making her presence felt on our team, being with her family always reminded her of how close she was to the other side. Though she did not fully understand it yet, her father was an alcoholic, as were a good number of her cousins, aunts, uncles, and grandparents. Alcohol was so ingrained in all of their lives that Peggy simply knew no other way, though as a 16-year-old, she had not yet touched a drop of liquor herself. It wasn't so much that she was afraid of becoming an alcoholic, though genetics being what they are, she should have been. It simply did not appeal to her in high school, and besides, she had more important things to do—like work on her jump shot.

But alcohol infused her very existence. The relative who was perhaps closest to Peg was her grandmother Margaret, whom Peggy adored for her blunt, brash sense of humor and no-nonsense attitude. She always had her hair done and her nails polished, the picture of the prim and proper widow—except for the can of beer next to her. "Honey, go get me some more," her grandmother would cajole, and so on any given day, Peggy could be seen trudging down busy Dempster Street, lugging a case of beer and reasoning that it sort of counted as a workout.

One time when Peggy was 10, she asked her grandma if one of her uncles who had died was an alcoholic. "No," her grandma replied, "he was the finest drunk around. He drank nothing but the finest whiskeys and wore the finest suits."

Adults all made an impression on Peggy, one way or another, and Mrs. Mulder was in the process of unwittingly making one of the biggest. At our team banquet the previous spring, she had given each one of us a copy of *The Prophet*, the classic book of poetry by Kahlil Gibran, and written personal inscriptions of inspiration to each of us. Unlike most of us, Peggy actually read hers and treasured the book of aphorisms on such topics as love and giving, joy and sorrow, work and pleasure, marriage and children, teaching, friendship, pain, and beauty.

It didn't do anything for her jump shot and she was still awkward on the court, all elbows and knees. But she was improving as we began our second half of league play with a raging flu that swept through the team and left us with six players for our game at Maine West. It hardly mattered, as we still won by 50. In one week's span, we had defeated Glenbrook South 77–21, Maine East 74–49, and Maine West 76–26, the last two games on the road.

Even weak opponents did not seem to drag down our game, as often happens. In one sequence against Maine West, the game in which we had just one player on the bench because of the flu epidemic, Bridget hit a short jumper in the second quarter and picked up a foul. She missed the free throw, but Connie darted into the lane for the rebound and shoveled it to Peggy, who then dumped it to Karen for an easy lay-in and a four-point play to make the score 28–7.

Still in the first half, Connie scored on three consecutive steals off our press followed by full-court driving layups. Then, as the trailer on yet another steal and fast break, she followed her own miss to give us a 44–9 lead at the half. We scored in bunches the scoreboard operator could hardly keep up with, and it demoralized our opponents.

We were so sure of ourselves that we even seemed to intimidate the refs, like the time when the ball bounced off one of our players and out of bounds. Everyone in the building could see it had touched our player last. But bold as could be, Shirley reached toward the female official and snatched the ball before anyone had a chance to think about it. Shirley was so confident that even our opponents failed to argue as we quickly scored off the inbounds play.

It seemed we could do no wrong.

Arlene Mulder, meanwhile, felt like she could do nothing right.

Almost every game, her husband, Al, would show up with their two daughters, Michelle and Alison, now 10 and 6. Alison, wearing her little homemade Niles West cheerleader outfit, would crawl between her mother's knees as she sat on the bench, Mrs. Mulder oblivious to this as she coached but eventually sending her back up to Al in the stands. Al was clearly carrying the load at home these days, and though he did so willingly, it weighed on Mrs. Mulder.

"Daddy only combs the top of our heads in the morning," Michelle told her mother one day.

It was adorable and funny and might have made her laugh had the circumstances been different, but instead it made her cry, which she always did out of sight from her family and from us, sometimes in her car on her early morning drives to school or coming home, also in the dark.

At first, it had just been a few months of coaching tennis. Then later in the winter, there were a few months of basketball season. But now basketball started earlier and lasted longer, and in her first trimester, she was wearing down. Sometimes she would be so exhausted, Al would tell her not to drive home at all, and she would simply plop down on the trainers' table in our locker room. She didn't need much sleep, but she could doze off anywhere at a moment's notice. During her long commutes to school, she had a recurring conversation with herself: *I'm a lousy mother, a lousy wife, and I'm probably not doing a good job teaching or coaching. I'm trying to do too much and not doing a good job of any of it. Am I really doing this for the right reasons?*

The truth was that she loved almost every minute of coaching, and she felt selfish for it. At least this pregnancy would eventually give her some time to think. At the pace we were going, there was precious little time for that either.

We were not particularly worried about the Waukegan East game on February 9 as we took the school's first trip there since '75, but suddenly, the adults were all talking about our safety. It was the first time we had ever played the predominantly black school at their gym, and despite our earlier 75–38 victory, we had heard from opponents that their gym was a "tough place to play." It was also the most unusual place we had ever played, with the first row of bleachers raised about 15 feet above the floor and a railing all around, giving us the feeling that we were foreign invaders battling before a hungry crowd.

That attitude, the fear, and the reputation we'd heard about were steeped in racial prejudice. If you'd asked any of us if we feared or distrusted black people or if we flat-out did not like them, most of us would have unequivocally said no. And in our hearts, we would've believed it. But there was no question that we looked at our Waukegan East game differently from the rest. While it was not the only predominantly black team we played, the school's reputation—at least from what we heard and perceived—was that they were rougher, maybe even played dirty, and that going there was somehow dangerous.

Indeed, it was easily the most physical game we had ever played. We won, 67–53, but shot horribly and came out of it angry at what we thought was a lack of control by the officials, as two Waukegan East players had actually challenged Connie and me to a fight after the game.

The home crowd was dissatisfied as well, appalled in part, we assumed, by the apparent ease with which a team that was smaller, slower, and apparently in possession of fewer skills than their players had won. They were also furious at the disparity in free throws, as we converted 21-of-34 from the foul line, while the Bulldogs were 3-of-12.

We dressed quickly and quietly afterward, and then Mrs. Mulder came into the locker room and told us we would have a police escort to our bus. A school official had asked if we'd like one and she figured if they were offering, she'd accept.

"Are they kidding?" Connie asked no one in particular. And we all laughed nervously.

But when we emerged from the locker room and walked outside, a seemingly angry group of Waukegan East fans had gathered, and we huddled together and hustled onto the bus before the driver peeled out, leaving the crowd behind.

Was it a case of fervent basketball fans getting emotional over a tough loss to a conference rival they thought they should beat? Or were they frustrated and angry that we felt we required police protection? Most likely, they were just basketball parents waiting for their kids like our parents did, and we had let our imaginations run wild. Whatever it was, Mrs. Mulder preferred to downplay any racial angle as we muttered among ourselves that we were the victims.

Whomever we played by this point, it was safe to say they were especially motivated to knock us off. Glenbrook North was next, and though the game was in our gym, Mrs. Mulder cautioned us that we would be facing another angry team out to avenge an earlier defeat. And unlike Waukegan East, Glenbrook North really should have beaten us the last time we played, considering they had led the entire game and were up by 10 points with less than two minutes left when we suddenly snatched an unlikely victory.

The Spartans were 5–1 and in second place in the Central Suburban League South behind Niles West, now 7–0 in conference play. But they were missing their top scorer, and we poured it on, outscoring them 20–4 in the third quarter to expand an 18-point halftime lead to 34. Shirley, Connie, and Bridget each had 14 points, and Shirley was all over the boards with 13 rebounds. Peggy scored 10 points off the bench and we won in a rout, 65–28.

After another easy victory over Maine West, 77–23, we were 15–0 overall going into our second tournament of the season, the Libertyville Invitational. We were psyched up for another tournament, greedy to collect another trophy en route to the big one at the end of the season. But our sophomore guard, Barb Atsaves, had other things on her mind.

Barb had sprained her ankle during the Maine West game, and besides worrying about whether she could play in Libertyville, she wondered how she was going to try out for the cheerleading squad the next day while wearing a big ACE bandage on her leg. The spring tryouts determined who would be cheerleaders for the next school year, and Barb, despite the ACE bandage, made the squad as expected. But it was clear to her now that she had to make a decision. Cheerleading and basketball practices were going to conflict, and she was already well aware of how Mrs. Mulder felt about other commitments.

In the end, Barb chose basketball over cheerleading, but it was not without significant anxiety and some not-so-subtle peer pressure by her fellow cheerleaders, who wondered aloud why in the world she would want to be a jock instead of a cheerleader. Barb's ankle and psyche recovered in time for the Libertyville tournament, which promised to bring as much stiff competition as Evanston had, with some of the top teams from our surrounding conferences competing.

That said, we still coasted through our first two contests with a 71–35 victory over Zion and a 55–33 win over Maine North. Looming in the bottom half of the bracket were Libertyville, Hersey, and Maine South. Hersey, 13–9 and fourth in the Mid-Suburban League North, eventually knocked off both Maine South and Libertyville to get in the title game against us.

Again, Mrs. Mulder warned us not to take our opponent lightly. Despite their record, Hersey had defeated two former conference champs that season in Crystal Lake and Buffalo Grove. We listened and tried to heed her warning. But unlike the Evanston tournament, when we had actually enjoyed sitting around the locker room all day waiting for the title game, our game against Maine North started at 10 a.m., and we were cold, stiff, and tired by game time that night.

It showed immediately with a poor shooting start as Hersey took a 24–21 lead at the half. We came back to life in the third quarter, as Shirley had nine points to help us outscore Hersey, 17–6, and take an eight-point lead into the final quarter. But that's when Hersey's 5-6 junior, Debbie Barnd, took over. In a shooting slump to that point, Barnd suddenly led her team on a 10–2 spurt, including 7-of-7 free throws, which tied the score at 40. Barnd then fed a teammate for a layup and iced the victory with a final three-point play.

At 45–44, we still had a chance when Judy went to the foul line with 18 seconds left. But she missed the front half of the one-and-one and failed on a last-second shot attempt.

Afterward, Judy was inconsolable, though not in the way a lot of kids would be inconsolable. There were no tears, just a stubborn, surly silence. We pleaded with her to stop punishing herself, tried to assure her that it was our crummy shooting the entire night and not her free throw that lost the game for us. But she remained mute. Instead, she took off her shoes and in the now-empty gym, picked up a basketball, walked to the foul line in her stocking feet, and took aim.

"Judy, come on," said Shirley. "What are you trying to prove? Stop it. We win as a team and we lose as a team."

But Judy ignored her, bounced the ball deliberately, then shot. And just as we knew she would—just as we had done at an 80 percent clip as a team all season long—she lofted up the perfect free throw, barely rippling the net as it went through.

She then looked at us solemnly and walked off. It was silly really, the whole thing, and silly for us to be mourning a loss that in the long run would do nothing to affect our chances of going downstate.

Judy knew that, just as we all did, and minutes after thinking her world had come to an end at age 16, she was smiling again at the absurdity of it all. Now feeling much better, she decided that as long as she had her socks on, she may as well slide off the gym floor and into the locker room, and so she did. Except that she miscalculated slightly, veered off course, and landed in a pile of debris that was exposed when the bleachers were pushed back. As she got up, wrinkling her nose and wondering why she felt wet, we collapsed on the ground in hysterics, for as best as we could tell, Judy was now covered in someone else's vomit.

Mrs. Mulder wondered why we were wiping tears from our eyes and giggling as we boarded the bus, but she didn't question it. Apparently, we had already put the loss behind us. Still, as we returned to school that night, our coach worried about how we would respond from that point until regionals in two weeks. She also worried about how we would respond to the news that she was pregnant and coaching her last games with us.

But she also knew there was no hiding it any longer. She was entering her second trimester with her third baby, and she had clearly "popped," or so she told Jean Armour when she asked for her advice. She also asked Mr. Schnurr and a few others, and they all agreed that she needed to give her team enough time to digest the news and get used to it before the postseason began.

And that was now.

"You were right," she told us as our bus cruised through the dark suburban streets, "when you made the point about our team being a seed that has grown all season. Mr. Schnurr told you that at the beginning of the season and it was in your last poem to me, and that development is something that reflects our hard work."

Our eyes began to glaze over. We had absolutely no idea what she was talking about.

Finally, without actually using the word *pregnant*, she spat it out.

"We're having another baby," she said.

And she was leaving us.

At 16, 17, and 18 years old, this was a lot for us to process. Of course, there was the instant embarrassment and revulsion every kid feels when digesting the notion that their parents, or in this case a parental figure, did what they had to do to have a baby. Then there was the common sense reaction to be happy for this person whom we cared for and who was experiencing one of the true joys of life. That lasted for about five or six seconds, followed by the selfish teenage reaction—perhaps the overriding emotion, for me anyway, which centered completely on me and how this would affect my life. And I didn't like it. Not one bit.

Someone joked that the kid's name had to be "Westley" for Niles West, and Mrs. Mulder promised that if she had a boy, Westley it would be. It was one great big joyous moment.

I looked around at the seniors, resentful as hell.

Of course they're happy for Mrs. Mulder and excited about the news, I fumed silently. What did they care? They were graduating. We would win the state championship together and then they would all go out contented and victorious, without a second thought to the rest of us they would leave behind. She said she was going on maternity leave but we all knew better. She wasn't coming back, and I felt betrayed. At least my mother had trained me well enough to pretend I was happy.

We were now 17–1 following the Libertyville tournament with four games left before regionals began. Once again, we handled Glenbrook South and Maine East easily, winning by an average of 41 points, but had two tough foes remaining in Mid-Suburban League North champ Buffalo Grove and good ol' Maine South.

We had the best crowd of the season for the Buffalo Grove game, but again we came out flat. Connie was especially uptight after spotting DePaul women's basketball coach John Lawler in the stands.

"It'll be fine," I told her before the game. "He already knows how good you are. There's no added pressure."

I probably could have chosen not to use the word *pressure* in any context. She had been writing to various colleges all season, inviting coaches to come watch her play, sending them film of our games. But aside from DePaul, she was getting almost no response, and it was starting to make her nervous. More than that, it made her realize that we would have to make it downstate for coaches to actually see her in person and for her to have any chance at all at a scholarship.

When Buffalo Grove senior Joyce Gallagher hit a last-second jumper to hand us our second defeat of the season, 44–42, Connie figured the DePaul coach was probably ready to award Gallagher a scholarship on the spot.

In one 10-day span, we had lost twice and were officially in a slump, at least for us. Mrs. Mulder used the fact that it was exam time and that we were all good students as an uncharacteristic excuse to reporters. But she worried that the baby news had thrown us off. All that was left now was Maine South, the same Maine South that had run out to a 17–0 lead against us earlier in the season before we pulled out a four-point win. Of course, that was the night we had warmed up by watching Bridget goad Holly Andersen into running through Maine South's gym wearing their mascot's head. Just a guess, but that might have fired them up.

This time, we had Parents' Night to motivate us, really just another excuse to try to get more people to come watch us. The seniors' parents were given flowers and introduced on court before the game; it was all very sentimental and sweet, and it apparently put us in the perfect frame of mind to crush Maine South, which we did, 73–50, in our regular-season finale.

CHAPTER 12

The Mighty Susies and Other Technicalities

IT WAS A SATURDAY NIGHT before regionals and Mrs. Mulder, as she often did, hopped into her car to scout a future opponent. Her kids weren't asleep, but she had been able to make them dinner, so for the moment anyway, all was good and guilt-free. She tuned her radio to WCLR, a Top 40 station, and wound her way out of Arlington Heights, the shortcuts to virtually every school in the northern and western suburbs of Chicago as familiar to her as a trip to the grocery store she had no time for these days.

She made these excursions on her own, her husband, Al, as always, looking after their daughters, and she never told us. Nor did we ask. We figured she got her information from opposing coaches or from the occasional film we were able to obtain. She didn't think we cared much one way or the other. She imagined her players were enjoying their off-night as most teenagers would—out to a movie with friends, on a date, or better still, she hoped, at home watching television in their pajamas.

When she arrived at the game, however, she found the majority of her team in the stands, as Shirley and I had hopped in a car as well that night and met Connie, Peggy, Judy, and Karen, figuring we could get something valuable out of watching a future opponent.

"What are you girls doing here?" Mrs. Mulder asked, not altogether pleased. She did that pursed lips thing she only pulled out when really angry, while we squirmed in our seats like we were caught in the back of a VW van with a heavy metal rock band. Her mind raced. What would her players gain by actually watching our next opponent without her filtering that impression as she always did? And what would the opposing team think? Maybe this would fire them up even more. This was not in the game plan, and Arlene Mulder always had a game plan.

But as we sat together and watched, she realized that this was not a fun Saturday night out for us. We studied their defense and memorized their offense and began to formulate a strategy on our own. And so our coach stopped worrying—at least for the time being.

The next week, we were the subject of a long feature story in the *Lerner Life* suburban newspaper, previewing our prospects in the state tournament and in regionals, where we were to face Niles North and then, if all went as expected, St. Scholastica. Jim Braun, the sports editor, had become our official chronicler along with Susan Sternberg of the *Suburban Trib*, and on this occasion, he also wrote about our desire to go to Champaign, with "the opportunity to compete with Kojak and Love Boat on prime-time television."

We smiled to ourselves at the thought of playing on "prime-time television" opposite *The Love Boat*, but this was no laughing matter. The memory of last year's supersectional loss to Hinsdale South never completely left our thoughts. Unlike last year, Mrs. Mulder noted repeatedly, we were the hunted, and there was nothing each of our opponents would rather do than knock off the team now considered one of the favorites for the state title.

Just as she continued to harp on the fact that everyone was

gunning for us, Mulder also continued to promote the team concept. But as the season wore on, she abandoned that strategy and simply insisted on mentioning every single one of us in every article. And local writers knew better by now than to push one of us over another, lest they be turned down in their next interview request.

"Every time we take the court, we know we have 10 girls," Mulder told Braun. "It doesn't allow them to be selfish."

We entered the postseason 20–2, averaging 66 points per game while allowing just 42. But a stark reality hung over us as we began the 1978 girls' state playoffs. Our coach was leaving us. And with every game, our seniors could be looking at the end of their athletic careers. But this only motivated us further. We would win it for Mrs. Mulder. And we would send our seniors out as champions.

Regionals were held at Niles West, and the bleachers were filled nearly all the way to the balcony for our first game against Niles North. We had no real worries about our Skokie neighbors just a few exits down the Edens Expressway, and we had no reason to as we notched an easy 64–34 victory.

St. Scholastica won a two-point squeaker over Evanston to set up the regional final two nights later. It would be our first step in the postseason, a new theme Mrs. Mulder had invoked, this idea that every game built on the step that came before. The gym was near filled again, and we were ready for JoAnn Feiereisel and the mighty Susies.

Yes, the *Susies.*

For years, many high school and college women's teams were not given the same nicknames as the guys' teams. Instead of the Warriors or Spartans, it was the Warriorettes or Spartanettes, or worse, the Lady Spartans, as if somehow that made it OK for girls to compete. More ladylike. We hated that. We had played St.

Scholastica twice before over the last two years, and they always played us tough, but their nickname never escaped us. In their defense, they had little choice in being an all-girls school or the Susies, but still, we had our principles.

The night of the St. Scholastica game, one of Niles West's school administrators gave us each a rose dyed green for St. Patrick's Day. But we were in no mood for roses. We filled out goal cards for the game, and Bridget and Diana both wrote BE MEAN in large capital letters across their index cards. Bridget added, "Don't get mad at myself, push harder, be intense."

Then she went out and broke Feiereisel's jaw.

Well, not intentionally or anything. But in a mad scrum for a loose ball in the latter stages of a game that began with Bridget trying to wrestle the ball out of Feiereisel's grasp, the St. Scholastica star ended up sprawled headlong on the floor.

Bridget was getting tougher every day, but she wasn't that tough. As we clapped her on the back, encouraging her aggressive play before realizing that Feiereisel had actually injured herself and that she would, in fact, be taken to the hospital by ambulance with a dislocated jaw, Bridget recoiled in horror. "I wasn't trying to hurt her, I swear," she wailed, trying to convince teammates who did not need convincing.

We wondered if this was the official end of her mean streak.

In the end, we cruised to our second consecutive regional championship with a 65–42 victory over the Susies.

Bridget may have been somewhat subdued, but we didn't let that stop our celebration. No one had a ladder ready for us to cut down the nets and so, once again, we hoisted each other up on the taller girls' shoulders. I stood on Shirley without the slightest thought that maybe putting 100-plus additional pounds on the shoulders of our leading scorer was not the smartest idea. It did not occur to Shirley either. The moment was too sweet, our emotions too overwhelming to think very rationally. But unlike the year before, we looked ahead almost immediately.

"We're happy we won," Connie told reporters, "but this isn't our ultimate goal."

We all solemnly nodded in agreement. And apparently, the rest of the school was in sync with us because they didn't seem satisfied with just a regional title either.

All around us, our classmates and teachers joined in our effort to go downstate. Bridget's accounting teacher put up a transparency on the overhead projector each day with our scores and next games. Mr. Karbusicky did the same thing in history. Signs started going up in the halls, and kids whom I had barely spoken to all year suddenly smiled at me or whispered words of encouragement in the back of Mrs. O'Reilly's Spanish class.

Connie's boyfriend, Bob, hid in the back with me, where we always had a great time discussing basketball and butchering the Spanish language. Bob had started doing stats for Mrs. Mulder and had convinced his friends, like many of the upperclass boys, to follow us. We had wanted a crowd and now we had it.

The school provided a fan bus to sectionals at East Leyden High School, and it filled up quickly. We would be playing Elk Grove, the Mid-Suburban League South champ, in our first-round game, and we knew that they, like so many of our opponents, would outsize us. But we also knew that with every game, we seemed to not just improve our offense or defense or both but to become more dimensional.

Connie was now showing the same aggressiveness on offense as she showed on defense. Confident now of her foul shooting, she drove the lane whenever there was an opportunity and was the only one on the team who had developed an actual jump shot. I wanted dearly to be able to jump then shoot, just like the pros and the boys did it. But hard as I tried, my jumper was more of a jump-and-push, and so I had to settle for set shots. My brother Barry urged me to at least get the ball up over my head, à la Jamaal Wilkes of the LA Lakers, despite the fact that as a 6-foot-6 professional athlete, Wilkes had a slight advantage over me.

Though Barb was only a sophomore, her shot was already a thing of beauty as she hoisted it back over her head, her hands in perfect position, the rotation of the ball consistent, her follow-through a textbook example of how it should be.

By now Barb had begun asserting herself offensively as the shooting guard and had established herself as a bona fide starter, though I remained in the starting lineup. My job was to bring the ball upcourt and to set up our offense from the point-guard spot. But Barb got plenty of minutes, and Mrs. Mulder, using her system, was able to keep all of us happy and involved.

Elk Grove had a center-oriented offense keyed around their 5-11 senior Carole Pollitz, who averaged 16 points per game. They also relied on their 5-11 senior forward Kim Richardson, who averaged 20 points in regionals. But they weren't ready for our array of full-court zone presses—we were now solid with six different looks—and we made them pay.

After clinging to a 19–13 lead after the first quarter, we outscored Elk Grove 23–7 in the second, limiting our opponent to just one field goal and forcing 20 turnovers for a convincing 74–40 victory. Bridget held Pollitz to 11 points, while on the defensive end, Pollitz drew four fouls in the first half and fouled out in the third quarter. Connie and Shirley were also in foul trouble, but Diana and Barb picked up the offensive slack with 24 and 19 points, respectively, while Peggy pitched in with 12.

A *Chicago Tribune* story that week centered on Bridget and her blue-collar attitude. "Niles West's Bridget Berglund doesn't get a lot of publicity," Reid Hanley wrote. "She just does her job. Her job isn't a glamorous one. She doesn't score a lot of points and doesn't do anything fancy. She just plays hard-nosed defense."

Bridget had arrived.

The sectional final was against Wheeling. Now we were two

steps away from a trip to Champaign, and I wrote about it in that game's poem:

> Climbing the steps toward total success will take
>   teamwork and desire.
> We'll work toward our goals while playing
>   tonight, then reset them even higher.
> We're still showing teams that have two or three
>   stars that they can't beat a team that has 10.
> Our spirits are high, our minds intense, we're
>   closer now than we've ever been.

Mrs. Mulder could have read my poems to herself and stuck them in a drawer, but she never did. She went over our opponent during her pregame speech and, then, maybe knowing that her message would always be incorporated into that game's poem, would end her speech by reading the poem aloud, slowly, clearly, and with the proper cadence. I would always blush, though she was not supposed to know that I had written them. But I was also pleased that she read them to the team and in just the right way.

Like so many of our opponents, Wheeling had a star player. Her name was Sandy Rainey, and though the 5-9 senior was still recovering from the effects of double pneumonia, she sure looked like she was healthy, scoring 24 points against Oak Park in their first-round sectional contest. Again, we would need Bridget to be tough.

Rainey, her socks drooping around her ankles, looked like a female "Pistol Pete" Maravich and showed us moves we had not seen before. In the second quarter, Wheeling led by as many as six points and were winning 27–23 with just two minutes until the half. But as we had all year long, we turned our defense into our most effective offense.

In a matter of just 20 seconds, Barb hit a jumper and Diana and Barb scored off steals. Wheeling tied the score at 29 just before intermission, but the momentum was clearly ours. In the first three minutes of the third quarter, we kept the pressure on and rattled Wheeling's backcourt, forcing multiple turnovers and outscoring them in runs of 10–0 and 18–4. Where there was a basketball, there were Niles West double- and triple-teams.

While an ultimately exhausted Wheeling team substituted just once the entire game, we used all 10 players as always and finished with four girls—Diana, Barb, Connie, and Peggy—in double figures, winning the sectional title 66–50.

"That's just something the kids do because they want the ball," Mrs. Mulder said to reporters of our defensive intensity after the game. "We play basketball from end line to end line. The only time you catch your breath on this team is on the bench."

Once again, we had reached the supersectionals, the Sweet 16 of Illinois girls' basketball. And less than 12 hours after accepting another trophy and snipping down another set of nets, we were back on the court.

Sitting in the stands before practice began the next afternoon, Connie casually folded up the newspaper.

"Sterling lost," she muttered to our coach.

Mrs. Mulder was not surprised. Sterling was Illinois' first-ever girls' state champs, winning the title the year before, and she had admitted to Braun earlier in the season that she thought the school in northwestern Illinois was making a fatal mistake by trying to pad their record while not scheduling any quality opponents, despite numerous requests by several Chicago-area schools.

But we didn't care about Sterling. At 24–2, the only thing that stood between us and a trip downstate was 26–2 Dundee from northwest Carpentersville. And no one was talking about our two losses anymore.

Dundee had beaten Central Suburban League North champion Waukegan West 76–72 in its sectional final, and unlike our games against Wheeling and other opponents of ours, this was not going to be a case of merely trying to subdue one key player.

In fact, though Dundee had two standouts in guards Pat Morency and Nancy Horgan, the Cardinals were a team not unlike us—small but quick, athletic, well-coached, and disciplined. Still, one of their losses during the season came at the hands of Elk Grove, a team we had beaten by 34, and that was hard to keep out of our minds.

We had several potential distractions leading up to the game. Two days after our sectional victory, the *Suburban Trib* announced its first all-star girls' basketball team, and we were one of only two teams to place two players—Connie Erickson and Shirley Cohen—on the team. Connie and Shirley also made the all–Chicago area team and with Diana were named all-conference as well.

Of course, Mrs. Mulder paid little attention to individual accomplishments and was not about to change now, and Connie and Shirley barely acknowledged the honors as it was not their style either. But there were five days between the sectional triumph and the supersectional game—too much time to think. Still confident we would be making the trip downstate, we allowed a niggling thought to reenter our consciousness.

We were confident in Mrs. Mulder. She had taken us this far. But soon the whispers of others, specifically some of the male teachers and coaches, became ours as well. Still reliant on Billy Schnurr for his help in practice, we wondered if we needed him on the bench for the Dundee game against Paul Judson, a coach who was, well, a man.

Judson was known for his ability to bully and intimidate officials. Gene Earl, the boys' freshman basketball coach, had been scouting Dundee for Mrs. Mulder at the request of Mr. Schnurr and let both of them know that Judson could dictate the tempo of the game from the sidelines if we weren't careful.

It was a full week before the game, which was to be played at Barrington High School, a suburb 30 miles northwest of our school, and Schnurr walked over to Mulder with two cups of coffee in his hands and sat at their usual corner table in the teachers' lounge.

"Arlene, this guy is going to be trouble," he said.

No explanation was necessary. She knew he was talking about Judson.

"You're probably going to have to draw a technical early to get treated fairly," Schnurr said.

She looked at him as if he were suggesting that she commit a felony, and she had the same sick feeling as she had had at the picket line.

"Billy, really?" she said. "You think that's going to be necessary?"

"It's basketball, Arlene," he said. "And yes."

The idea of Mr. Schnurr joining Mrs. Mulder on our bench had floated around before, and she never had an ego about accepting coaching help. In the early days of her coaching career, it was not uncommon for someone to walk through the gym, as Earl did one night, and point out something one of us was doing incorrectly.

Mrs. Mulder had stopped him as he walked away. "Any time you see us doing something wrong, feel free to correct it," she told Earl. "I'm not proud. I can use any help I can get."

She still felt that way. And the next day in the teachers' lounge, she brought their coffee over to their usual table and looked Schnurr square in the eye.

"Billy, I can use your help on the bench," she said as she sat down.

Schnurr was ambivalent. On the one hand, he was flattered that we felt we needed him. On the other, he did not want to undermine Mulder and did not want us to think his presence was necessary to get us downstate. "I'd love to, but you don't need me, Arlene," he said. "And I don't want to confuse the issue."

"But I bring you in to talk to them and it doesn't confuse them," Mulder insisted. "They know I'm their coach."

Schnurr had enjoyed his interactions with us more than he would have ever imagined. Many nights he would go home after one of our sessions still shaking his head. "They're so receptive and so hungry for basketball knowledge," he'd tell his wife about us. "I wish I could see 10 percent of their desire in my players." But he also respected his friendship with Mrs. Mulder and did not want to threaten her authority in any way. Besides, the decision had already been made for him.

Unbeknownst to Mrs. Mulder, our principal, Dr. Mannos, heard the scuttlebutt and went straight to Mr. Schnurr that week. "I know what people are saying, but this is Arlene's team, Billy, not yours," Dr. Mannos told him. "I won't let you sit on the bench."

"Arlene, I'll watch from the stands," Schnurr told her. "You'll be fine."

There would be no more discussion. Not from us and certainly not from Mr. Schnurr. Mrs. Mulder would coach as she always had. And we would walk into a frenzy the likes of which we could not have imagined.

CHAPTER 13

The Ultimate Slap

THE GYM WAS PACKED FOR THE GAME, a bigger crowd at 1,800-plus than we had ever played before by far, including more high school boys than you'd see at a typical homecoming dance. They had descended on Barrington High in carload after carload—football players, basketball players, band members, thespians, the gym rats not quite good enough to make their own varsity teams but who had helped make us better in scrimmages. These were boys I would not attempt to speak to in the hallway, but they were here for us, all of them.

We could tell by the noise alone how big the crowd was without taking a step out of the locker room. But the din outside the doors led to an ultimate sin inside.

Someone had handed Shirley a fake front page with a big bold headline reading NILES WEST GIRLS MAKE THE ELITE EIGHT, and we all cheered when she showed it to us, oblivious to the concept of jinxing ourselves.

Our parents apparently shared this lack of awareness.

Bridget excitedly explained that her dad had a few newspapers of his own and was passing them out to our fans. "When they announce Dundee's lineup, everyone is going to pretend to read the paper," Bridget told us in the locker room. "And then when we're announced, they're going to rip it up and fling it like confetti!"

Peg and I exchanged eye rolls, which was our fallback reaction to just about everything.

"Seriously?" I asked with just the right mix of "Really?" and "You've got to be kidding."

It didn't seem altogether cool, but we laughed along with the others, our adrenaline pretty much making anything seem funny and exciting. The locker room was loose, and that was a good thing.

But as we emerged from the locker room, Connie picked up on something immediately.

"Woman refs," she whispered.

We all sighed. We hadn't had female officials in regionals or sectionals, but we had occasionally run across some over the last three years, and it was rarely a good thing. Though we were all for equal rights, or at least we thought we were, it was painfully obvious that woman officials had a long way to go to catch up with their male colleagues. Refereeing was not just a skill but one that required instincts that could only be honed through experience, something these women just did not have yet. This, of course, was not their fault. It was a vicious cycle. They needed experience, just as we did, to get better. But in the process of gaining experience, they were setting the game back. Or, at least, we felt this way.

And it made little sense to Mrs. Mulder and to us that a game as important as the one that would determine who would advance downstate to the Elite Eight would be one in which they could afford to have woman officials gain experience.

Still, we felt we were more than ready. This was our fifth postseason game en route to the eight-team state finals. One more victory and the one word locked into our collective consciousness, the chant ringing in our ears, would materialize. *Downstate. Downstate.*

For the first time, that meant traveling 180 miles south to Champaign and the University of Illinois—the 16,000-seat Assembly Hall, which was the crown jewel of Illinois high school basketball and, until the previous year, the exclusive goal of every red-blooded boy in the state.

Now it was our goal. *Our* state tournament. And at this point, it felt like we could simply will it to happen. Just one more victory.

The year before, in the supersectionals against Hinsdale South, the moment had clearly overwhelmed us. But not now, we told ourselves. We would not be intimidated. Not by the crowd and not by our opponent, even with its celebrity coach. This was where we were supposed to be. With every early-morning run up and down the circular stairwell, we were sure. With every bus ride punctuated by our cheers: *Give me an R. Give me an* A . . .

It was one of our standbys. We would spell "Ray Rayner," the name of the host of a popular children's morning show in Chicago. Win a high school state championship in Illinois, and the newly crowned victors could expect an invitation to appear on his show.

What other girls' basketball team in the state was doing a Ray Rayner cheer? No one. So call us cocky. But then, what other girls' basketball team practiced on its own at five in the morning before the season began, we asked ourselves. What other team scrimmaged like we did against boys who blocked our shots and bloodied our noses and sent Karen Wikstrom to the hospital? What other team was so fixated on going downstate that one player not sprinting through one drill would draw the wrath of all the rest? And what other group of girls had this one ambition burned into their souls the way we did? If there were others, then they weren't as loud or as tough or as determined. Of this, we were certain.

And yet, at the moment, it was all slipping away.

We had swallowed up the Dundee Cardinals' press and had clearly shaken them early with our full-court zone press. But by the end of the first quarter, Shirley and Connie had each picked up three fouls, and even I was in foul trouble, which was unheard of, picking up my third with three minutes still left in the first quarter.

The second quarter had scarcely begun when Bridget was whistled for her third foul, and with 6:07 left until halftime, Shirley was called for her fourth.

Mrs. Mulder stood up, smoothed her dress, and politely addressed one of the officials.

"Come on, ref, call it evenly," our coach protested.

"Sit down," the ref barked back at her as she slinked back to our bench.

Everything Mrs. Mulder had heard about Dundee coach Paul Judson intimidating officials was coming true as he sauntered up and down the sideline like some slick politician stumping for votes, keeping up a running dialogue with the refs and smirking in our general direction. But four months pregnant and already feeling very tight around the waistband, our coach was in a foul mood and not about to head off to her maternity leave without a fight.

At halftime, the score was tied at 36, and in the locker room, a hint of panic mixed with blind rage had begun to settle in. Mrs. Mulder, a paragon of decorum and femininity, was clearly about to blow.

She inhaled and exhaled like a bull getting ready to spear some poor matador, as angry as we had ever seen her, and it somehow picked up our spirits a bit to know that our coach was as frustrated as we were. She tried to keep her mind on the game as she gave her usual halftime admonitions and adjustments, but she was planning her next move. And what we did not see as we jogged back on court was our coach cornering both refs outside the locker room, just out of everyone's sight.

This was not in her nature, and she knew it. She was not brought up to question authority, much less confront it. This was not the way she taught her players to behave. But she took a few cleansing breaths and launched in.

"This is against my principles," she began, her voice trembling with barely controlled fury, "but I'm tired of watching this. My team is better, and you're not giving us a chance. If you don't start calling this fairly, I'm not going to be responsible for my behavior."

Predictably, they said nothing, and Mrs. Mulder returned to the court. It was not the best speech she had ever delivered, but she was proud of herself for stepping out of character and defending her team. Still, she was shaken and so were we.

What aggravated us the most was that Connie's third foul had been whistled by a ref standing so far away she'd have been lucky to read the number on Connie's jersey. But we knew why she called it. She heard the slap. We all heard the slap. It was Connie's way of getting into defensive position, of getting herself psyched. She'd slap her thighs or the floor or both as she bent her knees and glared at her opponent. The ref heard the slap and assumed it was a foul.

This, not just the foul but what it represented, absolutely infuriated us. Why couldn't the woman refs raise the level of their game as we girls had raised ours? Why couldn't they keep up with us as we sprinted up and down the court? And why, in the name of everything that was sacred, could they not tell a self-inflicted thigh slap from a foul?

Afraid that Shirley and Connie were going to foul out, Mrs. Mulder opted to sit them for the entire third quarter, a decision that dramatically shifted the momentum of the game and knocked the wind out of at least one row of Niles West supporters, specifically Billy Schnurr and Walt Cocking, a guidance counselor at the school and a long-time high school basketball official.

Cocking was apoplectic. "Billy, what is she doing?" he wailed as Dundee pulled out to an eight-point lead. Schnurr and Cocking agreed that Mulder should have kept Shirley on the bench in the second quarter after she had picked up her third foul. But not in the third quarter. Not when her team needed her most.

Shirley was equally aggravated. She could keep from fouling out, she thought. Why couldn't Mrs. Mulder understand this? Not that she would ever put up a fight or, worse yet, pout on the bench. But sitting there next to Connie, it was all Shirley could do not to grab our coach by the shoulders and put herself back into the game.

Behind the unconscious shooting of Dundee's guards, and without Shirley and Connie's steady leadership, the Cardinals outscored us 20–12 in the third quarter to take a 56–48 lead into the fourth.

With Shirley still on the bench, Bridget fouled out 14 seconds into the fourth quarter. Diana hit two quick jumpers right after that to close the gap to six at 60–54, but for the most part, Dundee sneered at our press, breaking through and scoring a pair of breakaway layups to push its lead back to 10.

With Shirley about to implode on the bench and just 4:44 remaining in regulation, Mrs. Mulder finally sent her back in following a timeout. Immediately, Shirley scored off a pick on our inbounds play. But with 3:32 left, our captain and leader and the heart of our team walked off the court with her fifth foul. Once again, it was a questionable call, and as she left the game, Shirley stopped and, with an expression that conveyed all of her anger and frustration, her passion and will to win, pointed to our bench to rally us as the ref tried to hustle her off the court.

"We are *not* giving in," she shouted, "and we are *not* giving up." We all silently nodded in agreement.

Connie grabbed Shirley by the wrist and gently guided her toward the sideline. We didn't need a technical at that point.

Even trailing by 11 points as we were, with three and a half minutes left in regulation, this was not a situation that would have or should have made us panic. We all surely remembered pulling off a 10-point comeback in a game earlier in the season with less than a minute remaining. I knew for sure Connie was not thinking defeat as she squirted in on a patented drive. Diana followed with a steal off our full-court press and a layup, and Barb added another steal and a layup, cutting Dundee's lead to five.

While Judson played all of his starters without a rest, we rotated all 10 of our players, and it looked as if it was going to pay off. When Judson called a timeout with 2:44 left in regulation, his players were bent over, sucking wind.

I found a seat on the bench next to Shirley after also fouling out, and we kept the sweat going while cheering on our teammates. "Intensity!" we screamed at each other in the huddle, our buzzword taking on even more urgency, and we promptly narrowed the deficit to three. But Dundee guard Nancy Horgan responded with a jumper, and Pat Morency answered a pair of free throws by Connie with two of her own to keep Dundee's lead at five with 1:29 remaining.

Connie stole the inbounds pass, but Barb missed a layup. She made up for it, though, with another steal leading to a breakaway basket to trim Dundee's lead to 71–68 with 45 seconds left as the Cardinals' attempt at a four-corner stall appeared to be backfiring on them.

We caught a break when Dundee's center popped wide open for a shot and missed from short range. But a medium-range jumper by Diana rimmed out and Morency clawed away the rebound, drawing the foul with six seconds showing on the clock and all but crushing our chances.

As Morency strode to the foul line, in order to remove even the remotest possibility of fouling us, we could only surmise, Judson ordered his other four players to sit down on the court in front of their bench. We looked over in disbelief. This was the same guy who had been holding up giant posters with numbered plays written on them throughout the game, a weird tactic to be sure. But this was much weirder. And this showed us up.

We glared at him with eyes red and wet from fatigue and frustration as Morency calmly sunk both foul shots. On the bench now sat our entire starting lineup, all of us fouled out, angry and helpless, while on the court, Peggy scored one last lonely layup for a 73–70 defeat as we tried not to cry.

We had edged out the Cardinals in field goals scored, and our press forced a whopping 35 Dundee turnovers. But the difference in fouls—29 for us, compared with 13 for Dundee—was just as astounding and enough to offset their sloppiness.

At the buzzer, Dundee's half of the 1,800 fans crammed into the Barrington gym surged onto the floor, enveloping the players and their coach. Twenty-six years earlier, Paul Judson had teamed up with his twin brother, Phil, to give tiny Hebron High, with an enrollment of 99 students, the 1952 state championship over much larger Quincy in what was called the greatest Cinderella story in the history of Illinois high school basketball. Paul Judson went on to become an all-American at the University of Illinois. But he called this night "the most satisfying thing in my athletic career and just about the biggest thrill in my life," and you almost had to admire the guy for putting it into its proper perspective.

We moved like zombies toward the locker room, my gaze rising briefly from the floor and bouncing off Shirley's No. 45, a back so strong but now, I noticed, hunched ever so slightly. We sat in the locker room in silence. A half hour after the game ended, not a single Niles West player had showered, taken off her shoes, or peeled off her ankle tape.

Our warm-up suits would normally be picked up quickly, hung on hangers, and put in our special vinyl bags. But even they sat in a sad, neglected heap.

Shirley stayed in her uniform long after the rest of us, knowing it would be the last time she would ever wear the Niles West colors or, she knew deep down, any athletic uniform. The University of Illinois awaited, the hopes of a basketball scholarship long since passed.

But this was not about a natural end to another stage of life. The love of basketball had sneaked up and enveloped Shirley as it had captured all of us. This was not our birthright. We did not have basketballs dropped into our cribs. We did not love the game the way you do a sibling, with no real conscious thought of how it all started.

Our relationship with the sport was one that we coveted and pursued, then allowed to grow and deepen over time. Basketball was, in many ways, one of our best friends, dependable and fulfilling and intoxicating in its unpredictability. It gave us a feeling of belonging and security and confidence we so desperately needed during the angst of adolescence. Unlike the average high school social group or clique, we had a common goal that would not shake us, withstood petty bickering, and deterred all the usual grounds for rejection like the wrong hair or clothes or body type.

We had come to love and understand and appreciate the game the way boys did. And now for sure, we knew their heartbreak as well.

So did Mrs. Mulder.

But if she was thinking at all about having just coached us for the last time, she didn't show it. Instead, she had that look that had become all too familiar to us—the flared nostrils, the pursed lips—and she conducted an hour of postgame interviews without breaking form.

"I'm not saying that the officials were biased," Mrs. Mulder said, "just that these 10 girls deserved a better chance."

On the bus ride home, there was more anger than tears. But sitting in the second row, Shirley could not hold it back and broke down.

Mrs. Mulder slid in next to her, and they spoke in hushed tones.

"Why?" Shirley asked her, not expecting an answer. "It's just so unfair."

"But don't you see, Shirley?" Mrs. Mulder told her. "This is life. It's filled with these moments, things we can't explain, things that are unfair. And it's how we respond to them that's the important thing. You will get over this, I promise. It was never just about winning."

CHAPTER 14

Saturday Night Fever *and a Champaign Hangover*

THE NEXT DAY, Mrs. Mulder told us the school would pay for hotel rooms in Champaign if we wanted to go watch the team that broke our hearts further crush our spirits. And with all the enthusiasm of a group of kids about to take their ACTs, we once again made the pilgrimage to the state tournament.

There wasn't a thing we could say to the seniors, and we were a little surprised they even wanted to go. Shirley was still in shock, but she was going. It was almost as if she had to, like pulling that last bit of athletic tape off an ankle that had not been adequately shaved.

Once we got there we decided to inflict a little more pain on ourselves by going to take a look at Assembly Hall, the arena where we were supposed to be playing. It was so huge, it looked closer than it actually was, and we parked way too far away and a few parking lots removed from the main ones, as if that was our punishment and we were lucky just to be allowed into the place at all. Picking our way through a patch of tall grass and weeds, it felt a little like the scene in *The Wizard of Oz* when Dorothy and her buddies try to get to the Emerald City through the poppy fields. We half expected it to start snowing and for all of us to lie down and fall asleep.

Of course, when we finally got there, the arena was closed. Not that it was going to stop us. Eventually, we found an open door that was surely not meant for us, and over Mrs. Mulder's mild objections that "maybe we shouldn't," we let ourselves in.

The place was cavernous, even bigger than we had thought, and if possible, we were even more depressed. If last year's failure to make it to the Elite Eight at Illinois State in Normal was disappointing, this was misery. And as we made our way to the court, Mrs. Mulder nervously casing the joint for security guards, we could see ourselves there, in uniform, playing before our fans. If we could have gotten away with it, we might have tried to slip into the tournament and hope no one noticed.

Instead, we slinked out just as quickly as we had slinked in and checked in to our hotel. At that point, we had to find something to cheer ourselves up, and with time to kill, we talked Mrs. Mulder into going to see the movie *Saturday Night Fever*. Bridget, thrilled to be on the trip after not making it the previous year, told Mrs. Mulder she had a stomachache and was going to stay in her room.

In truth, her boyfriend, Scott, had just shocked her by showing up at our hotel with his roommate from Southern Illinois University, where they were freshmen. They had hitchhiked from Carbondale, roughly two hours away, to come see her.

Bridget was mortified.

It wasn't that she was not thrilled to see Scott. But any excitement she felt when she saw him standing there outside her room was instantly vanquished by her fear that Mrs. Mulder would see him and kill them both. Getting out of the movie bought her enough time to have a quick dinner and send the boys on their way, which she did long before we returned.

Most of us had already seen *Saturday Night Fever*, as it had been in theaters a while, but we wanted to go again, maybe even a little more so knowing that it came over the objections of our coach, who had not seen it and had not planned to. This was not her type of movie, to say the least, and if she wasn't already positive of this, it was hammered home in the first scene of the movie, when Tony, played by John Travolta, asked his boss at the paint store for an advance on his paycheck. He argued that most businesses paid their employees on Friday, rather than Monday, but his boss shut him down.

"This way you've got money all week," the boss said. "You can save for the future."

"Fuck the future," Tony replied.

"No, Tony, you can't fuck the future," the boss told him. "The future catches up with you, and it fucks you if you haven't planned for it."

Mrs. Mulder visibly cringed as we tried not to make her discomfort too obvious by staring at her.

From there, the movie only got worse and long before it was over, she told us she would wait for us in the lobby. We giggled to ourselves that our coach would be so naive as to be offended by a movie. But later in her hotel room, we weren't laughing.

We apologized for dragging her to the theater when we knew she probably wouldn't like the movie, but she waved us away. It wasn't about the movie, she said as she sat on the edge of her bed and we fanned out on the floor.

"I worry so much about my girls," she blurted out. "Michelle has become a latchkey kid, Alison is in daycare. Most days, they're asleep when I leave in the morning and again by the time I get home at night." She continued near tears over her guilt and fear. How could she be sure, she asked us, that her daughters would grow up morally and emotionally healthy in a world where movies showed young men engaged in a "gang bang" with an apparently willing young woman, except she left out the words *gang* and *bang*? How was she going to make sure that they did?

She was opening up to us in a way she never had before, speaking to us like adults, and we stared awkwardly at her for a moment, not quite knowing what to say. "You're a great mother," Shirley said, finally breaking the silence, "just like you're a great coach."

"Your kids are so lucky to have you," Connie added. "They know how much you love them."

I nodded along, not knowing quite what to say. It felt funny to be talking to her that way, but it also felt good and right, and we bonded as our coach sat on her bed, baring her soul.

The next morning, we went to watch the first state quarterfinal game between Dundee and Mattoon, and we had barely settled into our seats when the Cardinals ran onto the court and Connie spoke her first words of the day.

"I feel like I'm going to throw up," she moaned.

We all were a little queasy as we watched two teams that were not us warm up and their fans—not ours—launch into their school songs and cheers. Seeing Dundee's names on the scoreboard was almost physically painful.

"They're not even that good," I whispered to Peggy, and of course, she agreed.

"I hope they get crushed," she muttered back.

At halftime, we were summoned courtside to do an interview with Floyd Brown of WGN-TV. It perked us up and we felt very important as Brown talked about how so many people had expected us to still be playing.

Barb was thrust in front of the camera first.

"And what's your name?" Brown asked in his typical singsong delivery.

"Sophomore," replied Barb, at which point we nearly fell down laughing.

Shirley saved the school's dignity by being as naturally bubbly as ever, and Brown called her "Miss Congeniality," which further lightened our moods as we made our way back up to our seats. Then Mattoon beat Dundee, which made us feel even better.

On the way back home, after watching Joliet West take the second Illinois girls' state basketball title, I sat in the front seat of Mrs. Mulder's car with Shirley and resumed our conversation from the night before. It was late, pitch darkness all around us as we drove through the cornfields of downstate Illinois while our coach told us how it was to be a girl growing up on a farm in the 1950s.

She played the old-fashioned six-to-a-side girls' basketball, she told us, a version still being played in Iowa, and girls like her did not wear makeup or date at 13 or watch racy movies. There were nice girls and there were not-nice girls. "The way I was brought up," she said, "if a girl so much as used a tampon, she was no longer considered a virgin."

OK, maybe *that* we did not need to know, and I jabbed Shirley in the ribs as we tried once again to be mature and not laugh.

On Monday, I was back on the Niles West softball field with Barb and Judy, while Connie and Peggy retreated to the gym to play basketball with whomever they could find. In addition to her all-conference, *Suburban Trib* all-star, and all–Chicago area honors, Connie was also named to the all-state third team and was invited to try out for the USA Junior Women's Basketball Team in St. Louis in the summer.

For Shirley, her sense of humor and ours would come in handy. Pretty soon, Connie and I were drawing pictures in her yearbook of stick figures clutching their necks in the universal symbol for choking. And we all told her how much we would miss her.

We also thanked Shirley in our inscriptions: Connie, for teaching her how to drive the lane; Barb, for giving her the confidence to shoot; me, for keeping us all in line, for sharing laughs and tears. "Basketball was really everything, wasn't it?" I wrote.

We told her to never stop dreaming and promised her that

next year, we would win a state title in her honor and would bring her along as our water girl.

"Treasure your relationships and experiences always," Mrs. Mulder wrote to Shirley, "as I still hold that winning isn't everything. I'm sorry your dream wasn't realized, but I hope you felt that all the work (punishment) was worth it . . . "

Quietly, Arlene Mulder taught the last few classes of her career. She also took notice of an article in a local paper headlined FEMALE COACHES COMPLAIN: MEN MUSCLE INTO GIRLS' SPORTS and clipped it out. In the piece, female high school coaches in the area expressed concern that men would soon be pushing them aside.

"I'd rather coach three or four sports than to give one of the sports to a man," said Crystal Lake girls' basketball coach Linda Brady, who had led her basketball team to the Elite Eight. "Once the men come, the women will be out," Brady added. "They said once there was more money, better coverage and bigger tournaments, the men would take over. And that's what they are starting to do."

Brady contended that many men were starting to coach girls' teams strictly for the money. Also, the seasons were shorter and it was easier coaching girls, who were generally more coachable than boys.

Although Mrs. Mulder didn't know it, Bud Trapp had informally asked Billy Schnurr if he would be up for taking the Niles West girls' basketball coaching job, but he declined, not wanting the stress and strain of full-time coaching again. Trapp saw what happened with Paul Judson and had secretly hoped Schnurr would sit on our bench during the game. When Mr. Schnurr said he wasn't interested in replacing Mrs. Mulder, Trapp was sure that Gene Earl would be the man for the job.

Trapp already knew that Earl, as a lower-level coach, was one of his better teachers, and he liked his good ol' boy, southern Illinois charm. More importantly, Earl was not going to let anyone intimidate him, and Trapp, like many others, thought that was the difference between our going downstate and being denied once again.

Mrs. Mulder did not disagree with that notion, and she beat herself up over her unwillingness, almost inability, to draw a technical, stand up to Judson, and maybe give us the edge we needed to get past Dundee. But she was not about to be shy now.

After the Dundee loss, she spoke to Dr. Mannos and told him she'd like to have some input on the new hire. "They're losing three players, but they still have an excellent nucleus and some good underclassmen coming up," she told him, the "they" in reference to her team sticking in her throat.

"I agree, Arlene," Dr. Mannos told her. "We could have gone all the way this year. That Dundee game was stolen from us, and these girls need to be given every opportunity to achieve their potential. I'd like another woman to replace you, but she has to be qualified."

Mrs. Mulder was hoping for a woman as well. When she found out she was pregnant, one of her first calls was to Ann Penstone, the girls' basketball coach at Buffalo Grove High, asking if she would consider coming to Niles West. But Penstone, who had played basketball in the early '70s for the University of Illinois, where she and her teammates paid for their own uniforms and slept in dorm lounges on the road, said she wouldn't feel comfortable interviewing, and that was as far as it went.

Initially, Trapp was looking for someone who could teach dance and coach basketball because he had only one hire and two positions to fill, but he quickly realized those two skills were probably mutually exclusive in a male candidate. The problem was that there were not many woman candidates around school, and Mulder agreed that they should not give the job to a woman just because of her gender.

More and more, Mrs. Mulder was becoming resigned to the fact that Gene Earl would likely be our next coach, and though she didn't have anything personal against him, she wasn't overwhelmingly in favor of the choice either. She just didn't know Earl well enough.

"What do you think of him, Billy?" she asked Mr. Schnurr.

"He's a good man, Arlene," he told her, knowing that's what she needed to hear most. "He did a fine job at the sophomore level. It wasn't his fault they lost. If he had any talented players, I'd always take them away from him and move them up to varsity."

She nodded. "I'm sure he'll do a good job," she said quietly.

At that point, it hardly mattered what she said.

We also heard Earl's name bandied about, and one rainy spring afternoon, a bunch of us sat in the cafeteria lamenting a potential future with a man we knew nothing about except for the fact that he taught driver's ed, coached bad boys' teams, and was one of the teachers who yelled at us to stop goofing around as we boarded our buses after school.

"I mean, what are they thinking?" I demanded of Connie, who simply shrugged.

I turned to Peggy. "This guy is a loser. His boys' teams sucked."

"Worse than sucked," my ever-supportive friend and teammate replied, and right at that moment, Mr. Schnurr walked through the cafeteria.

"Pssst, Mr. Schnurr, Mr. Schnurr," we called, motioning him over.

We grilled him about Earl and what he knew about the hiring.

"Come on. You can tell us," Connie begged.

"Yeah, we won't tell anyone," I chimed in as my teammates tried not to laugh at the absurdity of that statement.

But Mr. Schnurr was purposely evasive and ended up shrugging and walking away with a smile, uncomfortable with giving us too much information.

We did not know it then, but we had already forgotten Mrs. Mulder.

It was considerably harder for her to move on. Still agonizing over our loss and second-guessing herself, she spent her last days at Niles West reading letters of consolation and congratulations, and cleaning out her desk.

"I'll miss you all so very much; it hurts to think about it," she wrote in my yearbook. "Thanks for being a part of my family."

I don't think any of us actually said goodbye.

CHAPTER 15

Big Whip

GENE EARL DIDN'T WANT THE JOB.

When Mr. Karbusicky greeted him the day after our supersectional loss as "the new Niles West girls' basketball coach," Earl replied in near horror, "No, I'm not. I'm not coaching next year. I've got a boy to watch."

He was referring to his son Dave, who was going to be a junior at Elk Grove High School and on the varsity basketball team, and Earl was determined to see him play, something he often missed out on in previous years while coaching. Bud Trapp was determined to get Earl to change his mind.

"You're taking the job," Trapp would tell him every two or three days that spring.

"No, I'm not," Earl would reply.

Despite the speculation, the school year ended without a new girls' coach, and we all went our separate ways, much more interested at that moment in our summer plans.

I opted to skip Mr. Schnurr's camp so that I could be a full-time camp counselor in Lincolnwood. It was not without considerable anguish that I came to this decision, and Connie was clearly annoyed when I told her, which was apparent more from her silence than anything she said. I felt I had no choice. Now that I was 16, I was going to be a senior counselor for the first time, and I was thrilled about my bump in (gross) salary to $80 a week. The job was tough to get, and I had been paying my dues as a junior counselor without a salary the previous two summers. As a JC, I was allowed to miss mornings the first two weeks to go to Niles West's basketball camp, but not now that I would be in charge of my own group.

I also returned, as I did every spring and summer, to softball, where I played center field for the Lincolnwood 16- to 18-year-old traveling team with Barb and remembered why I loved the game so much. I had made all-conference that spring for Niles West, and it had always been my best sport. Aside from basketball, I was never happier than when I was diving for sinking line drives in the outfield, then bouncing up and firing the ball home to nail an unsuspecting base runner.

I also continued umpiring girls' softball, as I had been the last few years, and with my burgeoning confidence, added boys' Little League baseball and women's 16-inch industrial league softball to my repertoire.

The women nearly broke me.

They were fresh off the assembly line at the nearby Bell & Howell manufacturing plant, and they were much more interested in emptying their cooler filled with Hamm's than in learning the finer points of the game like, for example, the infield fly rule. I realized this as soon as I called it, which I was very proud to have recently mastered. The women were not impressed. In fact, they were enraged that I would have the gall to call an automatic out on the batter when the shortstop dropped the ball, though the whole point of the rule was so a fielder wouldn't purposely drop it in order to get a double or triple play. With more than a few Hamm's in them by then, several kept up a steady round of obscenities for the next inning or so until I enforced another call I had just mastered—disqualification.

Informing the offending team after a couple of warnings that they had just forfeited, I walked—very quickly but with dignity— to the parking lot and got into my brother Barry's car, where I promptly—and not with dignity—burst into tears.

My brother, who paused briefly to tell a few women off, thought he noticed a carload of more angry women following us and briefly considered doubling back to the police station. But instead, we drove home and the women's car pulled into our driveway behind us. Instructing me to run into the house, which I gladly did, pretty sure I would never see my brother again, Barry stayed in the driveway talking to the three women. Soon, my mother and I were peeking through the living room curtains, and we saw the women walking toward the house.

"Oh, God," I said as my mom looked around for a weapon of some kind—and made sure the house was straightened up.

As it turned out, they came to apologize for their drunken teammates and were actually quite nice, my mother serving them fruit and coffee cake and forging a fast friendship as they settled in around our kitchen table.

Umping the boys was an adventure as well. In the first boys' baseball game I ever umpired—for 12- and 13-year-olds—most of the kids didn't see me before I donned my chest protector and mask and crouched behind the catcher, and clearly did not realize I was a girl. They didn't have any specific problems with my calls as I hustled down the first and third baselines and halfway to second to make sure I was in good position to make the call. They did, however, have a problem with my voice, which was high and a little on the squeaky side for a man, even a short one.

They mocked me incessantly as I made calls in my, well, feminine voice, and I tried to decide when would be the perfect time to pull off my mask and reveal my identity to the little brats. I wished I had long flowing blonde hair for real dramatic effect. But my light brown hair almost to my shoulders would have to do, and after the second inning, I pulled off my mask with as great a flourish as I could muster.

"She's a girl!" they yelled almost in unison as their coaches howled. And then the best part: "You're really good for a girl," they whispered as they came up to bat, obviously trying to get back on my good side.

When I wasn't dressed in drag, I continued my backyard routine of shooting and dribbling, adding jogging to my regimen, but I felt like Connie was still a little disappointed in me, and I knew Peggy was throwing herself into basketball as never before. In addition to basketball camp, they were playing regularly at the Morton Grove Community Center, along with incoming sophomore Holly Andersen and incoming junior Lynn Carlsen, and were getting great experience playing against guys. I joined them occasionally at night after camp.

Apparently, it was a gradual process gaining acceptance there. Normally, protocol required that you'd call out "Next," and your team would get to play the winners in the next game. So that's what Peggy and I did. Once. Twice. Three times as still another all-guys team would jog onto the court in front of us.

I had attitude and Peggy had height and attitude, and so we did what came naturally.

"Hey, you morons!" Peg yelled, instinctively knowing she would not get punched. "We yelled, 'Next.'"

"Yeah, that means, you know, next," I chimed in as they laughed at us and kept playing.

We soon figured out that the trick was getting a guy to agree to let girls play on his team and then having him be the one to call "Next," with the group taking the court before anyone could say anything.

This was the real game we had to play. That and jockeying with the ever-present wiseass, who would invariably yell out, "We're shirts, you're skins," to the team with the girls. With guys who didn't know Connie or Peggy or any of our teammates, it was always a struggle. But depending on the guys, some knew us and slowly came around, our notoriety from two supersectional appearances making it somewhat easier.

Peggy found it easier for several reasons. For one, no longer as awkward and all arms and legs, she had become solid, athletic. She was always quick, but now she was comfortable at a rangy 5-10; she was a solid rebounder and was developing a consistent jump shot from 15 feet out. She also became more secure off the court after she met and started dating her first boyfriend, Brett, one of the gym regulars.

But Brett or no Brett, basketball had become her one true love.

At his camp that summer, Mr. Schnurr paid extra attention to Peggy. After camp hours, he would hold a crutch over his head and make her shoot over it. At first, she struggled, still getting used to her newfound height and still shooting from her hip. But over and over again, Mr. Schnurr drilled her, forcing her to develop a shot above her head, imploring her to take advantage of her height. She loved the special interest Mr. Schnurr was taking in her and, like all of us, wanted nothing more than to get his approval.

She would go home and plead with her older brother Al—at 6-2 about the height of Mr. Schnurr's crutch—to guard her so she could shoot over him. Al was a top student, athletic though far from a star. He would go on to Michigan that next fall on an academic scholarship, and it was pretty clear to Peggy at that point that a scholarship of some kind would be the only way she would be able to go to college, too.

Peg was still crazy about Jerry Sloan, even more so after attending his camp for the second summer, and from him she would learn to play the game with a fierceness that was his trademark. As they had the summer before, Peggy and Holly would take two buses to get to Angel Guardian Gym, and afterward, it became a regular routine for Sloan to take them to his house, where they would play basketball in his driveway with his son Brian and his daughters, Kathy and Holly, none of whom were yet in high school.

Peggy also honed her skills on a team most of the Niles West girls played on that summer at Schreiber Park on the Far North Side of Chicago. We competed in a league against girls from Immaculata, Regina, and St. Scholastica and finished in first place after a tough 10-game schedule.

Peggy was gaining confidence every day, though she was still uneasy where Connie was concerned. Both came from the same junior high, where Connie had been one of the popular kids while Peggy had been part of the scenery, and Peggy always felt like she never quite measured up in Connie's eyes. Connie had a backboard and net in her backyard, right across the street from Peggy's house, but Peggy would dribble past, still too shy to walk out back and join in, and Connie didn't think to ask.

Connie was immersed in her own world. In July, she traveled to St. Louis for the Junior Olympic basketball tryouts and a spot in the US Olympic Festival in Colorado Springs the following summer.

Connie had a lot of work to do, and she looked forward to it, but this summer would also prove to be her most trying as a basketball player. That spring, a bearded substitute teacher whom Connie had never seen before and would never see again walked through the gym one afternoon while she was shooting and stopped to give her a few suggestions.

Connie was nothing if not open to criticism when it came to basketball, and so she listened intently as he told her she needed to change her shot. At the time, she was releasing the ball from behind her head with almost no arc. He told her she needed to improve her form and release the ball with better rotation. He worked with her no more than 15 minutes and encouraged her to practice it in the summer. He also told her that it would take time and discipline to change but that it would eventually make a big difference.

Connie knew what she had to do, and she knew where she had to do it. Like a writer going off to a secluded cabin in the woods to work on a novel, she had long since decided the South Balcony Gym would be the perfect studio to practice her craft, and for the previous two years, she had begged Mrs. Mulder to slip her a key that would get her into the school when it was locked.

Shortly before she left, Mrs. Mulder had finally relented. Connie was shocked and grateful and took the gesture very seriously. What it bought her was some coveted extra shooting practice during off-hours before a custodian would inevitably discover her, question how she got there, and shoo her out. But Mrs. Mulder had sworn Connie to secrecy and she, in turn, promised not to tell anyone on the faculty about it.

Connie also promised herself that she would not allow the favor to go for naught. She would take advantage of this opportunity by working harder than ever. She would prove that Mrs. Mulder's decision to buck the rules, which was so against her nature, was a worthwhile one.

And so, in the airless solitude of the little gym, minutes melted into hours and sweat mixed with tears of frustration as she tried to reprogram her brain to shoot properly and then to develop consistency. There were no words, no music, no outside distraction of any kind as she put up shot after shot, grabbed the rebounds, and shot some more—dozens of shots, hundreds of shots. Early mornings. Sunday afternoons. Late summer nights when her family assumed she was out having fun with her friends.

For the rest of the summer, she stole away to the school, shot in the fading light of her backyard, went to the community center when she could, and on a few occasions, joined Ricky Singer, one of the gym rats from school, on the playgrounds of some of the rougher neighborhoods in Chicago, where she was clearly out of her league.

By now, Connie could see her future or at least put her dream in focus. She wanted to play college basketball. She knew that it was within her grasp and that a scholarship would make it possible, and so she would not give up until it somehow became a reality.

The top women's coaches in the country were not exactly camped out at the Ericksons' doorstep, but this was hardly surprising. Women's basketball had come a long way since Immaculata University won the first-ever national championship for women in 1972, but it still had a considerable way to go. Recruiting was a piecemeal process, and Shirley's ill-fated attempts at making simple contact with the Illinois coach was a good example of the rudimentary state of women's college basketball.

Barb, who was still too early in her high school career to think seriously about a college scholarship but was already a strong candidate, had seen the Robby Benson movie *One on One* the summer before her sophomore year, and it scared her so much that she put the whole thing out of her mind. The movie was an embellishment of the ills of big-time men's college basketball, complete with illegal recruiting inducements and—once Robby Benson's character got to college and was considered not good enough—physical harassment orchestrated by the head coach with the intention of getting him to relinquish his scholarship.

I loved the movie because I considered Robby Benson a fox and because he was a guard like me. Barb, however, concluded that everyone who played college basketball was bribed and then beaten bloody.

In 1978, the Association for Intercollegiate Athletics for Women (AIAW) was still the governing body in women's college athletics, the NCAA being an early opponent of Title IX. Women's basketball was a rare sight on national television, and we were only two years past UCLA's Ann Meyers achieving the distinction of becoming the first female recipient of a full athletic scholarship.

We knew all about Ann Meyers as well as Nancy Lieberman, who played for Old Dominion and was considered the best women's basketball player in the United States. And that winter was to be the inaugural season of the Women's Professional Basketball League with Chicago one of the first eight franchises. They were called the Chicago Hustle, and on July 18 we watched as Rita Easterling became the team's first-ever draft pick. Finally, it appeared, we were to have some honest-to-goodness role models, talented women on teams with real names and real uniforms with no gimmicks, who could play and, more importantly, play in games we could actually watch.

All we needed now was a coach for our own team.

Gene Earl was clearly not thrilled with the idea of coaching girls. Or maybe it wasn't that as much as he felt like his job was being jerked out from under him all over again. The year before, the district had cut the driver's education department in half, and he was told he would be teaching girls' physical education. Earl was appalled. He liked driver's ed, had been teaching it for 13 years, and though two other male teachers would be making the move with him, he was bothered tremendously at being told to switch.

With no choice other than to relinquish his tenure and change schools, Earl made the move. And he hated it. To him, the girls were not serious about his gym class. They showed up to first-period class chronically late, with their turtleneck sweaters still on under their gym uniforms and whining about having to get sweaty.

If that wasn't bad enough, he was told he would have to teach a folk dance class, this for a man who couldn't do the two-step with his wife, Marlene. Horrified, he spent his free period observing the dance teacher, Josie Berns, teach her class, and whatever she taught that day, Earl would mimic in his class. If he missed watching Berns's class one day, he would teach the same thing he had taught the day before. He did not merely find it difficult; he found it unbearable.

This was not necessarily foremost on his mind when he considered whether or not to take the girls' basketball position, but it was not far off. In August, Earl took a car trip to New York with his wife, son, and daughter, and on the drive, the family discussed his new job offer. He asked Dave specifically how he felt about it, and his son said, "No way, Dad. Men coach boys and women coach girls."

"Tell Trapp you'll take it for one year," Marlene suggested, "and then you can tell him, 'Now I've done you a favor, you can do me a favor and hire someone else.'"

"What do you think, Dana?" Earl asked his daughter, then 12.

"Big whip," she responded.

Apparently, he was going to have to make this decision on his own. Then again, some decisions seem to be made by themselves.

Earl was Niles West's assistant golf coach, and in practice one day soon after school started again, Trapp told him that Dr. Mannos wanted to see him. "We're going to name you the girls' basketball coach," Mannos told him, apparently not interested in discussing the matter. Earl accepted, but what he did not tell his boss was that he planned to follow his wife's advice: take it for one year and then resign the post after the season. He did not advertise his new position or really say anything at all until two weeks after school had started, when he saw Connie and me running breathlessly toward him.

"You're going to be our basketball coach?" Connie asked. "Why didn't you tell us?"

"I can see you're happy about it," I added. "I see that twinkle in your eye."

Earl sized me up, unsure if I was being serious or merely a smartass. Of course, the latter was true, and he gave us a crooked smile and walked away.

He was starting to come around to the idea. After starting his coaching career at Niles West in 1964 with a $250 stipend for sophomore boys' basketball, he was slated to earn $1,500 for coaching us, the same salary Mrs. Mulder had received. But it was not the money that would permanently change his mind about girls and sports.

CHAPTER 16

Safe Haven

No one knew that Karen Wikstrom's father was dying. But then, neither did Karen.

Eric Wikstrom was a conservative man, loving and gentle but not overly emotional or demonstrative. He was born in Sweden and had met Karen's mother, Marianne, who was German-born, when the two were attending night classes—Eric to learn English and Marianne to learn bookkeeping and typing.

Mr. Wikstrom was a contractor, and soon after the couple married and he started a construction company, they adopted a two-week-old baby boy, Brian. Two and a half years later, they added a two-week-old daughter, Karen, to their family. Her mother would tell Karen how joyous they were to bring her home, and she grew up healthy and happy. She was a daddy's girl just as sure as she was anything, and she shared her father's soft-spoken manner.

Mr. Wikstrom was not an athlete, but he played catch with his son, taught his daughter how to shoot a basketball at the net he put up, and taught both kids how to drive a boat and water ski.

He showed interest in our team but, like many of our dads, could only be so involved. "That's good, honey," he would say to Karen when she told him we had won again, but he could rarely attend our games because of work.

He suffered his first heart attack when Karen was in fifth grade, and it seemed to her like he always had to watch himself. Her mom had had him on a special diet for as long as she could remember, but Marianne would make it a family affair with everyone eating healthy foods and watching their salt intake together. Her dad would take twice-daily walks, and Karen never thought much about it. It was just what Dad did. After breakfast and after dinner, Dad went walking.

I had gone to Karen's house a few times during our sophomore and junior years, and she had been over to mine. Her parents were sweet and her father seemed fine, but midway through our junior year, unbeknownst to most of her friends, he had another heart attack and a stroke, and for the next year, he spiraled downward.

Karen and her brother still did not realize the severity of their father's condition. Their mom sheltered them from the details by telling them simply that he was in the hospital, that he was going to be fine. Kids weren't allowed to visit the cardiac unit, and so Karen accepted what her mom told her. And when her father came home, she assumed he was back to normal. Her mother even encouraged Karen and her brother to continue their regular activities. When her dad had his first heart attack, Karen's mom had her give up ice-skating and horseback-riding lessons, as she was afraid to leave her husband to drive Karen. This time, Karen continued to practice with us, not mentioning anything about her dad.

But he was far from normal. He had arteriosclerosis and congestive heart failure and was growing weaker all the time. He became frail and eventually had problems with coordination, losing his balance occasionally, and struggled to put sentences together. Karen would occasionally become frustrated because he never seemed to finish a thought, and her mom would admonish her to be more patient.

One night in October, however, Karen did not want to go out as she had planned. She sat on the edge of her dad's easy chair, threw her arm around him, and told her parents she thought maybe she should stay home.

"No, no, Karen, go out with your friends," her mother told her. "Give your dad a kiss good night and go on out."

Marianne did not summon anyone until one in the morning. She stayed with her husband in their bedroom and waited until she heard Karen come home and go to bed. Then she called an ambulance and asked them to come in quietly, without sirens, so as not to disturb her daughter. Just as they were putting Eric into the ambulance, she woke up Karen and together they watched through the window as it drove away. She did not want Karen to see her father on a stretcher, leaving home for the final time.

Eric Wikstrom was 59 when he died on October 13.

Karen cried herself to sleep, and the next day, her mother told her she should play in her volleyball game that night. Karen did not tell a soul all day what had happened, but before the game, she quietly informed the coach. After the team won, she stepped to the side with her mom while the coach told her teammates about Mr. Wikstrom. Later that week, many of us from both the volleyball and basketball teams attended the wake at Simkins Funeral Home in Morton Grove.

I had never been to a wake before, much less looked into a casket, and I knew only one other father of a friend who had died. My friend Jane Segal's dad was just 40 when he died suddenly of a heart attack, less than an hour after we all watched *Marcus Welby* together when I was 10 and Jane 11.

My own father was just a couple of years younger than Mr. Wikstrom. And I remembered when I was little how I would lie on the couch with my dad, my head on his chest as I listened to his heartbeat, the steady *lub-dub* eventually freaking me out as I thought it might stop. It would invariably lead to the same story-line I had been privy to ever since I could remember, the one where my dad would wink and say to whomever was smiling at the little girl with the gray-haired father, "We had Missy to take care of us in our old age."

Everyone thought this was pretty funny, and I had no problem with it. I was the baby and, as far as I was concerned, both parents were going to live with me until all three of us were old and gray. "Will I still be your baby when I'm 40 and you're 80?" I'd ask my father. "How about when I'm 50 and you're 90?" calculating and recalculating until I was 100 and he was 140.

I was thinking of that more and more lately.

When Karen and her mom returned to their empty house, Karen's mother encouraged her to go to volleyball practice the next day and again the next, knowing it would be therapeutic. Basketball season was coming, and Karen had been looking forward to it. Sports would be her escape.

Gene Earl still wasn't sure quite what to expect, but his buddies on the faculty were giving him the business.

"Earl, you're a lousy coach if you don't take this team downstate," Otto Karbusicky whistled at him every few days that fall.

But that wasn't all they would tease him about.

"Earl," said Walt Cocking, "you're going to have to coach with your hands in your pockets."

He was more than a little nervous about that one.

Earl was a habitual fanny-slapper, like most male coaches were with their male players, but he knew enough to realize that was one behavior he would have to change when he started coaching girls. Would he forget and accidentally pat one of us, only to get slapped himself or worse, punched out by one of our fathers or hauled off to prison? He shuddered at the possibilities.

As for the coaching itself, the more he thought about it, the more he was looking forward to the season. He had not watched a lot of girls' basketball and assumed it would be boring the first time he watched our team play in our first-round sectional game last season. But as he watched that night, he found himself surprised that we handled the ball as well as we did and that the game was played at such a quick pace that it was actually exciting.

He had no plans to ask for anyone's help once the season began, but he consulted Billy Schnurr about our team before tryouts. Schnurr ticked off the top seniors and juniors and then dropped a bombshell. "You know," Schnurr said, "maybe the best athlete in the school is walking the halls."

He was talking about Diane Defrancesco. DD had not even thought about basketball since she was removed from the team. She had broken up with Connie's brother Chris, but we didn't know much else about what she was up to and neither did Earl.

He did not have to look far to find her. She happened to be in his PE class, and Earl asked her the day after he spoke to Mr. Schnurr if she was going to come out for the team. She told him no and rattled off a few excuses, and Earl didn't pursue it. He had learned years before that if you had to beg someone to play, you were inviting trouble and that was the last thing he needed.

Mr. Schnurr also told Earl about Becky Schnell, another player Earl had not heard of. Mr. Schnurr had her in camp that summer and, though she was an incoming freshman, felt she was good enough to play on varsity. Becky had just graduated from a class of 11 students at her parochial school and was enrolled at Niles East for the fall. Her older sister, Pam, attended Niles East and the Schnells lived in the East district. But Rich Schnell, Becky's father, wanted his youngest daughter to attend Niles West. A PE teacher and junior high coach, Rich believed Becky would not be able to flourish as an athlete at Niles East, a school with a girls' athletic program well behind West's, and that it would hinder her chances for a college scholarship.

Furthermore, he had been taking Becky to Niles West games since she was four, when the family lived in Morton Grove, and through his teaching job at Old Orchard had developed friendships with many of the coaches, including Billy Schnurr. Rich Schnell also knew Wes Gibbs, who for years had been the superintendent of District 68, which included Old Orchard, and was now the superintendent of District 219, Niles Township. Rich Schnell hoped that because Niles East was scheduled to close after the 1980 school year and because up until '78, parochial grade-school students had been able to select which high school they would attend, the school board would allow Becky to attend West.

So Rich sent a letter to Gibbs in which he listed all of these factors, including maybe the most important one. He told Gibbs that because of her unstable situation at home, Becky desperately needed basketball and that going to West would be crucial to her welfare.

Rich was thrilled when Gibbs granted her permission to switch to Niles West. Though Becky's grade school was small, her athletic résumé was already far more extensive than most high school girls who had come from the public school system. Becky began competing in track and field in second grade and, by fifth grade, had added softball, volleyball, and basketball. She had also played a rugged 20-game basketball schedule in eighth grade against other parochial schools.

Athletically, she had it. She had fluid mechanics on her shot and a veteran demeanor on the court. Off the court, however, she was a 14-year-old freshman from a class size smaller than that of the average basketball team. She walked into Niles West with its enrollment of 2,222 on that first day of school and could not, for the very life of her, find her locker.

After struggling with that, she wandered into the cafeteria and sat down at the first empty table she saw. "You don't want to sit there," said an upperclassman, informing Becky that she had just plopped herself down at the unofficially designated "burn-out table" and that was probably not where she wanted to be. In class, she struggled to find her way as well; especially daunting was freshman English, where on one paper, she received a −32 on the usual scale of 100.

But, like so many of us, sports would be her salvation.

She immediately found a home on the JV volleyball team, and one day that fall, even before basketball tryouts began, she was sought out by Earl, who told her she would be practicing with varsity when the season began.

I spent the fall learning how to drive and, like so many autumns previous, waiting for basketball season to begin. Connie and I played half-court games with the boys during 10th period before she had to leave for volleyball practice. That is, until one day when the volleyball coach, Mr. Beeftink, told her she would have to stop. Connie was nothing if not obedient to her coaches, but she told Mr. Beeftink she would quit volleyball if he did not allow her to continue playing pickup basketball. Next, she had a heart-to-heart talk with her father, who then had a talk with the coach, who told her the next day, "Fine, just don't get hurt."

That was actually not such an unreasonable request, as Connie had already developed recurring ankle problems. But just how she would go about avoiding getting hurt was a question we were not smart enough to answer. She just shrugged, and we kept playing.

We kept Shirley updated with a steady stream of calls and letters to the University of Illinois, where she had begun her freshman term. Shirley made one last run at the Illinois women's basketball team after meeting with her academic counselor and telling her about being stood up by the women's coach the previous fall. "I know Carla," the counselor told her. "I'll set up a meeting."

And so she did. And Shirley finally met Carla Thompson.

The coach claimed she had been there that day of the ill-fated meeting when Shirley and her parents waited for hours before going home without seeing her. Then she slapped Shirley on the back in a gesture of encouragement to try out for a walk-on position. Shirley nearly fell over from the force of the slap, and that was pretty much that for Shirley's basketball career. While she never expressed it in so many words, nor did any of us voice it out loud very often, the masculine image, in our minds, of women's intercollegiate athletics scared some of us off. Shirley had already joined a sorority, was taking a ballroom dancing class, and was ready to begin a new phase in her life. Playing for a coach who didn't want her—and who slapped her on the back like she was a linebacker—was something she decided she did not need that badly.

One weekend, Connie and I visited Shirley in Champaign, and she told us that Mrs. Mulder had written to her and sent her a birth announcement—Michael Albert Mulder (not "Westley") had been born August 4. Mrs. Mulder told Shirley that she planned to go to some of Niles West's tennis meets that fall.

Of the six returning varsity basketball players, I think I probably missed Mrs. Mulder the most, and even I hadn't thought enough to call and see how she was doing. Connie was focused solely on the task at hand, and that did not include reminiscing about our old coach. Barb was convinced Mrs. Mulder never liked her after the piano recital incident. Karen obviously had her mind on other things so soon after losing her father, and Judy was busy with volleyball and we rarely talked about our former coach. Like me, Peg didn't think of it and hadn't known Mrs. Mulder as long as the rest of us.

By the time the tryouts rolled around, some of us were convinced that Earl was going to be a typical male coach—a taskmaster short on sensitivity. We knew he'd be tough and probably insensitive to all of our little idiosyncrasies and rituals, but we kind of craved a tough approach, thinking maybe this was what we needed to push us over the top. After all, Peggy loved Jerry Sloan, and he was tough. But we also wondered how capable

Earl was, having only his previous losing records with the freshman and sophomore boys' teams to go by. And if that wasn't bad enough, that fall Earl walked around with a scruffy beard, which we couldn't stand.

Connie and I were also apprehensive about how this season's team was going to look. We wondered if Holly was going to be a younger version of the nonaggressive Bridget. And who could possibly replace Shirley's scoring punch and savvy at the wing spot? Karen was slated to start but another candidate who was emerging was junior Tina Conti.

I knew Tina from Lincolnwood. We played a little softball and her dad was a sweetheart who sometimes drove Shirley, Barb, and me to our morning practice sessions and had become a big fan of the varsity team. Like most of our parents, Mr. Conti was as far from a stage parent as one could get. Tina had initially made varsity her freshman year and was even given one of our cool new warm-up suits, only to be sent back down to JV after two games by Mrs. Mulder, who told her she needed to change from a two-handed to a one-handed shot. Tina didn't make varsity her sophomore year either, watching her good friend Barb make the team and contribute both years.

Tina was devastated both times. She had two older brothers, Rich and Dave, 7 and 10 years older than her, respectively, and Rich had played football and basketball for Gene Earl. But her father would not allow her to sulk, telling her that she should listen to the coach, do her best, and if she really deserved it, she would play.

Tina ended up as a standout on the JV team, and Mr. Schnurr helped her refine her shot so that by the '78–'79 season, she was ready. The seniors, however, still weren't sure what to make of Tina. Invariably, while we would be scrimmaging against some of the boys on one half of the court, Tina would be flirting with the others on the opposite side of the gym.

Earl settled on a final varsity roster of 13. Underclassmen Tina Conti, Holly Andersen, Becky Schnell, Pam Hintz, and Lynn

Carlsen made the varsity squad for the first time along with returning junior Barb Atsaves. The five seniors—Connie, Peggy,
Judy, Karen, and me—were back, and unlike Mrs. Mulder, who
saw no problem with having a senior or two play on the JV, Earl
elected to put the only other seniors who tried out—Nancy Eck
and Debbie Durso—on varsity.

It would not be the only situation in which Earl differed from
Mrs. Mulder philosophically.

In fact, soon the 44-year-old coach made it clear that we
would be leaving almost all of Mrs. Mulder's imprint behind. He
did not believe in allowing seniors to take up JV roster spots that
could be given to underclassmen who might one day help varsity.
But he pulled Nancy and Debbie aside during our first practice
and told them what they should expect.

"Now I want you two to understand that you will probably
not be playing much this season," he said bluntly. "If you have any
problem with that, you can still quit."

What was clear to Earl and eventually to us, was that he
would continue to coach as he always had. Unlike Mrs. Mulder,
who believed in picking the 10 best players for varsity and utilizing her entire roster to build depth, Earl knew immediately that
he would choose a starting five and would keep that group intact,
barring illness, injury, or ineligibility. Further, he knew he would
be rotating in one or two regular substitutes and the rest would
play sparingly. And he knew after the first three days of practice
that Nancy and Deb would not play at all, barring the last minute
of a blowout.

Neither ever complained. Deb was happy to be a part of the
team and figured she could only improve by practicing with the
best players. Nancy was like a grown woman in a teenager's body,
with all the sensibilities of an adult, and likewise did not rock the
proverbial boat.

Earl was looking for three main things—quickness, shooting, and height. The fact that I possessed only the first would

have given me a clue as to how he felt about me, had he shared these favored traits with us. Ironically, as a junior, Connie had possessed only quickness as well. She had everything else going for her: great passing abilities, an innate talent on defense, intelligence, floor leadership. But she did not consider herself a great shooter and she wasn't until her summer of reckoning in the South Balcony Gym.

As for height, Earl was going to have to get used to that deficit. He now had Holly, at 5-11, in mind for center and Peggy, at 5-10, as our undisputed starting power forward replacing Diana Hintz. But after that we dropped off pretty dramatically in the height department. He already envisioned Tina, at 5-7, as his eventual starter at the wing spot. He liked that she was left-handed and could handle the ball well. Though Barb, at 5-6, was of average height for a high school guard, she certainly was not tall, and neither was Connie, who was listed her senior year at 5-6 but still wasn't more than a hair over 5-5.

Whatever nervousness Earl may have had over our lack of height, however, was quickly assuaged by what he saw in practice. Never had he walked into a gym for a practice to find that his entire team had already started without him, but that's what he found us doing the first day. He also found that first week that most of us stayed on the court well after we were dismissed to practice free-throw shooting, run laps, play three-on-threes, and whatever else we could do before getting kicked out by the freshman boys' basketball team or rhythmic gymnasts or anyone else who needed the gym.

But what Gene Earl found most interesting about coaching girls for the first time in his life was that we were a much more mature group than he was used to. The two-time Sweet 16 Niles West girls' basketball team not only worked exceptionally hard but we actually listened to what he was saying. Now he was dealing with mostly 17- and 18-year-old girls who were clearly more serious than the 14- and 15-year-old boys he was used to coaching, most of whom seemed interested primarily in pulling each other's shorts down. Or up, depending on the situation. Even at 14 and mid-wedgie, those same boys tended to believe they knew everything there was to know about basketball. And even after three years of playing among the elite teams in the state, we did not.

Our hunger, that word Arlene Mulder had drilled into us and then used as a constant barometer, was intact and as strong as ever. Though we were apprehensive about our new coach, Peg and I in particular, we all wanted to know what this man had to tell us. We were, in fact, desperate for someone new to share with us exactly where he thought we stood and what we needed to do to win a state championship. We were no more satisfied with two supersectional berths than we had been with one. And now the seven seniors who remained were infused with the same sense of urgency that Shirley and Diana and Bridget had had festering inside them last year.

And so, as we took this collective leap of faith with a man we knew so little about, we seemed to agree silently to give him the benefit of the doubt. When Tina secretly cried in the locker room every time Earl screamed at her in practice, we told her to suck it up. When Peggy got elbowed in the mouth on a rebound and spewed blood into the water fountain, we laughed it off when Earl yelled, "Peggy, spit out the Chiclets and get back in the game." And when we practiced an inbounds play intended to set up a last-second shot and I fired up an air ball only to have Earl glare at me sarcastically and announce, "Isaacson, if you have the ball and we need one shot to win, we're in deep trouble," I did not flinch.

I did, however, complain to Shirley. In a running dialogue we kept on a cassette tape mailed back and forth between Lincoln-wood and Champaign, I informed Shirley that I was pretty sure our new coach couldn't stand me. And I also thought his coaching style and expectations of our collective basketball IQ bordered on condescending.

Just the same, if this was what it was like to be coached by a man, then we would become tougher, stronger, and less sensitive in the process, just as we had become when we scrimmaged with boys for the first time. In turn, Earl grew more impressed with us by the day. One afternoon, Judy ran into practice uncharacteristically late and with an excuse that our coach did not want to hear.

"Drop and give me 20," he barked at Judy as we looked on, stunned at this form of discipline.

"What is this, the Marines?" I whispered to Peggy. But we never took it further than that, and neither did Judy, who jumped up upon completing the push-ups and said, "Sorry, Coach, won't happen again."

Earl was amazed and impressed with Judy's response. When he had inflicted a similar punishment on boys in the past, he would invariably get an annoyed or at best defiant look that said, "I'll do your damn push-ups all day."

Even the most seemingly innocuous moments began to make a lasting impression on him. One day we were in two lines for a practice drill when he began to show the first girl in each line what they were doing wrong. Instinctively, we fanned out around him, making sure we were all able to see.

Driving home that night, Earl found himself smiling. "They're so receptive, this is really a joy," he told Marlene when he got home. "I really feel like I'm teaching them."

He could not get over it.

CHAPTER 17

Earl's Girls

GENE EARL WAS A HICK. From his easy smile to his corny humor to the way he pronounced *school* "skyewl," he screamed southern Illinois, and he was the first to admit it.

The oldest of five children born to George and Faye Earl in Zeigler, a coal mining town of about 3,000 people, George Eugene Earl Jr. came into the world on October 1, 1934, as the country was beginning its long recovery from the Great Depression. He joked that he never knew he was poor until he moved to Chicago and "got rich," and he remembered fondly a childhood filled with sports, friends, and few responsibilities.

Other than the bankers and the barbers, all of the men in his hometown, including his father, worked in one of Zeigler's two coal mines. When World War II began, George Sr. worked 20 to 25 days in a row to support the coal production for wartime consumption. Meanwhile, Gene, as they came to call him, played with his two younger brothers and two younger sisters, his only real jobs filling the coal bucket at night to warm the house and taking his siblings to the movies.

At Zeigler High School, Gene received nine varsity letters, excelling in football, basketball, and track. Routinely, he would make the honor roll at the beginning of school only to fall off after the first six weeks, much more concerned with sports and hanging out at the local pool hall with his buddies. Based on his athletic prowess, he was invited for a campus visit to Southern Illinois University but decided he had had his fill of studying in high school and was not interested in going to college. It was 1952, two years after the Korean War had started, and Gene wanted to enlist.

Like his buddies, he knew that by avoiding the Army, he would not be sent to Korea. But after some convincing, George Earl agreed to sign the papers that would allow his oldest son to enlist in the Navy at 17, reasoning that it kept him out of the coal mines and that Gene could attend radar school, learn aircraft mechanics, or be trained in any number of other vocations.

The Navy, it turned out, would be almost as carefree as Gene's childhood. After boot camp in San Diego, he went to Norman, Oklahoma, for aircraft repair school, then spent 27 months in Northern California at Moffett Field, which was situated between San Jose and Palo Alto. The extent of his sea duty was a 12-day stint that included 11 days tied to the dock and the 12th day crossing under the Golden Gate Bridge.

To a small-town innocent, the service was a constant education. Once, while Gene was standing at the rail of the docked ship, police came on board to investigate the suspected buying and selling of illegal narcotics by sailors. Gene asked an older sailor what was happening and was told "drugs."

"What're drugs?" he asked the sailor, who walked away in disbelief. The only drugs Gene knew of were the pills his mom sent him to fetch from Mr. Green, the town druggist, and that couldn't be what they were talking about.

Discharged in August of 1955, still two months shy of his

21st birthday, Gene had the idea that he wanted to go to college after all, study to be a civil engineer, and build big highways and buildings. But after his first drafting class at Southern Illinois, he realized he would never be an engineer and instead majored in social studies with a minor in physical education.

In '56, Gene married Marlene North, a girl from nearby Carterville whom he had met two years earlier while on leave from the Navy (Gene's best buddy was dating her best friend at the time), and the couple had their first child, David, in April of 1962. By then, both Gene and Marlene were on staff at a high school in downstate Sesser, Illinois—Gene teaching economics and geography and coaching basketball, and Marlene teaching English. Gene then moved on to Bridgeport, also close to both of their hometowns, where he taught PE and American history.

Gene Earl's first teaching job at Sesser paid him $4,800 a year. At Bridgeport, his salary rose as high as $6,300. But when his high school coach and mentor became the first chairman of the boys' PE department at the brand-new Niles North High School in Skokie, Gene knew he would soon be making the trek upstate— and hitting the big time. Soon enough, he was hired to teach driver's education and to be an assistant football and track coach at neighboring Niles West for the '64–'65 school year, and he received a whopping $3,000 above his salary at Bridgeport. But the best part was that every week, it seemed, he got a raise. They would add cafeteria supervisor to his duties and bang, raise him $100 and free lunch. The next week, it would be bus supervisor and another hundred bucks. A week or so later, they gave him indoor track and another raise.

At 30 years old, Gene Earl was in all his glory.

But life, as it so often does, intervened, and two and a half years later, now with David, four, and a daughter Dana, 13 months, Gene and Marlene's idyllic suburban world was shaken.

It was the spring of 1967 and Gene was finishing up the school year when doctors told Marlene that the lump in her breast was nothing to worry about. It was a Friday when they removed a section of tissue in routine surgery and sent her home. On Monday, she was told she had cancer.

Gene's first thought was instantaneous. "Here I am," he said to himself, "with a four-year-old boy, a one-year-old daughter, and no wife."

Marlene underwent a radical mastectomy, which meant the removal of one breast along with the underlying muscles and lymph nodes, followed by skin grafting. Her summer was spent in bed while both Gene's and Marlene's mothers took turns traveling from downstate to help out while Gene learned how to be a full-service dad, handling meals, baths, and diaper duty.

He was teaching summer school by then and might have taken off work except that his family needed the $1,000 stipend. When doctors told them they believed they had removed all of the malignant tissue, Gene and Marlene told themselves they were over the worst.

And it seemed they were. Until four years later in the summer of '71, with David now nine and Dana, five, when doctors found a malignant growth they estimated to be the size of a grapefruit on Marlene's ovary.

They said the new malignancy was not related to the previous one and, again, that they thought they had gotten it all. She would have to receive cobalt treatments, they told her, but her prognosis was good. Still, the mood was grim in her hospital room the day after surgery when Marlene looked at her husband of 15 years and asked plaintively, "Gene, what are we going to do?"

He knew what she meant. But they had never had the conversation, had never talked frankly about the worst-case scenario before. Not after their last scare and not this time. And Gene would have no part of it. "Dammit," he told his wife, "we're going to raise two kids; that's what we're going to do."

And that was that. No more discussion. No other alternatives. He would not hear of it. And Marlene followed his lead.

By fall 1978, Gene Earl's outlook on many things had changed. When he first moved up north, he envisioned himself as a varsity football coach at one of the big suburban high schools. But after a few years as an assistant coach at Niles West, he found he could experience all the joys of coaching without the headaches a head coach had to endure, and he soon allowed his long-held dream to fade away.

Now, suddenly, he was the man in charge. And not simply in charge, but in charge of a team with outrageous expectations. A state championship? Did these people know how hard that was to achieve with more than 600 schools competing? Sure, these girls he was now entrusted with coaching were working hard and seemed talented, but how did he know exactly how we stacked up to the other teams in the state? And suddenly, after years of installing Billy Schnurr's offensive and defensive systems with the freshman and sophomore boys, he was now left completely to his own devices with the girls.

How much would he change us? How much should he?

In the end, he took what we already knew was a well-oiled motion offense and tinkered. Instead of one big post player, two forwards, and two guards as we had last year with Bridget, Shirley and Diana, and Connie and me, we had two post players in Holly and Peggy, and ultimately three perimeter players in Connie, Barb, and Tina. We'd pick and we'd move. Pass the ball and pick away from the ball, or pass and screen for the ball. If one of us had a free lane to the basket, he wanted us to take it. It was simple. He wanted both his players and the ball to move faster than the defense.

Defensively, we would continue to press full-court, adding to an already heavy complement of zones several more variations under Earl. If we missed on the offensive end, we would drop back into man-to-man. Otherwise, we would scramble and trap, forcing turnovers and converting them into easy buckets. On court, the transition from Mrs. Mulder was an easy one. We got it. The system suited us, and the newcomers picked it up quickly.

Off the court, it was still going to take a little time.

Earl was still a little shocked at the way we did things, and our music topped the list. At the beginning of every practice while we warmed up, shot, and ran drills, and at the end while we ran sprints and shot free throws, the record player was on. It was as old as the school itself but it did the job, playing our favorite albums and 45s—The Beach Boys, Barry Manilow, Queen, with "We Are the Champions" quickly becoming our new anthem, Styx, Elton John—infusing us with added energy and giving practice a rhythm all its own.

It was as second nature to us as pulling on our socks and lacing up our shoes. It did not alter our concentration or interfere with our work. Rather, it inspired us like old friends giving a favorite pep talk, and in our minds, these voices would accompany our journey as they had from the beginning. But that did not mean that Earl understood, and he rolled his eyes a lot.

It was the same thing with all that infernal cheering we did. After practice, during timeouts, and especially on the bus, the never-ending patter psyched us up, bonded us. We did not believe, as the boys were trained from birth, that you screwed on your game faces several hours before competition and did not take them off until you were back home.

We talked. A lot. We teased the coach and each other; gossiped about boys, parents, teachers, and teammates; and chatted about movies and TV and whatever else struck us, whether we had a game in two hours or had just finished one. We talked about our opponents, too, but even for our most formidable foes, there was a looseness that we carried with us, that perhaps all good teams did, and that confounded our coach at first.

"Give me an *R!*" one of us would yell, and we would be off, spelling the name of Ray Rayner.

Earl was floored. You didn't talk about what you were going

to do *after* you *won* the state championship any more than you talked about the opponent after your next game. But there were Judy and Barb, drumming on lockers and bus seats, the rest of us bopping our heads and singing merrily along. I would not be writing poems for every game anymore. It just didn't seem natural after Mrs. Mulder left. But it was left to me to pen a team song and so, with a little help and no other inspiration handy, I did, to the tune of *The Brady Bunch* theme song:

> Here's the story
> Of a group of Indians
> Who were looking for someone to coach their
>   team.
> All of them had just one dream
> To go downstate,
> And they worked hard to win.

> Here's the story
> Of a man named Earl
> Who was looking for a team that he could coach.
> He had experience
> In the game of b-ball,
> Yet he was all alone.

> Till the one day when the girls met this fellow,
> And they knew that it was much more than a
>   hunch
> That this group could one day be state champions,
> That's the way we all became Earl's Girls.

How our nickname, Earl's Girls, started, no one really knew, though it was so painfully obvious, it probably occurred to someone within minutes of his hiring. One of Earl's friends on the faculty may have uttered it first, and before long, it seemed, we were no longer the Niles West Indians but Earl's Girls. Even though I was the one to write it, I couldn't stand the Earl's Girls song. Neither could Peggy.

I mean, how could a man who had barely begun coaching us be given ownership of the team? It bugged me. Then there would be the occasional comments in articles, like one in the *Chicago Sun-Times* in which Earl said he did the school "a favor" by accepting the job. He tried to praise us for our work ethic when he was quoted as saying, "The girls approach practice with a high degree of intensity. The boys would say: 'Do we have to practice?' But the girls say: 'Can we practice longer and more often?'"

But then he would still put his foot in his mouth, as he did with comments like, "I think they've made me a better person and a better coach, too. For example, the boys could complain and I wouldn't take enough time to understand their problems. Now I take time to listen. I try to be more understanding. The girls are more emotional and seem to have more problems than the boys."

I brought the *Sun-Times* to school the next morning and shoved it at Peg in case she may have missed it.

"That's great," she said. "So now we're mental cases."

Peg was not particularly big on authority. It wasn't that she was disrespectful. Not with Mrs. Mulder, anyway. She was, in fact, in utter awe of our former coach from the first day she met her, hoping only to have the chance to play for her one day.

But she didn't trust Gene Earl.

Pretty quickly, we both had our doubts about him, resenting, in particular, the relationship Connie seemed to be developing with him. There was no tangible evidence, but to Peggy and me, Connie was being way too chummy with this man whom we still did not know enough about, and he seemed to have already identified her as the star of our team.

Common sense should have told us that Connie *was* the star of our team. Though she was not the leading or even the second-leading scorer or rebounder (Peggy was), she led us in steals and assists and was our captain, our undisputed leader, and our best all-around player. Anyone could see that. But it bothered us that this team was already losing its egalitarian ways, and the harder Earl tried to bring Peggy into the fold, the more suspicious she became.

At first, it began as a joke. Earl, who possessed the belly of most middle-aged men, would tell us to run laps around the gym, and Peggy would mutter, just under her breath but loud enough for him to hear, "How about we just run around you?" I encouraged it because as the season started and Barb was officially made a starting guard—a move that was justified and one I had seen coming for a long time—I had a pretty good feeling that for the first time in my high school career, I would no longer be a key contributor to the team.

I was not wrong. Early in the season, Earl pulled Becky aside and told her, "If the game is on the line and I need a sub, I'm going to use you. If the game is not close, I'm going to use Missy." I did not know this at the time, but I did know, not so deep down, that my coach had little faith in me, that he could not see into my heart the way Arlene Mulder had, that he could not tell that with every fiber in my body, I was invested in this team, and that before he had even known who we were, I had wanted to win a state championship more than I had wanted anything in my life.

Peggy knew all of this and she felt for me, even as we both should have been celebrating her own two-year ascent from a kid who was scared to even try out for basketball to the starting forward on one of the best teams in the state.

When Earl tried to be nice to Peggy, she read it as phony, that he was trying too hard, that he just didn't get it. And when he lost his temper, he was just like most men she knew, maybe even the one she really didn't. Either way, she was suspicious. And you could hardly blame her.

When she was in sixth grade, Peggy and her little brother

went to court with their mom to tell a judge that they wanted nothing more to do with their father. When her brother refused to go into the judge's chambers, Peggy was sent in his place to talk to him. She told the judge that Al King scared her, that he broke their windows and knocked down their doors and beat them up. She told the judge she was terrified of her father and did not want to see him anymore.

"And you call yourself a Christian?" the judge bellowed at her.

"I am a Christian," Peggy stammered.

"Christ forgave. Why can't you?" he responded.

Peggy ran out of the courtroom and straight into her mother's arms, sobbing.

"You son of a bitch!" her mother yelled at the judge.

Her father had recently survived a fire, and Peggy's family heard he had received a large settlement from the insurance company.

Apparently, the family concluded, Al King had put the money to good use.

CHAPTER 18

Dreidl, Dreidl, Dreidl

WHILE SOME OF THE WONDER we had experienced at receiving our first uniforms and real leather basketball shoes may have abated by this season, we still appreciated any strides we made that brought us closer to total equality with the boys.

We had finally discarded the plain, dark red jerseys we wore for home and away games and got brand-new road uniforms—red shirts with white short sleeves and red stripes and INDIANS emblazoned across the chest. We also had matching shorts that were miraculously and mercifully looser-fitting. If those weren't cool enough, we had bestowed upon us actual practice jerseys—reversible, just like the boys'. Unlike the boys' shirts, however, which were sleeveless mesh, ours were short-sleeved and two layers—white on one side, red on the other—of heavy cotton jersey material.

But they just couldn't quite get it right. The heaviness we could tolerate. And we were thrilled they were cotton and not polyester. But because they were cotton, it was not humanly possible to wash the shirt without the red side bleeding onto the white side. Even for my mother, who prided herself on flawless laundering, there was literally no way to avoid what none of us saw coming. After years of trying and coming pretty close to making people forget we were girls when it came to athletics, there we were, on the brink of greatness, wearing pink practice jerseys.

Of course, each of us thought our mother was the only one to make this heinous mistake, and so none of us could bear to tell anyone else what had happened the first time we washed them. We all came out of the locker room with the red sides out, hoping against hope that maybe Earl would let us all keep them that way. When he didn't, and the white team retreated back into the locker room for a quick change, one by one we realized we were now all part of this embarrassing pink sorority. We laughed, but not much.

There was always the sense that as far as being treated equally with the boys, there was something just out of our grasp, as mystical and magical as the spacious varsity boys' locker room we always heard about but obviously never got to see. Same with the boys' weight room, the school's only weight room, though we could at least pass by and peer into the large smelly cave just off the gym. It wasn't as if any of us were dying to walk into a place so acutely male-dominated that it literally reeked of testosterone, or at least really bad BO. Nor did we want to develop huge muscles like men, which was the only option we saw.

Though the first national powerlifting competition for women had taken place the year before, girl high school athletes did not do strength training. It did occur to us in a vague way, however, how lifting weights might be beneficial. We realized that one reason we found it so difficult to hoist jump shots like the boys was that we were simply not strong enough. Sure, we found our own ways to build up our legs, sitting against whatever wall we could find until our quads burned and tears sprang to our eyes. And we took great pride in our vertical jumps, though we saw only barely perceptible improvement in that area. There were also the early-morning stair circuits and lateral slides. But those were intended to develop endurance and agility, and we did almost nothing to build upper-body strength.

And so we'd glance at the boys' weight room and walk on by, no real clue of the benefits that many of us would find in our 40s and 50s but that were so elusive to us now. For the time being anyway, we had business to attend to. On December 16, we opened the season at home with Crystal Lake South, a team we had never played, seen play, or heard of because the school had recently opened. Not that we were particularly nervous.

Earl, however, was beside himself.

Not in his entire life dating back to his own high school career could he remember butterflies the magnitude of which he experienced before the Niles West–Crystal Lake South game. He had not scouted our opponent and did not possess our confidence that unfamiliarity was probably a good thing. More than anything, he was afraid that we would come out looking awful and sloppy, that other teams, coaches, teachers, students, towns-people, and lord knew who else would take one look at this stumbling, bumbling group and wonder what the new coach had been doing for the last month.

"I don't know what's going to happen tomorrow," he told his wife the night before the game. "But I hope I don't get run out of town when it's all over."

Good thing he never let us know what little faith he had.

After three trips up and down the floor, he calmed down. For one thing, we were playing a sagging man defense and the Crystal Lake coach yelled out, "They're playing a matchup zone," so Earl knew he wasn't going to be outcoached at least. We led 19–11 at the end of the first quarter. In the second quarter, our defense held Crystal Lake to three points to take a 38–14 lead at the half, despite a twisted ankle and early foul trouble for Connie.

It was 65–20 after three quarters, and we ended up winning 83–30.

OK, thought Earl, so maybe all that singing isn't such a bad thing.

Addressing us after the game, he couldn't hold back. This was really fun, and he didn't mind telling us so. "Gang," he said in his parting remarks, his voice rising to the level he used to get our attention in the gym, "it's GREAT to be a winner."

We all jumped in alarm. Then laughed.

I had fully expected to see Mrs. Mulder at our game, and if anyone would have asked her eight months earlier, she'd have thought she would have been there as well. But she began having second thoughts after Gene Earl took over. For starters, he never called once to ask for her input or to invite her to attend a game, and she took that as a sign that she should stay away.

It was not her style to stand on ceremony, but that is not how she viewed it. Instead, she told her husband, she felt sincerely that she had to let the new coach bond with his team. And she feared that in light of the fact that none of us had called her either, her presence could be a distraction. No, she determined, it was best if she stayed home. And we went on without her.

Next up was Hoffman Estates, and Earl again started Karen at the wing spot. He had intended to start Tina in the last game, but unfortunately for her, though happily for the Conti family, her brother was getting married in Florida that weekend, and hard as she actually tried to convince her parents that her presence was not necessary, she could not get out of it.

If Earl considered getting nervous again, it took even less time to reassure him in a game we led 23–0 after the first quarter and won 74–40.

Almost on a daily basis, however, he was still confronted with plenty of other things to make him uncomfortable. With a wife and 12-year-old daughter at home, there was reason to believe he had been desensitized to certain things. But it was with great horror, during the Hoffman Estates game, that he opened our first aid kit looking for tape and instead found a half dozen tampons spilling out. For several seconds, our coach kept his head buried, unsure of where to look and not look. No one had told him about this when they were trying to get him to take the job. What other surprises, he shuddered, were hidden around the next corner?

For now, it was only Maine South, and for that he had to be relieved, though it was a team that always shook us a little. Maybe it was that, more than any other team, Maine South reminded us of ourselves. In the early days, their team had arguably better talent, was more experienced, and possessed the same type of intensity and hunger we had. Their players were also cocky with their striped socks and their flashy warm-up routines, and it was just that way they had of acting as if they could beat us any time they really put their minds to it—especially on their home court—that threw us.

Trouble was, they were right.

The Hawks had packed their gym on this night, the biggest regular-season crowd we had ever seen, and they were getting to Connie, which meant they were getting to us. By halftime, she had picked up three fouls, all drawn on blind picks at midcourt that sent her and her defender flying as she backpedaled on defense. Earl shouted at us to warn Connie that the picks were coming, and he was getting madder by the minute.

Although he was adjusting to the differences between coaching girls and boys, we had not adjusted to the level of his voice. It could best be described as something between bellowing and screaming, and was generally preceded by an ear-piercing whistle he accomplished with thumb and pinkie inserted between his teeth, causing pain to every person in the gym and, quite possibly, small animals in parts of rural Illinois. He told himself that he needed to be heard. And, as players had done to their coaches since the beginning of time, we often made him crazy.

On one series, Holly saw a pick coming and attempted to call it out, but Connie didn't hear her over the din of the crowd and got creamed. Under the basket on the next play, a Maine

South player went over Holly's back on the defensive rebound, and as Holly walked back downcourt to shoot her free throws, Earl let her have it.

"Holly!" he yelled as loud as we had ever heard him. "I told you to call out the pick! You have a tongue in your head? Well, you *use* it!"

Holly turned a few shades darker than the color of our uniforms, marched to the free-throw line, and in her anger, missed the front end of the one-and-one. At halftime, all 5-11 of her cornered Earl. "If you scream at me," she scolded, looking him squarely in the eye, "I'm going to get my Norwegian dander up, and I'm not going to play any better."

"Uh, OK," said our startled coach, who dialed his screaming down several notches after that.

In the end, we escaped Maine South with a 75–73 victory. Despite their picks and their flopping—which resulted in Connie picking up four fouls and playing just nine minutes, and Barb picking up her fourth foul late in the game—we established a 14-point lead early in the fourth quarter and held on. Toward the end of regulation, we went into a semi-stall offensively, packed in our zone defensively, and per our coach's instruction, did not foul and stop the clock. Maine South's outside shooters scored over the zone, but it was one of those games that was not as close as the final score indicated.

Just the same, Peggy was apoplectic and disgusted with Earl's celebration of our win.

"What are you so happy about?" she snapped at him.

It was only our third game, but already we were having the kinds of problems winning teams avoid, the minor griping we had never had before with Mrs. Mulder. While she would not allow individual statistics into either the newspapers or our collective consciousness, that was apparently of no concern to Earl. He didn't care if stars emerged or if one girl was getting more attention than another. If it bugged some of us, Peggy, as usual, would be the one to express herself. And more often than not, her frustration would be taken out on our new coach, who did not quite know what to make of his players standing up to him.

Connie knew she was the cause of some of the conflict and suspected that her developing relationship with Earl was the root of it. She had taken to calling him "Coach," which was standard stuff on boys' teams, and if we had thought it through, it was probably not especially egregious to refer to your coach as "Coach." But it seemed, to Peggy and me anyway, that it represented a special bond forming between the two of them that the rest of us didn't have and, frankly, that Peggy and I weren't ready to have with him yet. At the same time, Earl recognized that the leader on his team was Connie, and whether real or imagined, subtle or not, we felt he was starting to treat her preferentially as well.

Connie was no dummy, had picked up on the vibe, and tried making fun of him like Peggy did, telling him he was "going to the home" when he was forgetful or said something that struck her as senior citizen–like. But coming from Connie, it came off as cute and not disrespectful, and soon it became a team thing to yell, "Going to the home!" at our coach, just as it had become his routine to yell after each victory, "It's great to be a winner."

But finally, she had a talk with him. "You've got to do something," she told him during one of her free periods. "Everyone thinks you're favoring me. Maybe you can ream me out once in a while."

Earl did not wait long. The next practice, at Connie's first minor transgression, he barked, "Erickson, go run a lap," as we looked at one another in shock. He had never called her "Erickson" before, much less made her run a lap, and as she passed him, she mouthed, "Thank you," in his direction.

That problem apparently solved, Coach Earl moved on to his lineup. That week after the Maine South game, he reviewed our stats and noticed that while Karen had scored eight points in the first three games combined, Tina, who was playing behind her, had scored nine against Maine South alone. He also decided that while Karen gave us a little more height inside and potentially better rebounding, Tina brought a little more quickness and ability to help break a press. He envisioned Tina quickly inbounding the ball after an opponent's basket, rather than Peggy, who currently handled that duty. If the opponent was employing a full-court press, Tina's first option would be to get the ball to Barb in the middle, who would quickly shovel it off to Connie, streaking downcourt. Peggy, a great defensive player herself and also fast, was then available at the other end.

Any of our guards was capable of breaking the press alone. But if Barb or Connie were caught in a trap, Earl loved the idea that Tina, a lefty, could go strong on the dribble up the left side of the court. Karen could rebound, but she wasn't a ball handler. And Tina possessed a scrappiness that, although annoying to those of us who had to practice against her bobbing head and flailing elbows, was effective, especially in our defense.

Tina was still adjusting to Earl's yelling, as we all were, and she privately fretted that Karen and Judy didn't like her because the two were friends, both seniors, and all three were competing for the same starting spot. But rather than talking to any of us about it, she often poured her heart out to her guidance counselor, Walt Cocking, whom everyone called "Doc."

Every day, she popped in for at least one visit, chatting about everything from basketball to boys to our off-court chatter. She thought nothing of sharing this information with him. It felt like privileged communication—like doctor-patient or lawyer-client. He was a good listener, always dispensing wise advice, and Tina wasn't the only one on the team who talked to Doc. Little did she know that Earl and Cocking had an unspoken agreement. Whatever Tina told Doc, Doc would tell Earl—our coach's own private pipeline into our locker room, which none of us, including Tina, ever knew about. If, for example, we emerged from our

inner sanctum with a new nickname for someone based on confi-
dential, potentially embarrassing information, Earl knew exactly
what we were talking about. Or if he didn't, he would a day later
after consulting with Doc.

Great.

Not that we were necessarily opposed to exposing embarrassing information. Humiliating each other, which had long
been a favorite pastime of healthy teenage boys, had now inched
its way across the gym to the girls' side. Almost nothing was out
of bounds if it meant getting a laugh, which became clear the day
I whispered to my supposedly good friend Peggy that I wanted a
nickname.

Everyone else seemed to have one—Peggy was "Japes" and
Karen was "Wik." Connie had even bestowed one on a freshman,
as she had begun calling Becky "Rookie" or "Rook." And I wanted
one. I even offered a few suggestions like "Eyes" for Isaacson. But
no sooner had the words come out of my mouth than I knew it
was a big mistake. Peggy's face lit up as if I had just told her that
I saw Coach Earl in a dress, and I knew what was coming next.

"Hey, you guys!" she screamed, and I knew that shushing her
or even socking her would not be an effective deterrent at this
point. "Missy just *asked* for a nickname. And she even made
some up."

As I slinked away, I realized that nothing was sacred in the
gym. Once we started playing with the boys, we were bound to
pick up some of their bad habits.

We still scrimmaged with the odd group that Earl gathered up
from guys who hung around the gym. But now we had graduated
to playing against the freshman boys, an actual organized team of
players who had some real talent for the game. Granted, most of
them were smaller than and not as strong as most of the senior
gym rats we loved and were used to playing, but the freshmen ran
their plays and their defenses against us and had the advantage of
having practiced and played together. We looked at it as a real test.

So, apparently, did their coach.

The young coach of Niles West's freshman A team had something of an ego and was not quite sure what to make of these games. Officially, we did not keep score, but the coaches knew exactly who was winning—and usually it was us. This did not sit particularly well with the boys' coach, who did not think girls of any age should beat his boys. Whenever we would get the better of them, he'd grumble to his players, "They're just a bunch of good shooters and passers," as if that was supposed to make them feel better.

The boys desperately wanted to win and gave us their best, but they also shook their heads respectfully when, time after time, Connie or Peggy or Barb would spring off a pick and drain a 15-footer. And by the end of the season, the freshman boys would be among our most loyal fans.

All we had to do now was stay healthy, emotionally and physically.

Despite the fact that we now had our own athletic trainer, Tulla Terpinas, Connie's ankle problems were not getting any better, and it seemed every other day, one of us would hit the court clutching an ankle. On this day, it was my turn.

It was a half-court scrimmage early in our practice, and after going up for a shot, I came down on the foot of Tina, who, with an expression of utter innocence, acted as if she had established perfect defensive position. In my view, she had moved right up under me so that I had no place to land and my ankle nothing else to do but roll. And as she stood there, her arms straight up in the air as if I had committed an offensive foul, I was filled with anger. And pain. I collapsed on the court, making a scene the likes of which I'm pretty sure no had ever witnessed before.

Granted, it hurt, and I was scared as I clutched my ankle, which I was sure had snapped in at least two places. But a gamer I was not. I liked to think I was. And in many situations, I took nasty tumbles on the court only to bounce up and continue playing. But this time, I rolled around and immediately began spewing a string of obscenities worthy of a longshoreman. "Goddamn son of a—," I screamed, words spilling forth that I myself had never said before, and soon I was vaguely aware that no one was comforting me, afraid, I'm sure, that like Linda Blair in *The Exorcist*, my head might soon start spinning.

I stopped squirming long enough to see Coach Earl walking over to me very slowly, probably intending to see if I was OK, but he was so overwhelmed by my language that he chose instead to react much like you would when slapping a person in shock.

"Hey!" he yelled. "Come on, that's enough."

So much for Mrs. Mulder's nurturing.

By that time, I was sure Coach Earl simply did not like me. I blamed a personality clash on my dwindling playing time—I was now entering games in the second quarter and making a few appearances in the second half but never in crunch time and almost always without any starters on the court. "Even if you put Connie on the floor with the bottom four players on the team, she would struggle," I half rationalized, half whined to Peggy. "It's not a fair judge of my talent."

I wondered if my absence from camp the summer before had hurt my standing. I also wondered if Becky had an in because of her father. I wondered a lot of things, some rational, some not. And most I only discussed with Peg. It was the kind of petty stuff you only tell a good friend, and I poured forth, as both of us had convinced ourselves that our new coach was not only insensitive to us but also maybe even prejudiced.

"I heard that some of the boys from Lincolnwood who played for Earl said he treated them worse than the other guys because they were Jewish," I whispered to her one day.

This was not the first time a Jewish kid from Lincolnwood had ever quietly leveled that charge against a teacher at Niles West. To some of us, anti-Semitism was a vague accusation you could toss around without having any real proof, and it was often suspected, even without an outright charge. Peggy thought this Earl theory was very interesting.

She would routinely make comments about Jewish people being cheap, driving Cadillacs, and having big noses, and I let this slide in the interest of humor. If, for example, while riding on the team bus she spotted a group of Hasidic Jews walking down the street in long coats and beards, she would invariably yell out, "Hey, Missy, do you know them?" and I would laugh along, the only Jew on the team that season and not the least bit offended.

In my heart, I knew Peggy did not mean harm. And in my heart, I knew Gene Earl was not anti-Semitic. But one day, we took it a little too far.

It was right around the holidays, and after a couple of spirited rounds of Christmas bus songs, which I happily joined in on, I started singing "Dreidel, Dreidel, Dreidel," one of the few Hanukkah songs I knew. We were all having a great time until Coach Earl, apparently annoyed at the noise level on the bus when we were supposed to at least be pretending to concentrate on the game at hand, stood up and yelled at us to shut up. Only it sure seemed like he yelled at me to shut up since I was the only one singing at the time.

Being at the very back of the bus afforded Peggy and me some anonymity, and so Peg took advantage of this opportunity by pretending to cough while yelling out, "Jew hater," through cupped hands.

I'll never know if Coach Earl heard us. I can only say that after a brief moment of satisfaction that Peggy had actually said what I had been thinking, I felt instant remorse. And I never made that accusation again.

CHAPTER 19

Let It Snow

BECKY SCHNELL WAS NOT THE TYPE OF KID to try to draw attention to herself. If anything, Peg and I used to joke, we weren't even sure she could talk her freshman year. Nevertheless, she was somehow thrust into the spotlight, whether it was having her name in the paper, developing a close friendship with Connie, or getting knocked out cold while naked in the locker room.

In her defense, this was not something she had planned, at least not the naked part. And probably not the concussion part either. But there she was, after walking just a little too fast coming out of the showers, sprawled unconscious on the floor of the Evanston High School girls' locker room.

It was our third straight appearance at the Evanston holiday tournament, and we had just wrapped up our third consecutive title with a 78–46 victory over Fremd. Coach Earl was in the coaches' hospitality room when he was alerted that one of his players had had an accident, and he was not about to let the little matter of a girls' locker room stop him from attending to one of us in need.

"Cover up 'cause I'm comin' in!" he bellowed, putting that booming voice to good use.

"Stay out. Stay out. I'm fine!" screamed Becky, who was coming to and surprising us with a decibel level we had never heard from her before.

Fortunately, Coach Earl only got a few steps in the door when common sense prevailed. But he did make Becky tell her parents what had happened, and a trip to the emergency room revealed that she had suffered a minor concussion.

Otherwise, the tournament was a rousing success.

We had taken apart Resurrection in a first-round game, 81–43, and defeated Regina the next day, 58–36, to send us into the title game. Regina did not represent our finest moment. In fact, after taking his starting lineup out in the fourth quarter of what seemed a sure victory, Coach Earl put all five back on the floor and had us go into a stall with three minutes to go in the game. We ended up scoring just one field goal in the fourth quarter and missing seven free throws, but we still won by 22, a sign that we could still dominate on an off-night and that Earl had absolutely no faith whatsoever in his bench. As the season wore on and wore down the confidence of most of his subs, this fact was not lost on us.

But Coach Earl already had his sights firmly set on the big picture. And after a surprisingly easy victory in the tournament final against a Fremd team that none of us had forgotten had annihilated us in our season opener two years before, our coach approached the referees. They were two brothers who he knew were from the downstate Galesburg area, and he had a feeling they might be able to quell a niggling concern.

"So, how do we stack up against the other teams you've seen in the state this year?" he asked, trying to sound casual.

"You can play with 'em," one of the brothers said, and that was enough to make Earl feel at least a little better about his 6–0 team.

After the tournament, we still had a week of Christmas

vacation left and our coach was content to take off that Monday, Tuesday, and Wednesday, but obviously he did not know us very well yet. We wanted to practice. With very few exceptions, we always wanted to practice. And if he expected applause after his announcement on the bus that he'd see us on Thursday, he was quickly set straight.

"Coach, you must not want to win bad enough if you don't want to practice," Connie lectured him.

When he showed up in the gym that Monday, he found half of his team was sniffling and sneezing and the other half coughing, and again encouraged us to go home or at least take it easy. No one moved. "Do what you want to do," he said, taking a seat in the bleachers and opening up a newspaper. Half of us got up a three-on-three, while the others shot at the side baskets as Earl simply shook his head. Some things, he realized, were not worth arguing about.

It had begun snowing over the weekend, not exactly breaking news for Chicago in January, except that it did not stop. Soon it had a name, the Blizzard of '79—very original—and while our classmates looked forward to winter vacation being extended, all it meant to our team was a little more inconvenience getting to the gym and for me, further delay in taking my driver's test and getting my license. To Coach Earl, it meant four hours in his car for the 12-mile drive from his home in Elk Grove for still another practice we insisted we had to have.

But this was nothing new to us. Almost every winter, there were at least one or two snow days, and we still managed to practice. That most cars in Chicago were buried entirely did not dawn on those of us with garages and parents who were easily badgered into driving us to the gym.

My father took great pride in his driving abilities, particularly in bad weather. And he never said no to a request from one of his children to be driven someplace, particularly to school. On one of these snowy excursions to Niles West for practice, Peggy, who had slept at my house the night before, ended up in our car and our car ended up, after an unfortunate turn, on a snow-covered set of railroad tracks, to which my dad seemed oblivious.

"Um, Dad, what are you doing?" I asked him as he stopped at the railroad crossing, put on his right blinker, and turned *onto the tracks*. Though death, for all we knew, could have been as close as the next speeding train, Peggy laughed so hard in the back seat that she nearly hyperventilated. I laughed at first too, out of sheer nervousness and the absurdity of it all, but not for long and not because I was afraid of getting killed.

"Shut up, Peg," I yelled at my good friend as she continued howling.

It just wasn't funny. Not anymore. I thought back to several weeks earlier, before winter break, when we were playing at Hoffman Estates. The school is in the far western suburbs, 24 miles from our house and a 40-minute drive on a good day. But this was not a good day. I wasn't overly worried when my parents weren't there by warm-ups or even tipoff, but I was nervous when they hadn't arrived by halftime. Then, in the fourth quarter, I saw my mom, red-faced and unmistakably annoyed, rushing into the gym, a dozen steps ahead of my sheepish-looking father.

I didn't mention it to my teammates during or even after the game. But the second I walked through the door that night, I demanded to know why they were so late.

"We were in Iowa," my mom said, shooting an angry look at my father.

Accustomed to my mom's sense of humor and her penchant for sarcasm and exaggeration, I would have laughed. But I saw their faces and knew right away she wasn't kidding. Apparently, they had gotten lost and continued west on the interstate, and though I doubted they actually made it all the way to Iowa, which was a four-hour trip, I imagined they had been well on their way. My dad shook his head and headed upstairs, and after that, either my sister, brother, or sister-in-law drove them to games more often while I silently noted that my parents were getting worse.

My father, now bewildered by both the bumpy road and the lunatic in his back seat, turned off the tracks and somehow made it to Niles West. But I was more than a little worried about him, and I opted not to share the latest adventure with my mother.

The Blizzard of '79 was actually a seemingly nonstop series of snowstorms that blanketed the Chicago area with 88 inches of snow from December 31, 1978, until February 28, 1979. But the worst of it was the more than 20 inches of new stuff dumped on the city between Friday night, January 12, and 2 a.m. Sunday, January 14. It brought back memories of the Chicago Blizzard of '67 (you'd think they'd come up with a new name this time around) when, as a kindergartner, I was allowed outside to play in the backyard one day during the storm, only to become buried up to my nose. My brothers, taking a break from jumping off our roof to yank me out by my arms, pulled me right out of my boots, which were not retrieved until the spring thaw.

This time, my teammates and I were actually careful not to do anything teenage stupid, like flinging ourselves off our roofs. Peggy had other things to think about during our time off, like how she had none. Peg did office work at the Julia Molloy Education Center for children with multiple disabilities and often jogged the five miles to and from Niles West in the snow to accommodate work and practice. But she never complained. Her boss would clip articles that had Peggy's name or photo and tape them on the walls of her office, beaming like a pseudo aunt while Peg ate it up.

By the time the Maine West game rolled around, we could barely contain ourselves. It was a home game, and blaming the snow for the almost nonexistent crowd, we unleashed a month's worth of pent-up energy in the 72–30 victory.

The other reason for the lopsided score was one thing Coach Earl picked up on as he watched the Maine West coach handle his team that night. It was nothing any of us would ever have noticed, but Coach Earl, who always paid a little more attention to the rare male coach he ran up against, spotted it immediately. The man was thoroughly disinterested, even disgusted, Earl determined, as if he had been given the job as punishment. And for someone who once wondered himself how much passion he would have for coaching girls, our coach was offended. How dare this guy demean his girls and the game by acting as if he did not want to be there, Earl thought to himself. He would not forget either the man or his attitude as we brazenly ran up the score against our ill-prepared opponent.

We would close out the month at home against Maine South, the second of what would eventually be four meetings against our conference rivals, and we were determined to finally assert our dominance after beating them by only two points last time.

Their sophomore guard Sally Petersen had scored 22 points against us in our first meeting, 18 coming in the second half, and Connie was bent on stopping her. It was our best game all year. It seemed everything we did worked, and we played with an intensity level even our coach had not seen from us before. We led 44–27 at halftime, and avoiding the inevitable third-quarter letdown that often afflicted us after a big first half, we came out in the third quarter with even more energy, scoring 30 points en route to an 86–58 blowout. Sally Petersen finished with four points.

Coach Earl delivered his usual postgame remarks with notes on things we needed to work on—there weren't many in a 28-point win—and then added what was clearly his new post-victory catchphrase. "Gang," he shouted, "it's great to be a winner!"

It was funny and, OK, maybe even sweet, and we all laughed.

With another home game against Maine East the following week, it occurred to us that for an 8–0 team, we were still falling far too short in attendance. Once again, we took to the campaign trail, counting on our scrimmage buddies as well as our teachers to spread the word. Peggy's homeroom teacher, Mr. Fitzpatrick, did his part by not marking his students tardy if they could produce a ticket stub from one of our games. Whether it worked or not was hard to tell, but we were still a little bitter about our unsupportive student body.

I was also still contending with my own bitterness over my decreased role. For two seasons I was a varsity starter and a significant presence on our team, and suddenly, it seemed, I was invisible. I continued to work hard in practice, still convinced that I could somehow prove myself to Coach Earl. But there was never any carryover from effort or performance in practice to playing time in games, and it was really starting to get to me.

At home, my mom listened sympathetically to me complain, and my father vowed to say something to Coach Earl, something we all knew he would never do and I would never let happen.

So frustrated was I that I actually screwed up the courage to go ask the great Billy Schnurr for advice. It seemed like a good idea until I was standing in front of him with no script to work off of. "Hi, Mr. Schnurr," I opened cleverly. "I was just wondering, I mean, if you think, if you've noticed, you know, I haven't been playing much and is there anything you think I should be working on?"

I was expecting a little sympathy, possibly even some outrage on his behalf that Earl was not playing me more. But as I looked up at him, I suddenly had the sinking feeling he might not throw open his arms and give me a hug. "This is a great team," he said. "Hang in there and enjoy the journey. It should be one heck of a ride."

This was not exactly what I wanted to hear.

Next, I tried to talk to Connie about it, but she seemed disinterested, urging me to focus on our goals, to suck it up for the team. "It's all about the team," she said. "It's not about any one of us anymore but working hard and sacrificing for the good of the group."

"I feel like that's what I have been doing, and he's not noticing," I said, realizing I wasn't getting anywhere with someone I considered to be one of my closest friends. I felt betrayed. It was hard not to resent Connie's growing friendship with Becky, who hung on Connie's every word like an eager puppy. Becky considered it one of the great moments of her life the first time Connie called her to come to the community center and practice with her, and she was blossoming under Connie's guidance. This only made me more jealous of Becky and angry at Connie.

But I wasn't the only one who was quietly seething. Karen thought she had finally arrived as a starter the first three games of the season but had also seen both her playing time and Earl's interest in her game diminish. Independently of each other, we both tried talking to our coach about our respective plights. "I've been playing you less to give your ankle time to rest," he told me when I approached him.

Yeah, right.

Karen's conversation on the gym balcony was a little more contentious, ending with Karen storming off and Earl calling after her, "You're the one who wanted to have a conversation. You're not going to hurt my feelings any."

So far, not exactly a touchy-feely season.

My last stab at finding empathy came with a late-night phone call to Champaign, which also did not go the way I had hoped. "Are you kidding, Miss?" Shirley lectured me. "Do you know how much I would give if I could still be on the team? Do you realize how lucky you are that you have another chance at state? Stop complaining and enjoy it while it lasts."

I stared at the phone for a long time after hanging up, debating whether to throw it across the room or cue up my old Carpenters album and listen to "Rainy Days and Mondays."

It was time to get new friends who understood me, I thought. Or maybe, possibly, it was time to stop feeling sorry for myself. I still adored basketball, loved practice, and respected my teammates. And so I continued to do what I had been doing, playing hard in practice and sitting on the edge of my seat during games, ready to go in. Even when I knew I wouldn't.

As a sign of my revitalized attitude, I decided there was no better time to write new lyrics to another sitcom theme song, this one from *Laverne & Shirley*:

> We're gonna do it
> We're going all the way this year
> We're feeling great, we have nothing to fear
> We're gonna make our dreams come true
> Doin' it our way.
>
> Straight ahead, no looking back
> We see our peak, come on, let's pack
> We're gonna end up in Champaign
> Doin' it our way.
>
> We've got it all it seems
> Never heard the word *impossible*
> This time, there's no stopping us
> We're gonna do it.
>
> Using our skill and self-esteem
> We are a classy team
> We're gonna make our dreams come true
> And we'll do it our way, yes, our way,
> Make all our dreams come true
> And we'll do it our way, yes, our way,
> Make all our dreams come true,
> That's what we'll do.

It was only February 1, practically an entire season left, and Maine East was next up. After juggling the wing position among Karen, Tina, and Judy, Coach Earl had finally settled on Tina as his starter. We beat Maine East 73–42, but our performance was far below par. Aside from our usual stellar defense, we contributed to what was the sloppiest game of the season to that point, replete with turnovers and poor shooting on both sides.

The worst part, though, was that Peggy went down in the second quarter with a badly sprained ankle that initially looked to be a season-ending injury. Her showing up in a walking cast the next day did nothing to improve our outlook.

After a victory against Maine West, in which we overcame an embarrassingly uninspired first quarter to outscore our opponent 50–18 in the second half and improve our overall record to 13–0, a Maine West player told a reporter, "Well, at least we only lost to them by 40 points."

That victory, however, was better remembered for what happened afterward. Coach Earl, who by now had grown somewhat accustomed to waiting at least a half hour longer for us to shower and dress following games than any boys' team he had ever coached, was especially tested on this night. For whatever reason, it took us even longer than usual, so long that the Maine West coach—the same man who earlier had offended Coach Earl with his patronizing attitude toward coaching girls—turned out the lights in the gym and left him sitting in the dark, waiting for us.

Our coach was not in the best mood after that and was even more annoyed when we pulled into the Niles West parking lot only to find the door to the school locked. Because the bus could not be maneuvered over grass to the next closest entrance, Coach Earl and the bus driver jumped out in the dark and ran off to find an open door. Especially giddy after the big win and bored by the five-minute wait, we wondered if Coach Earl would notice if the bus was not in the exact same spot when he returned.

Judy was first behind the wheel, driving it a few feet, followed by Pam, who moved it a few feet more, and finally Holly, who lurched it forward again. Some of us had the maturity to not participate in this dangerous and childish stunt, those like Peg and I, who chose instead to egg on the culprits while acting as lookouts. Meanwhile, Lynn Carlsen decided she was in grave danger and bailed out the rear exit, setting off a buzzer in the process.

Somehow, we all managed to get off and get into the school without Coach Earl noticing what had happened. But the next morning, a plan was hatched by Peggy and me to once again ensnare the most gullible among us—Holly—in a practical joke.

It was actually quite easy to pull off as Holly did not feel well that morning and was not in school that day. We firmed up the scheme during the day, and after practice Peggy called Holly and told her that Earl had found out that three players had driven the bus and that Judy and Pam had already confessed. "He wants the third person to come forward," Peggy said with dead seriousness. "Otherwise, he said we are all going to be held responsible. You may not be allowed to take driver's ed next year, but I think he knows it's you, Holl, and if you confess, you might get off lightly."

The key to the joke's execution was that Coach Earl, by now familiar with our warped sense of humor and willing to be an amazingly good sport, was in on the gag and waiting when Holly came in trembling the next day, ready to spill her guts. "You know," he bellowed at her in mock anger, "we can keep you out of driver's ed until you're 18."

Holly heard the giggling shortly after shedding her first tear, as we all came spilling out behind the bleachers. It was both a real bonding moment with our coach and a perfectly executed plan. Now if only the rest of the season went that well.

CHAPTER 20

Perfect Shmerfect

THE CAPTION UNDER THE PHOTO of Connie driving to the basket was a typo, of course.

A forgetful copy editor was supposed to insert an actual number. But instead, after the sentence "Niles West guard Connie Erickson has done it all this season," were the words "The 5-6 guard has compiled a zillion points, rebounds, assists and steals."

Connie couldn't win for losing. If she refused to do interviews, which she tried to do at first this season, it looked like false modesty. If she talked, there she was in the headlines where she had never intended to be. Or in a caption scoring "a zillion" points.

Sitting on the bleachers before class with the paper on her lap, Peggy rolled her eyes. She had become accustomed to seeing her name in stories that read: "Connie Erickson put on a spectacular display for the Indians, finishing with 10 points, eight assists and six steals, while Barb Atsaves was deadly accurate from the floor with 14 points. Peggy Japely chipped in with 22."

Local writers like Susan Sternberg and Jim Braun were having a field day without Arlene Mulder there to shield her players from them. Suddenly, Connie was showing up as the subject of feature stories, though always reluctantly and, without exception, always crediting her teammates. Peggy, meanwhile, was a late bloomer, a player no one had really heard of before her senior season. And indeed, we had been playing well as a team during Peggy's absence with the ankle injury.

Maybe the only good thing about her being sidelined was that it forced others to pick up the slack. Peggy had been averaging 17.5 points per game at that point, and Holly had her best game of the season in a victory against Glenbrook South, finishing with 19. Judy, who had been starting in Peggy's place, also stepped up, scoring 17 in our victory over Waukegan East.

But we missed Peggy's height, her rebounding, and her defensive presence, and we knew we would not get very far in the postseason without her. She normally guarded the other team's best big girl, and against Glenbrook South, that would have been Colleen Monckton, who scored 27 points, including 10 in the fourth quarter alone.

Peggy was happy we did well while she was out and never outwardly sulked on the bench, just as Karen and I were happy we kept winning despite our own personal frustrations. But as Connie and, lately, Barb started getting more attention, Peg felt left out.

She was not the only one.

Connie's brother Chris, who already had the inherent challenge of distinguishing himself in a family with 11 kids, now had the added burden of having his twin sister on the brink of stardom. Chris was on the varsity football and basketball teams and was a fine athlete in his own right. But through no fault of his own, his time at Niles West also coincided with a down period in boys' team sports while the girls' programs were still new and exciting and, in the case of every team Connie was a part of, wildly successful.

The natural competitiveness between twins had increased to

the point where Chris, who seemed to be growing more and more withdrawn, would not even acknowledge Connie if they saw each other in the hallway, and it bothered her a lot. She never shared her feelings about Chris with any of us. She was still going out with Bob, so she had him to talk to, but mostly she was intensely focused on basketball as we all were.

It was weird how jealousy was affecting our team this year when it had never reared its head before. But we kept it under control, for this season was also destined to be the most special of all, and somehow every one of us was starting to feel it. Or at least I was.

When the *Spectrum*, our high school yearbook, asked the seniors three months before graduation to write down all of our accomplishments from our four years at Niles West for the senior survey section, I had the audacity to add one more regional and sectional championship to the tally as well as "One State Triumph?!"

Peggy glanced over my shoulder with an arched eyebrow as I added the "?!" in as a disclaimer, but then we had every reason to be confident as we headed into the final stretch of the regular season and the Libertyville tournament. We were psyched up, as we always were for tournaments, but especially so for this one as it offered the chance to exact a little payback on Hersey. We always loved tournaments, but this time we felt there was no team on our schedule capable of beating us. We were in the top bracket, slated to meet Hersey again in the championship if everything went according to plan.

After a three-week absence, Peggy was back for our first-round game against Wheeling but didn't start and played sparingly, scoring eight points in a ridiculously easy 77–33 victory. Next up was Maine South, against whom we now had a five-game winning streak, dating back two seasons. Experience should have told us that, aside from our last meeting, most of our games against Maine South were competitive and that the Hawks had enough talent to give any team a run. But with one eye on Hersey, we got sucked into one of the oldest sports pitfalls around—looking ahead.

After we jumped out to a comfortable 24–15 first-quarter lead, Maine South clamped down in a man-to-man defense that limited us to five points in a physical second quarter that left us with a three-point lead at the half. The margin was the same through three quarters, when we led 43–40. But we played scared in the second half, playing not to lose instead of our usual aggressive style, and it cost us in the end.

Connie, Barb, and Peggy fouled out, and Judy had four fouls as Maine South made 29-of-40 free throws while we were 14-of-18 from the line. Still, Becky was poised to be the hero of the game when she hit two free throws with nine seconds left in regulation to put us up by two at 52–50. But with one second remaining, Kathy Spychala, a 5-7 junior reserve for Maine South whom none of us had ever heard of and who was triple-teamed where the center court line meets the sideline in our 1-3-1 half-court zone trap, heaved up a prayer only to see it swish through, sending the game into overtime and the Maine South cheering section into delirium. Maine South took advantage of its instant momentum as we scored just one basket in the overtime period and lost our first game of the season 58–54.

As we shuffled wordlessly toward our locker room, Coach Earl unleashed his frustration on the referees for the lopsided free throw totals, walking away just short of being sorry for something he said. We took no comfort in his defense of us, nor did we take much interest in what he was saying. We were awash in self-pity and self-doubt, and for the next hour or so anyway, we played it for all it was worth.

In stage whispers, Peg and I had been critical on the bench about what was happening, second-guessing Earl's coaching being the main topic of conversation, and clearly we had not been very subtle. Becky had silently dubbed us "Snip and Snot" and wondered why she, a freshman, was seemingly more mature than a couple of seniors.

On the bus ride to lunch before we had to return for the third-place consolation game, Coach Earl stood up and gave us an it's-not-the-end-of-the-world speech that we sort of appreciated but pretty much ignored. "Come on, gang," he intoned. "It's one game. One game. Now you get back up, dust yourself off, and go back out there."

In a row by herself, Connie sat sobbing in frustration, distraught that our perfect season would be marred by the likes of Maine South.

Coach Earl walked down the aisle and stood in front of her. "Trust me," he told her, "you are not going to remember this when you're giving birth to your first child."

It was sort of an odd thing to say and an even odder thing for a teenager to hear, and Connie laughed through her tears at the absurdity and awkwardness of it, lightening the mood.

If we were going to prove that we were a high-caliber team, there was no better way than to show how we rebounded from a dramatic loss. And fortunately for us, we had only a few hours to deal with the sickly taste of defeat. Still, a short team meeting felt necessary, and in the locker room before playing Libertyville in the consolation game, the seniors took the floor, delivering the message that we had come too far to let the season derail at this point.

"Whatever petty differences we may have, whatever personal gripes, now is the time to put them aside," Connie began.

"Remember what we're here for, what our goal is," Judy all but shouted at her usual football coach volume.

As I sat there, I knew Connie was talking about Peggy and me, and I felt bad. I didn't want to be a cancer on the team. I certainly had never viewed myself that way, and I thought I had largely put my own grievances aside. The worst part was that I had always considered myself to be a leader, but I also felt in no position to be a leader from my place on the bench.

Connie's biggest fear was that we would let one loss spiral out of control, but we were still furious about the Maine South game when we took the court against Libertyville, and as adept at breaking a press as we were at pressing ourselves, we cut through our opponents' defense like their feet were shackled and raced out to a 24–12 first-quarter lead.

Still, it turned out to be a tough game, exactly what we needed, as one of Libertyville's guards got hot, leading the Wildcats on a 17–8 run to pull them within three points at the half. They outscored us again in the third quarter, trimming our lead to 47–45, but we hung on for a well-earned 65–57 victory that instantly restored whatever confidence we may have lost for the few hours after the Maine South loss.

Earl determined, as he had during Christmas vacation, that we needed a break from practice as the regular season wound down, but once again, he gave in and let us have a shortened workout without his supervision. Hard as we tried, we could not help but look ahead again to Hersey, which had defeated Maine South in the finals of the Libertyville tournament and loomed as our second to last game of the season. Despite the distraction, we managed to dispatch in orderly fashion both Maine East, 62–49, and Waukegan East, 84–52, but our nerves were again frayed for our game against one of the very few teams we feared.

We played Hersey at home before a healthy number of loyal fans that was still nowhere near what we felt we should be drawing, and Hersey did not disappoint. After scrapping to a 12–12 first-quarter tie, they led by as many as 12 points in the second quarter and took a 33–25 lead at halftime as we filed into the girls' PE office. It was the first time all season we had trailed at halftime.

Under Earl, we couldn't hold our halftime meetings in the girls' locker room for obvious reasons, and sitting on desks and sprawling on the floor as we normally did made the tiny office feel even more cramped than usual. The bickering began as soon as we closed the door. Coach Earl generally gave us a few minutes to cool down by ourselves before he came in and addressed us, and we used our time on this night to yell at each other. Peggy was particularly incensed, snapping at no one in particular that she was open inside and not getting the ball, while Connie shot back that if Peggy were open, she'd get the ball and furthermore, she was getting sick of her complaining.

Peggy was mid-rant when Earl walked in.

"Shut up!" he shouted so loudly that we all jumped. By now, we had heard him raise his voice plenty of times, but this actually scared us, and he immediately calmed down. "Peg, if the guards don't think you're open, you're not going to get the ball," he said. "The point is, we need to play in sync. We're down eight points and we're not going to get it all back right away, so don't be in a hurry."

He paused and stared at us.

"Look, we're going to whittle this lead down and then some-one is going to get a key steal or an offensive rebound, and we're going to win this game," he continued. "But it might be in the last 15 seconds, so be patient."

Pleased with himself and his speech, Earl watched his ornery team take the court and proceed to wipe out Hersey's lead in the first minute and a half of the third quarter. Our full-court press was perhaps the best it had been all season, and suddenly, a team that looked quite capable of beating us in the first half crumbled, unable even to get the ball past half-court.

It was the biggest turnaround Gene Earl had ever experi-enced with a team he had coached, and he sat back on the bench and enjoyed it as we outscored Hersey 22–8 in the third quarter and won 61–53.

If he was not fully convinced of it before, Earl knew it then. He had a damn good team.

We were now 20–1 and that week, Jimmy Baron—a senior

who was the PA announcer for our games, starred in our school plays, and wrote for the *West Word*—ended his account of the Hersey victory with a personal aside: "In this reporter's opinion, it is a shame that such a tremendous team as the girls' basketball squad cannot draw a respectable-size crowd. Hopefully, Niles West will someday learn to appreciate a winner."

We finished the regular season at 21–1 after defeating Glenbrook North 61–45, finally arriving at the long-awaited post-season. Regionals were at New Trier East, while Niles West was hosting sectionals.

After spending the last 12 months looking forward to getting back to supersectionals and having the chance to wipe away the frustration and sadness of a long two years, we would approach this state tournament as we had been trained. We would look no further than our next opponent, our next game. And we would barely notice that one of our teammates would not be a part of it.

CHAPTER 21

Joy Is . . .

WHEN HE LEARNED THAT he could take only 12 of his 13 players to the state tournament, Gene Earl did the fairest thing he could think of to resolve the issue.

He flipped a coin.

It was not an obvious pick between Nancy Eck and Debbie Durso for the last spot on our postseason roster, but it was obvious to Coach Earl that it should come down to the two seniors as to who should stay and who should go.

Only Nancy was present as he flipped the coin that would break one girl's heart. She called it and lost and, in her disappointment, asked if instead of simply cutting her from the team 22 games into the season, she and Debbie could take turns dressing in uniform and sitting on our bench while the other was relegated to the stands.

Earl agreed, and it was determined that since Debbie won, it would work backward. If we made it to Champaign and the state finals, Debbie would dress for those games. He found out that the roster for supersectionals had to be the same as the one in Champaign, so Debbie would suit up that round as well. For sectionals, which Niles West was hosting, it would be Nancy's turn. And Deb would dress for regionals at New Trier East.

It was far from ideal, but it was done, and Nancy, as she always had, obeyed authority and went along with the plan without so much as a whimper. Meanwhile, not one of the rest of us paused for more than a second to consider how this might have hurt both of them or whether or not there was a better solution.

Regionals were before us, and the Niles West student body was reminded yet again that we were a team worthy of their support. Our smattering of male fans—the boys who scrimmaged with us, assorted boyfriends, and the boys, like Jimmy Baron, who had been watching us closely—marshaled their forces and others fell in line. Football players said they would be there and an ad hoc pep band called the Super Sax was assembled.

We were not particularly worried about our first-round opponent, nor should we have been, as we easily defeated New Trier West 63–26. Glenbrook South was next, and though we had beaten them in two previous meetings that season, Titans coach Kay Sopocy told reporters she thought her team had outplayed us in all but two of the eight quarters and that they had one coming.

Their top scorer, Colleen Monckton, had scored 25 and 27 points, respectively, in the other two games, and though we were always concerned with trying to neutralize her, we also knew that Peggy had missed both of those meetings because of her sprained ankle. We were at full strength now and nothing, we believed in our hearts, could stop us, least of which Glenbrook South.

Whatever petty bickering we had done during the season had been set aside, and we went into the playoffs as one, rolling to the regional title in our most dominating victory yet over the Titans, 75–47. In addition to forcing 19 turnovers off our press, we held Monckton to 16 points. Their second-leading scorer was shut out.

If anyone doubted that Connie and Barb formed the best

backcourt in the state, they had not watched them in the regional final, where they combined for 35 points, 14 assists, and 13 steals. Peggy poured in 20 points to lead all scorers, and as we cut down our third straight set of nets celebrating a regional championship, it was not with the same giddiness as in the past but with a firm resolve that said we had not even begun to finish the job for which we came.

Looking ahead to sectionals at home, we could feel our school being swept along with our momentum, and we were hearing rumors that school officials would actually have to use the upper balcony of the gym for the crowd they were expecting. Not so swept up, however, were the varsity cheerleaders, who were asked to cheer at our sectional opener against Maine South and declined, saying they were busy.

Though we had every reason to be apprehensive about facing Maine South in our first-round sectional game, we were as confident and eager as ever to play the Hawks for the third time this season, especially because they were the only blemish on our record.

Much to our delight, the predictions were correct and our gym swelled to near capacity, which—combined with the excitement of the moment and other flu symptoms—led Tina to lose her lunch in the drinking fountain under the basket during pregame warm-ups.

The mere thought of Tina barfing was enough to send me racing for the nearest toilet, and Peggy, who eagerly informed me of Tina's unfortunate illness, found this hysterical as we tried to keep our minds on the task ahead and keep our distance from Tina.

I was still seeing spot time, usually in the second and third quarters, but I also fully expected to be summoned at any point in any game, and I was ready if it happened. Even as Dr. Mannos greeted my parents that evening and told them that he was mystified as to why my playing time had dropped off so dramatically this season, I went through warm-ups as always, as if preparing to start, my simmering personal disappointment far behind me.

Before our biggest home crowd of the season, we scored the first basket of the game and never relinquished the lead. A pair of baskets by Peg extended our advantage to 13–4, and superb passing by our offense, which sliced through Maine South's zone defense, left us with a 36–20 bulge at the half.

The game was physical, as was usually the case against Maine South, but overly aggressive officiating reminded us that girls were only allowed to be so physical as Connie was limited to seven minutes of playing time due to foul trouble.

In the end, it was Barb's shooting, Holly's rebounding, Peggy's all-around dependability, and the strength of our bench, led by Judy and Becky, that carried us to a 69–55 victory and set up a sectional final against Oak Park.

Oak Park was 26–0, taller than we were at all three positions in the frontcourt, and not a team we had played before or with whom we shared any common opponents as a basis to compare. But we knew tall usually equaled slow and easy to press, and we were at home before a crowd that now had standing room only.

Despite clinging to a 29–27 lead over the Huskies at halftime, we sensed we had them right where we wanted them. Our press took its toll against our dog-tired opponents as we built a nine-point lead in the first two minutes of the second half and never looked back. We led 51–33 after three quarters and outscored Oak Park 40–19 in the second half to win our third straight sectional title 69–46.

Barb and Peggy finished with 22 and 18 points, respectively, while Connie and Tina had 11 apiece. We celebrated afterward, though our immediate thought was on our supersectional opponent. Debbie Durso's immediate thought was on her job, which had shifted from a reserve guard in street clothes to the person in charge of putting "We Are the Champions," our unofficial theme song by Queen, on the courtside record player while we cut down the nets. In her haste, the well-played record started skipping, sending Deb into a mild panic that she had blown her one sectional responsibility. The playing of that song had become almost as important as our pregame warm-up routine, our wristbands, and our collective psyche.

Debbie could laugh it off, as she knew at least she would be joining us at East Leyden High School for our supersectional matchup with undefeated Glenbard West. Nancy, on the other hand, quietly took off her Niles West uniform that night for the very last time.

In typical fashion, she never complained.

We had five days, or until the next Tuesday, to think about our next game, and we studied film of our opponent as if for a final exam. Unlike in our first days watching grainy game films with Mrs. Mulder, both the film quality and the surroundings had improved as we now watched in an empty classroom. There was not a single doubt in any of our minds that this was our year, and yet, if we had allowed ourselves to really think about it, we would recall that we had had the same feeling the previous two years, and no one had to remind us how those supersectionals turned out.

How this was going to be different, we did not discuss, but then we didn't have to. Clearly, we were a superior team this season. Connie was more experienced, a better shooter, an improved passer, a more confident floor leader. Barb, now a starter, had developed into one of the best pure shooters in the state. Peggy, who only two years ago had hesitantly tried out for basketball for the first time and began last season on JV, was now a dominant rebounder and money from 12 feet and in. Holly and Tina, who spent all of last season on JV, were now bona fide varsity starters, dependable and tough-minded and also capable shooters.

Defensively, we were the best team in the state, or at least that's what we believed. Connie and Barb had hands so quick that their victims often never saw the steal coming, and Connie's anticipation was scary, as if she had crib notes telling her where every pass was going. Our press was a thing of beauty. Everyone in the state knew about it, and yet they still couldn't stop it. With

Peggy intimidating the inbounds passer and Connie and Barb lying in wait, most teams couldn't get past half-court on us. And if they did, there was Tina ready to pounce with the double-team as 5-11 Holly, arms outstretched and face scowling from the lane, hung back, knowing that her teammates would soon recover and join her.

After 25 games and, for most of us, two or more years of running stairs and scrimmaging at five in the morning behind us, we could say with confidence that no team in Illinois was better conditioned or more in sync. While Pam, Lynn, and Debbie may have lacked the experience of Judy, Karen, and me, they were prepared and well-schooled from practicing against the best starting five in the state. And Becky, despite her continued shyness off the court, just never seemed flustered.

While it remained something of a frustration for me to watch a freshman continue to reap the benefits of years of hard work for which she was not present, Becky was impossible to dislike. Though I wouldn't necessarily admit it, I finally saw what Connie had long seen in Becky—an eager-to-please, sincerely sweet kid who, despite my occasionally thinly veiled disdain, wanted nothing more than to be my friend and a good teammate. And it was while squeezed next to her on our bench as we yelled ourselves hoarse, laughed, and slapped hands during regionals and sectionals that I began to genuinely like her back.

Our next game was billed as the best matchup of the eight girls' supersectionals. At 26–0, Glenbard West was one of only three undefeated teams in the state along with Chicago Public League champ Marshall—expected to win their supersectional and meet our game's winner in the state quarterfinals—and downstate Sterling, which had gained fame as the first-ever Illinois girls' state basketball champion in 1977.

Our game was also hyped for its individual matchup at guard between two *Suburban Trib* all-stars: Connie Erickson and Glenbard West's 5-4 senior playmaker Beth Stevenson.

Both of our teams employed a vaunted full-court press to force turnovers and convert them into easy fast-break baskets, and both teams loved to run.

Coach Earl was already subtly working the refs in the papers, saying that the officiating would be key and subtly suggesting that he could only hope they would allow us to play our usual aggressive game without taking the ball out of our hands. None of us forgot how we lost last year's supersectional, with all five of our starters fouling out in a crushing three-point loss to Dundee. But most of us had conveniently forgotten about Arlene Mulder and never considered how the loss might still be eating at her.

Busy with her new son, Michael, now seven months old, and Michelle and Alison, now 11 and 8, Mrs. Mulder still had not attended a game of ours and still had not had any signal from us or from Earl that we wanted her to come. But that did not make her sudden withdrawal from us any easier for her to bear. Though we missed her at first and eventually felt betrayed by her absence and what we felt was a lack of support, it simply never occurred to us to pick up the phone and call our old coach.

Most of us had sent notes of congratulations and baby gifts— or at least our mothers had—after Michael was born. But calling a teacher at home? Even for a former teacher, the thought was unheard of and especially now that we were so intensely focused on the task at hand, Mrs. Mulder was far from our thoughts.

Even Peggy had begun to appreciate, if not exactly love, the quirky, good-natured charm of Gene Earl. He still got on our nerves occasionally with his down-home colloquialisms, but he was forever a good sport, accepting our teasing—even when Peggy would openly mock his chubbiness—our bossiness, and our ever-changing moods with humor and patience.

He was our leader now. We were Earl's Girls, whether we all loved the moniker or not. And it was Gene Earl, as much as Connie and Barb and Peggy, who was going to carry us to the place of our dreams.

March 27 was the final obstacle. Super Tuesday, as they called the Illinois basketball supersectionals, was Tainted Tuesday as far as we had come to know it. But no longer. This time, we told ourselves, we would not be outplayed or psyched out, cursed by officials, or dictated by curses of any kind. We would neither be intimidated nor overwhelmed nor even particularly moved by the occasion.

Glenbard West officials had called Niles West that week, asking for more tickets because they had already sold out their allotment. We were convinced that would result in a gym dominated by opposing fans, which no longer hurt our feelings but might, we felt, give Glenbard West an advantage that we would prefer they not have.

But we would not allow it to defeat us before the game had begun. We would march into the East Leyden gym and take what was rightfully ours, what we had sweated and worked and fought and cried over for three long years.

Susan Sternberg of the *Suburban Trib* likened Niles West versus Glenbard West to "other super match-ups such as boy meets girl, the 1975 World Series and good against evil. It's the game girls' basketball followers have been waiting for—the one featuring the two best teams in the suburban area."

"Determination isn't going to win it," Coach Earl was quoted as saying, "but it will help."

So would experience, and finally we could say we had the advantage in that department over almost anyone we faced. Not only had we played in pressure situations but we had both failed and ultimately triumphed in many of those situations. We were battle-tested and savvy, and we seldom choked, which would make Shirley proud.

One member of our team who was not particularly experienced, however, suddenly began to feel like it.

As we dressed before the game, Becky thought she might throw up, kind of like she felt before our first game of the season when she spent the afternoon baking cookies with a friend, then promptly lost hers. She kind of felt like that again, a "What-am-I-doing-here?" refrain ringing in her head. And in the locker room, she eyed the giant pickle jar filled with dextrose tablets that we lugged to every game. No one particularly noticed that up until that point, Becky had avoided the pills like rat poison. She knew they weren't rat poison, but she was reasonably sure they were dangerous narcotics of some kind, and even the endorsement of her mentor and idol Connie could not have convinced her otherwise. But her first supersectional could, and she quickly choked one down, thinking she surely needed it for what was in store.

When we walked out of the locker room, we were struck by one thing and were quickly relieved. One side of the gym was solid green, the other a massive wall of red. The Niles West turnout was unlike anything we had ever seen. It made last year's supersectional showing look like a junior high pep rally. The roar was spontaneous and deafening and brought tears to the eyes of the older girls.

They were all here. Finally. For us. The same girls they wouldn't allow into the Boys' Gym three years earlier were overcome by a roar that lifted us up and carried us onto the court.

Our hearts were hammers inside our chests as we performed our ballhandling drill, each backhanded behind-the-back flip eliciting cheers. We could not be any more ready. So psyched was I, it was all I could do not to run out for the opening tip.

Glenbard West was no fluke. The Hilltoppers shook off a 26–18 first-quarter deficit and kept it a game most of the way. But it was clear which was the dominant team. When we weren't forcing them to take low-percentage shots over our 1-3-1 zone, we were forcing 15 turnovers, mostly off our press, in the first half alone. We held a 44–31 lead late in the half despite playing the last four minutes before intermission without Connie, who had picked up three fouls.

Peggy had already scored 16 by halftime when we led by 10,

and in the third quarter, Coach Earl called off the press, hoping a man-to-man defense would suffice and save Connie from further foul trouble. But Glenbard West closed the margin to four once and to five two other times before Connie took control.

A steal for a layup, followed by another Erickson steal and a feed to Peggy underneath helped us mount a nine-point third-quarter lead as we shot 10-of-19 from the floor and held on to the momentum. As we held an eight-point lead in the final minutes of the game, Connie and Barb simply took the ball out of the Hilltoppers' hands, directing a four-corner stall that left them frustrated and flailing.

And as we closed out the 71–64 victory, the familiar chant began, garbled at first as the Niles West half of the gym got in sync, and then clearer. And louder.

We are going. We are going. State, state. State, state.

Connie finished with 17 points, and once again, it was Peggy, chipping in her usual underrated 23 on 10-for-12 field goal shooting, who carried the day.

On court at the final buzzer, Connie found me and I found Peggy, and together we found Judy and Karen, the five seniors who understood better than anyone how truly sweet this moment was as the crowd poured out of the bleachers, enveloping us in a giant group hug.

"They were the quickest and best passing team I've seen all year," Glenbard West coach Emily Mollet told reporters on her team's sideline, shouting to be heard over the din.

Hinsdale South and Dundee, supersectional slayers of years past, were a long way away. And so was Marshall, our first-round opponent in the state quarterfinals in Champaign only three days from now.

We had taken a disciplined, methodical approach to finally breaking through our supersectional stumbling block, and now we acted like the kids we were, giggling and dancing and hugging each other again and again. Connie slipped one of the nets around her neck like the familiar jewelry it had become, and it fit her perfectly.

Since our loss to Maine South when we had committed one of sports' greatest sins in looking ahead, we had stayed focused. We were veterans. We knew better. And then our coach called us over to the bench, pulled off his tie, unbuttoned his sweaty dress shirt, and tossed them aside. Forced to keep his sport coat buttoned up all night so as not to reveal his secret, he could now bare all. Underneath, he was wearing a white T-shirt that read JOY IS WINNING A SUPER SECT.

Even Peggy had to laugh.

CHAPTER 22

Why Not Us?

OUR LOCKER ROOM AT East Leyden just happened to lead into both the gym and the school's swimming pool, a sign from above, some of us felt, that we should cap off our celebration by jumping in. So what if we didn't have bathing suits, hadn't received permission, and our bus, our coach, and most of the 3,000 fans who had come to see us were waiting for us to come out?

We were celebrating, the pool was private, and most importantly, it was there. And so we jumped in, some of us still with our uniforms on, some in just bras and underwear. And everyone was forced to wait for us to finish, including the janitor who had come in to clean and stayed to watch despite our shrieks.

The next day, we were back in class pretending we were paying attention, a nervous energy fueling us as classmates and teachers greeted us with hand slaps in the hall and a steady stream of "Congratulations," and "Good luck at state."

Before we left for Champaign on Thursday, there was another pep rally—and this one was spectacular. Far from our usual apathetic Niles West affairs in which those students who did show up only did so to miss class and yawned louder than they cheered, this one had the pep band and cheerleaders, TV cameras and newspaper reporters, and the entire student body and faculty. We promised to bring them home a title, and they roared their approval, sending chills up and down each one of us.

But the cheerleaders were a contentious point. Though we never had a problem with the group as a whole, we felt insulted by what we viewed as their disinterest all season, particularly in the postseason. Our coach was just plain annoyed. Now that we were actually going downstate, playing before an Assembly Hall crowd and a television audience on WGN, the cheerleaders were interested in coming, they said. But Coach Earl gave their supervisor a firm "No thanks," and we left them behind.

It was a strange sort of reprisal. They were our peers. Some were gymnasts and on the track team, athletes themselves and our friends even. They were not, by nature, the sort of prissy girls we could easily detest. But in drawing the line that day, we somehow stepped away and symbolically separated the girls who cheered from the girls who played. We played. And we didn't have much patience for the rest. Not now anyway. We had business to do.

Our first stop on Thursday was the Rantoul High School gym, not far from the Illinois campus. Coach Earl knew the athletic director from his downstate days and had arranged a practice there since we could not practice on the Assembly Hall floor. It was a smart move, and we wondered among ourselves if Marshall, our quarterfinal opponent, was as prepared as we were. Sweeping through the school and into the gym, we felt like celebrities, big-city supersectional champs gracing Rantoul with our presence. What made it even better was the fact that the students all had to be in class while we practiced.

This could not be much cooler.

In some ways we felt we were carrying the hopes of not just Niles Township but the whole Chicagoland area, despite the fact that we were about to play the Chicago Public League champs. The night before our supersectional victory, we had watched Magic Johnson's Michigan State team defeat Larry Bird and Indiana State in one of the most closely watched and celebrated NCAA title games in history. But the big story of the tournament for us was Ray Meyer's DePaul team starring Mark Aguirre, which had lost in the NCAA semifinals to Indiana State.

DePaul's Final Four berth had captivated the city and suburbs and inspired us. We felt a strong connection to the school, as many of us had gone to both DePaul and Chicago Hustle games in DePaul's gym, Connie and Peggy were being recruited by the women's team, and Barb's father, Pete, owned the Seminary Restaurant, where Coach Meyer's players ate most of their meals and where we often dropped in as well.

The Blue Demons were heroes to us, and in our own goofy way, we felt like we were following in their footsteps. In another triumph for our area and even closer to home, Maine South had won the boys' state basketball title in Class AA (which was the larger of the two classes in Illinois boys' basketball), so we had inspiration seemingly everywhere we looked.

This was to be the third and final year of a single-class state tournament in girls' basketball. Participation was rising in the sport among member schools and topped 600 in '79 after numbering 475 for the first girls' tournament in '77. But we sort of liked the fact that we still had just one class. There would be no doubt as to which was the one top team in the state after this weekend, and we carried that cockiness all the way to the point when we turned a corner that Thursday night and approached the great white mushroom that was the University of Illinois Assembly Hall.

The 16,500-seat arena was already 16 years old at that point, but it still looked like something out of *2001: A Space Odyssey* to us. Rising seemingly out of the cornfields on the Illinois campus, it glowed from the under-mounted lights, almost beckoning us closer even as it was scaring the daylights out of us.

Clearly, those in Coach Earl's lead car urged him toward the building rather than continuing on to the hotel, which we had planned, and Miss Heeren simply followed. No one was sure what we were doing there, but then this was our goal, getting here, to this building, and so it seemed only natural that we would drive directly to the place.

It was already dark when we got out of our cars by the lower service entrance and let ourselves in. About half of us had been here for the tournament the year before, but we walked through the bowels of the building like astronauts navigating our way through an alien spacecraft, knowing as we did that at any minute a janitor could pop out from behind a corner and zap us. Coach Earl had little choice in the matter as we were clearly commanding this mission.

When we finally made our way to the court, which was one level below ground, we could make out enough of the place to tell how truly cavernous it was. We slowly circled the court, which we had not dared to do the year before. Then we stood on the free-throw line looking at the basket and the space behind it. It seemed like if you missed a shot, the ball would fly out into the great beyond, never to be seen again. I pictured an endless supply of basketballs at courtside, so they could shuttle one in every time a ball disappeared out of bounds.

Silently, Connie worried. What if all this confidence was just that? What if we were kidding ourselves here, in this massive place, with teams who believed themselves to be every bit as good as we were? But she also knew that our bravado was who we were, and if she showed her nerves, it could spread to all of us.

Coach Earl must have seen the looks on our faces because he took great pains to quell our fears.

"Gang, it's just like our gym back home," he told us. "It's just like every gym we've ever played in."

"Except the girls' gym," I whispered to Peggy, and she nodded solemnly.

"The basket is the exact same height," he intoned, "and baseline to baseline, exactly the same dimensions." Some of us wouldn't have minded some actual proof, since it looked the size of a football field.

"I feel like Neil Armstrong," Coach Earl said. "Like the first man to walk on the moon."

That Friday in Skokie, classes were officially in session but no one who went to school that day was actually taught anything. TVs were everywhere—in the cafeteria and the gym and the student lounge and classrooms that were largely empty. Kids stood around in clumps—those unlucky enough to have their own school or sports commitments keeping them from going to Champaign and those who may have professed disinterest but still found themselves gravitating to the TVs. The teachers had to be in school on Friday, and Billy Schnurr was no exception, though his PE class watched our 12:15 game against Marshall.

Doc Kusch, the women's basketball coach at Loyola University who was hoping to get both Connie and Peggy to play for him, had predicted a close contest in Friday's paper. Coached by the feisty Dorothy Gaters, Marshall was representing the Chicago Public League—whose champ got an automatic berth to the state quarterfinals in Champaign—for the second year in a row.

The Commandos featured 6-foot-3 sophomore Janet Harris, the Public League's best player. But as a team, they were an enigma. They were big and quick, and like us, they had an intimidating press. They won 58 of their last 59 games and at 29–0, they manhandled most teams on their schedule by lopsided margins. We saw the scores in the state program and "lopsided" actually did not do them justice—112–7, 111–21, 105–26, and 119–31.

It was ridiculous, like the Boston Celtics against Lincoln Hall Junior High. But we heard Gaters kept her starters in most of the games to run up the scores, and we knew that the rest of the Public League did not put up much of a fight. We did not know a heck of a lot more because Coach Earl had not scouted Marshall before our game. He simply hadn't had the chance. He did not tell us this. Instead, he read the papers for any helpful information and worried.

Inside the dressing room, so far from the court that it seemed we might have to call for transportation to get to the game, we were both calm and collected, thumbing through the state program, area newspapers, and telegrams from well-wishers, all while trying to contain the adrenaline that was threatening to exhaust us before the opening tip. Mostly, we were excited to let a brand-new audience—including those viewing on WGN-TV, which began broadcasting nationwide in October as a superstation—see what we were all about.

"We're sprinting onto the court," Connie and I yelled at our teammates, the idea being that we would carry that intensity throughout the game. Also that, well, we would look cool, flashy, and maybe even intimidating as we took the court. "Full speed!" I screamed for emphasis.

And that is precisely what we did. One small hitch on the way there, however.

As we were sprinting full speed—one of my best things—my adrenaline got the best of me, and I tripped, fell, then skidded facedown for several feet. If there was any question as to whether my teammates might be unnerved by this or by some chance stop to help me up, that possibility was immediately put to rest as one by one, they deftly hurdled over me.

I scrambled back up in one nearly fluid motion, and for an instant, I foolishly believed that maybe no one had even noticed. As we formed a circle for our ballhandling routine, I whispered frantically to Connie and Peggy and everyone else around me, "Did anyone see me? Did you see me? Do you think anyone else saw me?"

"Shut up," Peggy finally hissed at me as only a friend could. "No one saw you."

And I almost believed her as I glanced down, only to see most of the material from my warm-up pants missing from my left knee and blood dripping over the rest. Then I looked up at the stands and instantly spotted Shirley, one of my oldest, dearest friends, at the game to support her old team and laughing so hard she looked as if she might go into convulsions.

I had a sneaking suspicion that she had seen me.

As my knee swelled to twice its normal size—finally a game-related injury—the announcer introduced both teams, and we jogged to the free-throw line as our names and numbers were called. "Intensity!" we cried as we huddled up without our coach, just us, grinning for a long time at each other at the sheer excitement of it all, knowing exactly what was going through each one of our minds and coursing through each one of our bodies. We were really here.

Searing through Marshall's press and a team that was not nearly as quick as we'd expected, we led 14–0 before Janet Harris scored the first bucket for Marshall, five minutes into the game. By the end of the first quarter, we led 21–5, and by midway through the second quarter, we stretched the lead to 22.

Then we went to sleep for a while. Against their half-court press, we failed to score for the next seven minutes, allowing the Commandos to ease their way back into the game as they narrowed the margin to nine in the third quarter. By the time it was over, however, we outscored them 29–15 in the final quarter, winning 80–50 and forcing the Chicago champs into 34 turnovers and two technical fouls out of obvious frustration.

Because the state tournament was only three years old, it was relatively easy to set records, and we got off to a rousing start in our opener, setting new marks for highest point total, largest margin of victory, most free throws made (28), and most assists in a single game with Connie dishing out 11. Peg led us in scoring with 20 points, while Holly finished with 15.

For Marshall, the loss was bitterly disappointing to a team that felt it simply could not compete with the suburban schools. Gaters lamented afterward that they just did not have the budget to play a tougher schedule, and she offered the example of going to play Regina Dominican of north suburban Wilmette. Getting to Wilmette cost $200 for bus transportation, she explained, and in return, the school got a check for $37.50, or half the ticket sales. It cost the school nearly $2,000 to get to Champaign. Her team was a long way, Gaters said, from a state championship.

We were getting closer, but we weren't there yet. As she left the court, Connie held up four fingers as in "We're at least No. 4 in the state," and a player in the stands from an opposing suburban team that had not made it downstate leaned over the railing and chided her for being underconfident. Obviously, she did not know Connie very well.

Though it may not have been the most relaxing way to spend the rest of our day, we watched all three remaining quarterfinal games, including East St. Louis Lincoln versus Waukegan West and Oak Forest versus Bartonville Limestone, which tipped off at 8:30 Friday night. In between the afternoon and night sessions, we went T-shirt shopping. For us, though, this *was* relaxing, especially after winning our game so easily.

Back home, in the middle of Saturday's *Lerner Life* detailing our victory over Marshall, there was an insert telling readers that a parade to honor our team would be held on Sunday. It would start at the school parking lot at 2:30 p.m., when we arrived from Champaign, and it would wind through Morton Grove, Skokie, and Lincolnwood to be joined by marching band units.

If we had seen the paper, we would have laughed at the prematurity of the announcement. But not much. Next up was Oak Forest in the state semifinals, and on the blackboard in the locker room before the game, we all took turns doodling slogans like "Beat Oak Forest," "Sky," and the ever-popular "KA," short for "Kick Ass." "Sky" was especially important as Oak Forest boasted a towering and talented front line of 6-2 senior Karen Stack, 6-1 senior Nancy Galkantas, and her even more gifted 5-11 sister Sue, a junior. Oak Forest was now 26–1 after defeating Limestone 70–67 the day before in overtime.

In the two previous girls' state tournaments, the teams to defeat the Public League champion became the eventual champions. It was the very last thing Coach Earl would consider telling us, and it was just as well. Besides, he was too busy keeping the press entertained in Champaign.

Alternating between characterizing himself as "a dumb hillbilly" and "dumb as an onion" when he began coaching, Earl was quickly ingratiating himself to reporters who were normally forced to consider "We're going to give 110 percent" a colorful quote. One writer wrote that "Earl's pleasant low-key style made him a favorite among the sportswriters." This did not do us any immediate good, but we certainly were not being ignored either as we were quickly emerging as the favorite to take the title.

In the locker room before the game, our coach pulled out one of his favorite axioms. "The big take it from the small," he intoned, "and the quick take it from the tall." Oak Forest was big, but we had seen big before, and they had not seen a team as quick as Niles West. Besides, at 5-10, Peg moved better and faster than most guards. And we were pretty sure they had not seen a backcourt like ours before.

Oak Forest tried a box-and-one with its guard Tami Sender shadowing Connie, which resulted in shutting down Connie's point production but also resulted in Sender's picking up four fouls before halftime. Connie had detected the defensive strategy first and had jogged over to the bench in the opening minutes to tell Coach Earl, who instructed her to use Sender to screen off her teammates.

The tournament featured all-women officiating crews, and we were still unimpressed by their collective performance. We had been waiting since our supersectional loss to Dundee last year for the women to catch up to the level of the players. Games in Champaign were not merely closely called but were downright suffocating, dominated more by the refs' stoppage of play than by game action. Every touch was called a foul, every imperceptible slide of a pivot foot whistled for traveling, every pause in the lane was three seconds.

It was infuriating, and I could only imagine how it was coming across to first-time girls' basketball viewers. With their well-intentioned efforts to enforce the rules of the game, the woman officials, in my eyes and my teammates', were affecting the overall quality and entertainment value of the game. That said, I was proud of how we responded, in most cases quietly handing the ball over to the official after the whistle without so much as a stare, in a vestige of the Mulder days. And fortunately, their whistles were not affecting the final outcomes.

We led Oak Forest by seven at the half, and in the second half, we destroyed their 3-2 zone defense en route to a 51–35 lead after three quarters and an easy 68–44 victory. Barb and Peggy scored 18 and 17 points, respectively, while Connie was 5-of-5 from the floor, all in the second half, to finish with 17 points along with nine assists and eight steals. Just like that, we would be playing for the state championship. In less than eight hours, we would know.

After a dinner of McDonald's and a short rest at the hotel, we were back at the arena, a couple of hours earlier than we needed to be. While the starters tried to nap, I had just enough time to scratch out a pregame poem, my first of the year.

To Mean Gene:

Tonight's the night we've been waiting for,
We'll hit the boards and really soar.
We'll run and gun and play tough D,
The best in the state, they'll have to agree.
All our hard work and dedication,
Will finally pay off with some concentration.
We want it badly, so let's start with a burst,
Why settle for second when we can be first?

Let's go get it, the season's almost through,
We'll be state champs, our dream come true.

Love always,
Earl's Girls
1979 State Champions

Coach Earl smiled when he saw it. And again, no thought of a jinx occurred to me. At 32–1, East St. Louis was by far the most talented team we had ever faced. Four of its players had competed in the Class AA state track championship the year before, including Jackie Joyner, their 5-10 junior extraordinaire who was the two-time national AAU junior champion in the pentathlon as well as the Illinois state champion in the 440 dash and second in the long jump. They were talking about her as a "hopeful" for the 1980 Summer Olympics.

During warm-ups, we watched East St. Louis go through a normal layup drill that caught our attention significantly when Joyner leaped up, her hand above the rim, and tipped in a teammate's miss.

"Did you see that?" whispered Connie. "I've never seen a girl do that."

None of us had. To get above the rim and tip in a missed shot was routine for taller boys, but for a 16-year-old girl? Never. And we tried not to stare.

Joyner was averaging 18 points and 17 rebounds per game while her team averaged 85 points and allowed their opponents just 35. They were good. They were very good. But Coach Earl was not worried. Yes, they were big, and they were skilled. But their starting lineup, he thought, was not as deep as ours, and their big girls could not match Peggy's outside shooting. But there was still the matter of defending Joyner. Every major school in the country was already recruiting her as a two-sport athlete, and Coach Earl was rightfully concerned about her.

As he walked onto the court, he stopped to say hello to his parents sitting above the tunnel leading from the dressing rooms and heard a booming voice from above. Looking up, he saw a large man leaning over the railing.

"Hey, Coach!" the man yelled. "I sure hope you like losing."

Earl gave the man his trademark crooked smile and didn't say a word.

A record girls' state basketball tournament crowd of 6,832 was in attendance, at least half of which seemed to be from our high school. Sure, many of them had jumped on the proverbial bandwagon, but it was still cool seeing the sea of red that greeted us as we took the floor. Our parents were all there, sitting together in a section not far above the court, but this was no time for a pregame wave.

Connie was so revved up as we took a 10–2 lead in the first two and a half minutes of play that she began to hyperventilate and motioned to the bench that she had to come out. East St. Louis took the lead at 16–15 midway through the second quarter as Joyner went to work, but the Tigerettes rushed their shots and seemed to waste their talent in ways we couldn't understand from the bench. Their guards would break our press easily, for example, only to come to a jump stop just past midcourt and stall their offense.

Coach Earl nearly outcoached himself upon Connie's return when he called for us to go to a man defense with Connie on Joyner just to keep East St. Louis off-balance. Instead, on three subsequent trips up the floor, Joyner posted her up, scoring on turnaround jumpers until Earl abandoned his strategy and went back to our 1-3-1 zone. We quickly regrouped and, like our two previous opponents and most that season, the Tigerettes wilted under our defensive pressure with Connie and Barb keying steal after steal, and Peggy and Holly converting on the other end to build the lead back to seven at the half.

In the locker room, someone passed around cut-up oranges

as Coach Earl began his halftime speech. "Peggy!" he hollered. "You've got to box out Joyner."

"I am boxing out!" Peggy yelled back. "They're not calling over-the-back."

Trying to both make his point and, perhaps, express his frustration at Peg's stubbornness at the same time, Earl, who was holding a towel in his hand, went to slap it against his other hand and brushed it against Peggy instead. It didn't seem like anything to us, but Peggy flinched and recoiled, then reflexively threw the orange she was holding into Earl's face.

We all froze for a second.

"That's it, Japely!" Coach Earl shouted. "You're not starting the second half."

None of us knew what to make of Peggy's reaction, nor did Peggy. All she knew was that a man's hand was coming toward her, and her natural reaction was to defend herself. If her childhood had taught her anything, it was that.

We wondered what Earl would do. There wasn't much precedent on our team of throwing oranges at the coach. Would he really bench her to start the second half? We jogged back out uneasily, the most important 16 minutes of our lives beginning with uncertainty we did not need.

East St. Louis did not warm up at all before the start of the second half, their coach's speech presumably taking up the entire intermission, unless, of course, they had an orange-throwing incident in their locker room as well.

Coach Earl let the incident pass and Peggy started, as did Becky in place of Tina, who had twisted her ankle in the first half. A couple of nervous turnovers by Becky against the press narrowed the gap to five and threatened to give East St. Louis some much-needed momentum. On the sideline, Earl, like most coaches, shouted first for his players on the floor to calm down and then, for good measure, turned and yelled at our bench to watch the turnovers, as if we could do anything about them.

On the court, neither team could take control. Within the first four minutes of the third quarter, East St. Louis crept back to within two. But Connie pushed the ball upcourt following the rebound of a Tigerette miss, and Peggy quickly responded with a jumper to push the lead back to seven. Minutes later, six unanswered points for the Tigerettes closed the gap again, this time to two at 33–31, but once more our defense responded. A 7–0 run triggered by four straight steals followed as we took a 40–31 lead. East St. Louis would surge back to within five off a pretty jumper by Deborah Thurston.

But they would never get closer.

We led 44–37 to start the fourth quarter and opened it up to 14 at 51–37 on baskets by Barb and Holly, sandwiched around Peg's monster block of Thurston.

With just under a minute to play and the game in hand, Coach Earl started to empty his bench, and I suddenly found myself on the court. I slid into place in our zone defense and tried to absorb the reality that we were about to close out a state title—*the* state title—while also seeing if I could actually work up a game-related sweat in less than a minute. With 23 seconds left, the clock stopped with an East St. Louis turnover, and the WGN telecast went momentarily silent in anticipation.

"I'll tell ya, if he takes Connie Erickson out," said play-by-play man Tom Kelly, "you'll hear a roar that will rock the Assembly Hall."

"Here she comes," said Buffalo Grove coach Ann Penstone, doing the color commentary.

"Connie Erickson is coming out," said Kelly. "Connie Erickson."

The coronation had already begun for arguably the greatest girls' basketball player in the state, but as she walked off a high school court for the final time, it seemed to hit all 5-foot-5 of her at once. On the floor, Connie was often a blur, her body in a half tuck as she darted through traffic on the fast break, her expression one of complete focus and intensity as she crouched in her defensive stance. Not once had she allowed herself to stand out, to celebrate her own success or ours prematurely. But this was her moment, and as her right index finger shot high above her head, a smile spread across her face, an expression of complete and utter satisfaction as she walked into the waiting arms of our coach.

"She's getting a standing ovation from this entire crowd, Tom," Penstone said.

"They ought to carry her out on their shoulders," Kelly responded.

Connie had finished with a relatively modest 14 points in her final game, and 45 in three, but set a state record with a phenomenal 28 assists. As she walked to the end of our bench, leaning over with her hands on her knees as if to let it all sink in, Kelly announced Niles West's parade plans for the following day. And our crowd began its brand-new cheer.

This time, we could hear it clearly. All in sync. And thunderously loud.

"We are," they chanted, "state champs."

CHAPTER 23

April Fools

SOMEHOW I GRABBED the final errant rebound as the buzzer sounded on our 63–47 victory, but I didn't hang on to the ball. Instead, I flung it skyward, raced toward Peggy, and leaped into her arms, a sight we somehow knew was absurd even as it was unfolding, and we laughed hysterically as she called me a lummox. Connie hugged anyone and everyone she could find, beginning with one special person in the stands. Her boyfriend, Bob, was grinning widely as she came rushing toward him up the steps, only to be nearly bowled over as she brushed past him and into the embrace of Shirley.

In her dorm room at Brigham Young, Diana Hintz received a phone call telling her that her sister Pam was a state champion. And at Southern Illinois that night, Bridget Berglund learned the news that we had won from her sister Michelle, who was in the stands. In Skokie, Billy Schnurr snapped off his television with satisfaction and went to bed with a smile on his face. And in Champaign, lost in the mob of Niles West fans in Assembly Hall, her infant son on her lap and her two girls seated on either side of her, Arlene Mulder cried for all of us.

State champs.

Niles West principal Nicholas Mannos, one-time IHSA president and now an executive board member, the guy who stood at the podium with the other mustard-colored blazers and grimly handed out the championship trophies to other schools year after year, presented us with gold medallions hanging on red, white, and blue ribbons like Olympic gold medals. They may as well have been.

Dr. Mannos wore a smile we had never before witnessed on our principal, and we swelled with pride at bestowing on him this wonderful gift. "Ladies and gentlemen, it's indeed a singular honor for me to present to my school the first-place trophy," Mannos said. He praised our fans and congratulated our coach. Not a word, of course, about the role he played in winning us the right to be standing there at all. He asked Connie, as our captain, to step forward, and in typical form, she insisted all of us accept the monstrous first-place trophy together.

Next were the postgame interviews, and Earl was up first, with Floyd Brown asking him to what he attributed our victory. "Three things," Coach Earl began. "Outstanding talent. A great deal of determination by the kids. Hard work." And then with a wink and his famous southern Illinois drawl, he added, "And we shoot the ball pretty good, too."

It was actually four things, but who was counting other than all of us, giggling at our coach as was our custom.

Dancing off the court and into the locker room, we instinctively braced ourselves for more hilarity as Coach Earl launched immediately into a speech. "This is tree-mendous!" he shouted. "And it all started a long time ago with you girls. And it started just last November with me. No, not last November. It started last August when they said, 'This job is officially yours.'"

Sprawled around him on benches and the floor, we sat

transfixed as our coach paced and gestured as befitted the floor show it was. "This is tremendous," he said again as we windmilled our arms for him to get on with it. "It's the greatest thing that has happened to me, but I hope it's not the greatest thing that happens to you people in athletics. I hope it's one of the best. But I hope you have a lot of things like this that happen to you. I hope it gets greater and greater and greater."

He could have stopped there, probably should have, but clearly he was just getting warmed up. "I sort of feel like this old bum that took his hound to the dog show," he said.

"Is this punchline going to have the village idiot in it?" Connie asked, referencing one of Earl's recurring favorites, and we all broke up. By now, we were howling with laughter and pleading with him to stop, but that wasn't going to happen.

"It was where these rich people bring their purebred dogs, and one of them said to him, 'What are you doing? You don't expect to win any prizes, do you?' And he said, 'No, but I sure did get to meet an awful lot of nice people.'

"The best thing about this whole season is that I sure have met an awful lot of nice people," he continued. "Gang, it's tremendous. It's tree-mendous. You made it all come true for yourselves. I didn't know it was going to end like this. I hoped and I prayed and I knew we had an extremely good chance. But you made it all come true.

"Thanks, gang."

It was a sweet moment, even Peggy and I had to admit, and we all wiped away tears in unison until Connie broke in. "Here's to the best coach in the state. Hip, hip . . . "

"Hooray!" we shouted back.

"Hip, hip . . . "

"Hooray!"

"Let's hear it, Coach!" Judy screamed as we waited for the familiar call. And in typical booming fashion, he complied.

"It sure is GREAT to be a WINNER!"

After telling us to dress quickly—yeah, right—because we were going out for a steak dinner and he was "blowing the dough, baby," it seemed as good a time as any to break into the *Laverne & Shirley* theme song. We were nothing, after all, without our theme songs.

Give us any chance, we'll take it. Give us any rule, we'll break it. We're gonna make our dreams come true, doing it our way . . .

This time it was Gene Earl's turn to throw his head back and laugh.

After dinner, we headed back to the hotel just as midnight struck on April 1. Peggy and I looked at each other. It would be too easy. And as our teammates drifted in and out of each other's rooms, we hastily devised a plan. Mr. Karbusicky, our ticket manager and history teacher, it was decided, would be the lure. Well, not Mr. Karbusicky for real, but at least his name. It was not an elaborate plan, but at one in the morning after winning the state championship, we felt confident it would make our coach look silly and be good for a few laughs, and that was enough for us.

"Coach, Coach, come quick!" Peg and I yelled down the hall. "Mr. Karbusicky is in our room, and he's acting really strange. He won't leave."

"He's in his pajamas," I said, hoping to add a little drama.

"Yeah, and they have elephants all over them," shouted Peg as I shot her a dirty look that said she was going too far.

Fortunately, our coach had had just enough wine with his dinner to consider this plausible, and he came racing toward our room in his own pajama bottoms and undershirt, ready to rescue us, when half the team jumped out from behind the bed screaming, "April fool!"

It was childish and stupid, no question about it. But it cracked us up, and if there was any danger of our accidentally drifting off to sleep that night, someone absconded with the hotel security guard's handcuffs and cuffed me to Coach Earl, prolonging the laughs for much longer than either the coach or I would have preferred.

April fools.

Going on no sleep, we had only the cold and mist to keep us alert the next day atop the Skokie fire trucks that ferried us through the township. A half mile of police cars with sirens blaring and honking cars with streamers streaming trailed us through the streets, more brave souls than we would have imagined standing under umbrellas on street corners, waving as we drove past.

The temperature hovered in the upper 30s, but we huddled together unfazed, some of us in ski jackets, others in Niles West windbreakers, and tried to tell each other we would never, ever forget this moment. Some of us had our Kodak Instamatics and others had the Polaroid cameras where the photos came out instantly, and we gathered around to see the highlights as they unfolded.

Back at the gym, the bleachers and basketball court were full, TV cameras from Chicago stations capturing it all as we followed Connie, who carried the trophy through the crowd of about 1,500 to a podium set up on the baseline. We each said a few words, among the more memorable being Becky's proclamation that "I ain't a rookie no more."

It was all festive and fun and a great example of high school innocence and exuberance until the end, when Dr. Mannos started speaking and some of the students in the crowd began to yell for open halls, their chants becoming louder until his speech was nearly drowned out.

A few weeks earlier, Mannos had closed Niles West's hallways to student traffic during free periods because of excessive noise. His decision had been the talk of the school, and it was no real surprise that our classmates took this opportunity to exercise their First Amendment rights, but Coach Earl was offended at their timing and ordered us to walk out of the gym, which we did, thus ending the rally.

The next day's *Chicago Tribune* chronicled the walkout on page two of the sports section. Atop the front page of the section, above stories about the Blackhawks and White Sox, read a banner headline: EVEN NILES WEST'S CHAMPS CRITICIZE TOURNEY REFS.

A pullout quote from Peg read, "Lady refs call more chicken fouls than men. They don't really let you play your game. Men refs allow more incidental contact."

I had never heard Peggy use the phrase "incidental contact" when she was complaining about the refs, but it looked very impressive in print.

Discussion and criticism regarding the all-female crew of officials had been a sidelight during the tournament, with newly crowned state championship coach Gene Earl leveling the biggest blow in the *Tribune* when he said, "I know at least 100 male officials who are better qualified than the woman referees we've had throughout the final days of this tournament. Men have more experience, so they have to be better than this."

Not surprisingly, the fallout from his and other male coaches' remarks was swift. Earl was swamped with letters calling him a buffoon. The girls' athletic director at Buffalo Grove High School, a woman, accused him of setting back girls' basketball 100 years. The male secretary of the IHSA blasted him for his poor judgment, which Coach Earl responded to by citing his inalienable right to free speech.

One woman who identified herself as a junior high coach confronted Earl in person and told him men shouldn't be coaching girls' teams.

Despite the criticism, 20 years after he had started coaching at Sesser High School, where he compiled a three-year mark of 7–44 with the boys' varsity team, Gene Earl was a hero. At least they hailed him as such in the halls and over Niles West's PA system in the days and weeks following our victory, the first male coach to take a girls' team to the state title. The first basketball coach in Niles West history to win a state championship, period.

But the fanfare was not well received in at least one small corner of the gym. Listening to the accolades for Earl one day after we had won, Judi Sloan, one of the most respected coaches and teachers at the school, a gifted athlete in her own right and one of the toughest women around, sat alone in the girls' gym office and cried. She cried for her friend Arlene Mulder and she cried for all the woman coaches just like Mulder who would be forgotten.

When they named an award for Gene Earl, still another in the trophy case named for a male coach at the school, Sloan, a future winner of the Golden Apple Award for Excellence in Teaching, was discouraged. It wasn't that she had anything against Earl personally. He was a pretty tough guy not to like, and she respected the job he had done with us. But like many of her female colleagues, she simply wished he would have stopped during one of the many interviews and award ceremonies and thanked the woman who had laid the foundation for him, that at least one reporter would have taken note.

As for us, it all largely went over our heads—the rally walkout, the ref controversy, the woman teachers' sadness over Mrs. Mulder. For us, it was about getting new satin state championship jackets and milking every bit of our newfound celebrity. We were cool. Special. Or at least we thought so.

For Connie and Peggy, basketball would surely continue at the college level. Though Peggy's contribution was largely unsung, she had gone from JV two years earlier to first-team all-tournament and all-state honors. For Judy and Karen and me, there would be intramurals and club sports. Seeing my playing time decrease so dramatically my senior year cushioned the pain I had anticipated when taking off an athletic uniform for the last time. But so too did winning, leaving the five of us with a feeling of satisfaction and resolution that Shirley and Bridget and Diana never got to experience.

We were invited to numerous awards banquets that spring, attending with the likes of DePaul's Final Four team and the Maine South boys' champs. We received keys to our suburbs, got cash gifts from our banks, and traveled to Springfield, where we met Illinois Governor Jim Thompson and had a resolution presented to the Illinois legislature honoring us.

But it was our appearance on *Ray Rayner and Friends*, where we got to shoot layups at a basket on set; play with the show's mascot, Chelveston the duck; and introduce the next cartoon, that completed the dream.

When it came down to it, that's all we really wanted. Our very own uniforms, high-top basketball shoes, our names on a scoreboard. And in the end, a kids' TV show.

Give me an R . . .

Youth offered us only so much wisdom and so much perspective. But somewhere beyond the superficial symbols of success, we recognized this was life-altering, and we knew where it started—on the Little League fields where we could not play and in the gyms where we could not practice. On a tiny, poorly lit court in the balcony overlooking the Boys' Gym, Billy Schnurr told us we could do it. Arlene Mulder taught us to believe. And Gene Earl showed us the way.

Once girls, we were now athletes. Once athletes, we were now state champions. Forever.

EPILOGUE

I SHOULDN'T BE SURPRISED about what came next, when my teammates "grew up" and our coaches grew older.

As I think back, it makes perfect sense that Connie would become a hero to kids in her community. That Shirley would persevere and Arlene Mulder would lead and Peg would survive. That we would, as a group, fight through the tragedy and abuse that statistics said we would probably experience and somehow rebound, somehow remain standing.

In so many ways, what happened to us after that day in Champaign is what this book is really about. In so many ways, it is evidence of what sports gave to us, of what basketball, specifically, did 40 years ago to shape our lives today.

In wanting you to know what happened to all of us after 1979, I could have written another book, but not surprisingly, my editor frowned on an epilogue longer than the 23 chapters preceding it. Here is our compromise:

Arlene Mulder

ONE OF THE FIRST TIMES I interviewed Arlene Mulder at length for this project, she called from her dorm room in Cambridge, Massachusetts, where she was enrolled in the John F. Kennedy School of Government graduate program at Harvard. Among her fellow students were 68 elected officials, from state senators to representatives to mayors like herself.

For 20 years and five consecutive terms, Mrs. Mulder was the mayor of Arlington Heights, one of the largest suburbs in the Chicago area and the most populated village in the United States. Though generations of girls will never know what they missed by not having her as a teacher, she clearly found her true calling as a public servant.

After Michael was born, Mrs. Mulder still thought about returning to teaching. Though she loved spending time with her children and her husband, she felt a little like she had when she had gone from graduate school to motherhood a decade before—"drowning in domestic stuff and needing mental stimulation," she recalled. "When a part-time job opened up at Niles West in 1972, it allowed me to gain my self-esteem back." And when the opportunity came up in the summer of '79 to become a park commissioner, she dove in despite the fact that she "didn't know what a park commissioner was."

Two years later, Mrs. Mulder officially gave up her teaching tenure and was elected to the Arlington Heights park board, serving as commissioner and parks president through 1991. After two more years as a village trustee, she became the first woman to be elected mayor in the 106-year history of the village. And when she retired in 2012 as one of its most popular and respected elected officials, it was after 34 years of public service.

"I've never felt like a politician, and I never wanted to be," she said. "In most people's minds, they don't trust politicians. It has a bad connotation. It reminds people of empty promises not fulfilled, made before someone in office knew what capabilities they had and that you can't do it yourself." That was never her. She was a facilitator and consensus builder, both as a teacher and as a mayor. "I pull people together, and I try to encourage them to do what they can do well," she said.

When I interviewed her once in 2004, Mrs. Mulder at 60 was pure energy, her staff made aware of her arrival each morning by the click-clacking of her heels on the steps, which she always ran, eschewing the elevator. A grandmother of seven who turned a part-time job into a full-time commitment, often putting in 14- and 15-hour days and seven-day weeks, Mrs. Mulder became one of the most distinguished public officials in Illinois. She was also recognized nationally as a trustee on the executive board of the US Conference of Mayors, internationally as a leader on the issue of aircraft noise mitigation, and locally as a mayor known for her economic development initiatives and fiscal responsibility.

She loved us as much as her own children, she told me, but I think we always knew that. It was never about winning, she reminded me, and I know we were aware of that as well. It was about setting goals and striving to reach them, about working hard and playing together and knowing that whatever the result, we did it not as individuals but as a team. This for sure I remembered and clung to, even as Mrs. Mulder's ways seemed to become outmoded or unnecessary.

"I'm sorry," I told her. "I'm sorry if we never really thanked you. I'm sorry if you felt unappreciated, because it was your motivation that inspired us and carried us to the state title. It was your state title as much as ours."

She was very quiet.

"Teaching is bringing out what is already within the person," she said finally. "And sometimes it's just magic."

Billy Schnurr

AFTER RETIRING IN 1992, Schnurr ran the clock at Niles West basketball games for the next six years, and at one point, he helped design the new girls' locker room. Yes, a special locker room for the female athletes. In his late 70s, Schnurr was still playing tennis twice a week, working out at a local health club, and playing poker with Gene Earl, Jerry Turry—the former dean of students at Niles West and later three-term mayor of Lincolnwood—and some other former coaches and teachers.

Schnurr enjoyed dropping in on the occasional high school game, though he said he didn't miss coaching anymore. As was his way, he enjoyed a quiet, unassuming life with his wife of 60-plus years, Lima, their children, and their grandchildren.

Gene Earl

SURELY GENE EARL had to have gotten a kick out of it when our team was inducted into the Illinois Basketball Coaches Association Hall of Fame in the spring of 2004, and we had the best turnout by far for a team from our era. Later, back in a hospitality room at our hotel, our coach got up and made a little speech. This was nothing new to us, and we got ready to giggle. I was surprised that I felt really touched instead.

"I don't live in the past and I don't get depressed," he said. "But when the dust of everyday life covers your brain, memories of you 12 girls wash over me like a warm summer rain."

OK, so he was paraphrasing a country song by Kathy Mattea. The sentiment was there.

For Earl, who retired from teaching and coaching in 1990 after 26 years at Niles West, life has been easily filled with family, golf, traveling—mostly to play golf—and some work, mostly at a golf course. There was a brief return to coaching. In '97, a friend who was the Elk Grove girls' basketball coach asked him to be her assistant in her last year on the job, and he accepted, staying two more years to help the new coach.

But he missed his wintertime golf.

"There's no committee on what time do we get up, what time do we play, where do we eat that night," he told me in a 2006 interview. "I might just wake up any day of the week and tell Ma [his nickname of preference for his wife, Marlene], 'Hey, I'm leaving tomorrow.'"

In 2008, Marlene became ill while the family was visiting friends and relatives in southern Illinois on Labor Day weekend, and Gene insisted that she see a doctor when they got back home. The cobalt treatments that had saved her life when she was diagnosed with ovarian cancer 37 years before had now caused a blockage in her lower intestine. They were told it was inoperable, and eight months later, on April 1, 2009, Alyce Marlene Earl, 73, died at home with her family by her side.

After 52 years of marriage, Gene was on his own, making the occasional golfing trip to Florida and continuing to use the internet as a way to stay connected with his former players and old friends. Over the next three years, one of those friends he rediscovered was his high school girlfriend Sherrill Ferrera. "We'd send each other golf jokes and hometown news and whatnot," he said.

Gene and Sherrill now spend their summers at his home in Elk Grove and winters at hers in Ocala, Florida, where they play golf and volunteer two days a week for an organization that sends supplies to troops overseas and veterans at home. A six-handicap in his 70s, Earl was still shooting his age in his mid-80s.

After coaching our '79 team to a state title, his '80 team was upset in the regional finals, the year Jackie Joyner's team won the championship. The following season, he brought Niles West back to the Elite Eight, where they would finish in fourth place. And the next year, Becky Schnell's senior year, the team lost in the sectional finals to New Trier.

In his first four years as a girls' coach, Gene Earl's teams were 101–10. After that, they tailed off with several seasons at or near .500 before bouncing back with a 24–4 season in '88. Following that year, Earl was inducted into the Illinois Basketball Coaches Association Hall of Fame. He was humbled by the honor.

"Nobody would have ever heard of Gene Earl if we hadn't won the championship," he said. "The memories would have been there, but had you girls not won the ball games, I would have been just another unknown assistant coach. Jim Braun [the *Pioneer Press* sportswriter] said I came out of obscurity. I would have stayed in obscurity if I hadn't taken the girls' job. I wouldn't have been a basketball coach ever again."

When he saw Arlene Mulder at a '79 team get-together for pizza after I began writing the book, the two greeted each other warmly, with Coach Earl exclaiming in his booming voice upon seeing her, "I want to thank you, Arlene. If you hadn't gotten pregnant, I wouldn't be here right now."

It was clumsy, to say the least, but I fought back the impulse to spit out my Diet Coke because I knew what he was trying to say and that it was sincere.

"I had the utmost respect for Arlene and the way she worked at trying to learn to coach girls' basketball," he said. "The few times I saw her, she never acted toward me as though I got all [the] credit and she didn't get any. She left me in a very good position."

When he is introduced to someone new—particularly by another coach or to another coach—there still isn't a single time, he said, that the person doesn't preface it with, "Gene won a state championship." But, he emphasized, "I never used it as a tool to salve my own wounds. And I never brought it up to my other teams. Never."

But that doesn't mean he didn't think about it. Asked if he ever caught himself glancing at our state championship trophy in the glass case outside the gym in the years after we won the title, Earl did not hesitate.

"Every day," he said. "Unless I was in a real big hurry. But if I was just casually walking by, yeah, I gave it a look. I gave it a good look."

Shirley Cohen

SHIRLEY DID GET HER CHANCE to play on the Assembly Hall court. Competing in a one-on-one intramural tournament her freshman year at Illinois, she reached the finals and got to play at halftime of an Illini men's game. Not surprisingly, she actually won the thing, a distinction that would occasionally be mentioned at a party when someone remembered seeing her. But it was no substitute for making it there with us, and for all intents and purposes, it was the official end to her basketball career.

Still, college was a great time for Shirley. She majored in occupational therapy, joined a sorority, dated. After college, she moved back to Chicago and began a career specializing in treating patients with hand injuries.

The athletic drive never left her; she just channeled it differently. She decided she'd like to try bungee jumping and then did it on a trip to New Zealand. She traveled the world on outdoor adventure trips, parasailing, white water rafting, and skiing. She ran two marathons after the age of 40.

And every once in a while, her true competitive instincts would bubble forth. She'd make a diving catch in a flag football game or clobber a home run in a softball game, leaving men gawking. Once, Shirley visited me when I lived in Florida and, playing in a pickup basketball game at a local park in which we were the only women, we competed with all the intensity of a state championship game, recalling later the men looking on in shock.

In her early 40s and unmarried, she began thinking seriously of having a child on her own. Training with her friend Debbie for one of her marathons, Shirley confided in her, "Deb, if I don't do it now, I'm never going to do it."

"Finishing the marathon," Shirley told me, "was part of my

impetus. I thought, if I can do this, I can do anything." After five unsuccessful tries at pregnancy and one miscarriage, Jocelyn Emily was born on July 9, 2003.

Nine and a half months later, Shirley and Jocelyn met Gregg Katz. On their third date, Gregg gave Shirley her first-ever Mother's Day card. On their fourth date, he brought dinner over for the two of them, and for Jocelyn, a toy and a box of Cheerios. One day after they had been seeing each other for about six months, Shirley came home and there was a huge printed banner hanging above Jocelyn's crib. It read: GREGG AND I HAVE BEEN TALKING . . . AND I SAID, YES. NOW IT'S YOUR TURN . . . WILL WE MARRY HIM?

When Jocelyn walked down the aisle pushing a tiny pink shopping cart of roses, I thought I would lose it. When Shirley's parents followed, beaming, with Shirley between them, I did. I was far from the only one. Stealing glances at Shirley's closest friends, I saw we were all weeping.

It was not the way she had ever planned, but then whose life ever comes out exactly as planned? As Mrs. Mulder told her on the bus following that last loss to Dundee in Shirley's senior year, life would often be unfair, and it was how she responded that was the important thing. It was but one of the many lessons we learned from Mrs. Mulder, and one that Shirley carried with her, as near impossible as that would prove to be.

Gregg and Shirley thought they had their fairy tale. But in June of 2017, when they were then the parents of Jocelyn, 13, and twins Ethan and Jordyn, 10, Gregg complained of flu-like symptoms. A microscopic malignant growth he had had removed from behind his eye early in their marriage had metastasized to his liver, and less than three months later, Gregg was gone.

Once again, her friends wept, but we also knew Shirley. While there was no moral to the story and no consolation, there was Shirley's inner strength and ever-present spirit, and we continue, as always, to follow her lead.

Connie Erickson

AFTER TRANSFERRING FROM Southern Illinois to Northwestern her sophomore year in college, Connie continued her success on the court, as Northwestern advanced to their first NCAA tournament and Connie achieved all–Big Ten status at guard, her name still standing among the top 10 in single-season assists, as well as career assists and steals after just three seasons.

But nagging injuries plagued her. She was redshirted her senior year, held out due to a combination of injuries she felt she could overcome, and for the first time in a long time, she struggled with her self-image. "It was heart-wrenching," she described, "but it also ended up changing my life."

Only another athlete can truly relate to the feelings of isolation that an injury can create. "You feel like your relationships are out on the playing field," she explained. "It's the way you relate to others. I felt my personality was out on the floor, so I couldn't be who I was."

A guy on the football team with whom she had become friends, Kelby Brown, had graduated. She was struggling in an anatomy class. A close friend on the team seemed to be withdrawing from her and becoming better friends with another player. "I felt like the world was coming down on me," she said, "which is how it is in college. Everything is intense."

Her parents were there for her, driving their motor home to every game, even when she wasn't playing. The girls on the team called them "Mom" and "Dad." Still, Connie missed being involved, missed basketball, missed competing, missed the person she had been.

Finally, the team manager, a friend of Connie's, persuaded her to go to a Bible study meeting with her. Connie saw other athletes there. "And they showed me this unconditional love," she recalled. "They taught me who God is. It was a life-changing experience."

She and Kelby Brown had never dated. He was a card-carrying

member of the Fellowship of Christian Athletes and straight-laced. "That's why we never dated," she laughed. But when they met again after college, they were on the same page. And soon, they were in love.

After coming excruciatingly close to making the 1984 Olympic team the summer after she left Northwestern, Connie joined Athletes in Action and traveled to China. She also made plans to go to Barbados and play in a women's pro league that was just starting, but she blew out her knee playing in a rec league game the night before she was to leave.

Reconstructive surgery followed, and Connie accepted a graduate assistant coaching position at the University of Utah, where Kelby was the strength and conditioning coach. The two were engaged in October of 1984 and planning a July wedding but decided not to wait when a trip to Ohio State brought them to Kelby's hometown of Montpelier, Ohio, that winter. They called their parents at the last minute, found a church and country club, and were married there in December of 1984 before family and friends. Over the next eight years, their daughter and two sons followed.

To talk to Connie is to be inspired. She has coached on every level, from church league to AAU. She was a Division I assistant and coached her kids' prep school, Charlotte Christian, the alma mater of NBA star Stephen Curry, which Connie built into a state contender.

Connie went back to school herself, earning an associate's degree in computer integrations, began her own web design company, and laughed at the enormity of the task. "The confidence to be able to do that was probably based on being an athlete, just the whole experience," she said. "I was like, 'OK, sure, I can try this.'"

For 20 years, beginning in 1989, she and Kelby did missionary work all over the world but consistently in Ukraine, where they started a faith-based sports camp that continues today. Connie also volunteered in Charlotte-area schools, creating an after-school program for underserved kids that has seen tangible results in school performance.

"It has turned into such a great thing," Connie said. "It has just become part of who I am."

All the Brown kids played soccer and basketball and ran track. And her little boys grew to be exceptionally big and strong young men and, no surprise, extraordinarily athletic, both playing football and becoming academic all-Americans at Duke.

Torn cartilage and subsequent surgeries in both knees curtailed Connie's running and tennis playing. But she continued to ski, spin, hike, do Pilates, and, with Kelby, go white water rafting on a regular basis. And she doesn't discount some revolutionary future therapy for her knees that might allow her to play tennis again.

When I last saw our teammate and captain in the fall of 2017, it wasn't hard to picture her on the court again. And I remember a conversation we once had when she talked about coaching. "I would rather be out there on the court any day," she said. "I just enjoyed the game. I loved running down the floor, passing off, making something good happen."

Clearly, she's still a natural at it.

Becky Schnell

WINNING THE STATE TITLE the year she was probably least able to appreciate it represented the high point of Becky's basketball career. The season after our state championship win, Becky started on varsity, and the team lost by one point in the regional final. The next year, the team would return to the Elite Eight but would have to settle for fourth place, which felt like failure to someone who knew how it felt to win it all.

Becky's senior year, she blew out her knee in the third game of the season at Evanston. That team lost to New Trier in the sectional final, a game in which Becky—still not fully recovered from her injury—was able to play only a couple of minutes, marking the final appearance of her high school career.

"I was spoiled," she told me. "I thought, 'I'm going to do this the next three years,' and I learned the hard way it doesn't work like that."

Becky played basketball and softball at Mississippi College, but her heart wasn't in it, she said. And the summer after her sophomore year, she would lose her mother to pancreatic cancer at age 50. A decade later, as Becky was trying on her wedding dress, she thought of her mom. Phyllis Schnell was always horrified that her youngest daughter had no interest in going to prom or homecoming, that dresses were completely foreign to her.

When Becky's wedding dress came in before the big day, it was a good inch too small, and as she pulled it on for the final fitting, she was sure they weren't going to be able to let it out enough. "But somehow," Becky recalled with a smile, "the damn zipper just went up and I swear it was my mother."

Becky thought she had found her life's calling as a teacher and coach. She received her master's in education in 1988, coached at an elementary school in Skokie, helped Coach Earl with his Niles West team and his basketball camps, and took over for him as the girls' varsity coach following his retirement in 1990. She still coaches and teaches at our old high school.

"I always wanted to coach; it was always in me," she told me. "But I found out coaching is more than *x*'s and *o*'s and teaching. That was the part I loved about it. I loved practices, but all the other extracurricular stuff wore me down."

What also wore her down was the realization that even high school girls' basketball had become a year-round business. She lost some players who were recruited by private schools. She lost others to burnout.

"The teaching part of it was getting lost," she said. "The whole game had changed. We played for the fun of it. We were a team. . . . But kids now don't accept their roles, and they don't go out for teams if they think they might sit on a bench. And there's a lot more parental involvement—and not necessarily in a positive way. Now it's a job for kids."

I felt bad for Becky during our 25th championship reunion. Everyone who was married had kids, and Becky confided that she and her husband, Jeff, had been trying, going through "hard-core" fertility treatments for two years. "Having an athletic frame of mind, competitiveness was huge through this," she said. "It's just a never-give-up attitude. You're dealt something, and it becomes, 'OK, what's the next goal?' It felt good because sometimes I wondered if I still had it. To me, it became a game."

And when her doctor's office called on December 21, 2004, to tell her she was pregnant, she felt as if she had won. Becky and Jeff Tuecke welcomed baby Addison in August, their daughter's name an homage to Becky's beloved Cubs, who play at Wrigley Field on the corner of Clark and Addison.

"It was definitely the biggest success of my life," Becky said.

More often than not, it has been Becky who has played the den mother of our state championship team, doing the planning and organizing and encouraging when we have gotten together over the last few years. And as I worked on the book, it was Becky, perhaps more than any other former teammate, who seemed to be the most interested, the most encouraging. Part of it, I'd joke with her, was that she has the best memory of all of us because she's the youngest. She's also a helluva quote.

"When I look back, it's not the trophy," she told me once, "it's right now, you and me talking again. We have a reason to get back together. Looking at my other three years in high school, that's what makes it so special. Because of the state championship, we'll always have that bond."

It was impossible to disagree.

Holly, Judy, Tina, Barb, Karen,
Nancy, Pam, Lynn, and Debbie

OF ALL THE BENEFITS girls and women have gained through participation in athletics, dozens and dozens revealed through surveys and studies, there is this: on the 2017 *Fortune* list of Most Powerful Women, 65 percent played sports competitively in high school, college, or both. And a 2015 study by espnW and Ernst & Young found that 80 percent of female Fortune 500 executives played competitive sports at one point in their lives.

Of the 13 members of the 1979 state championship team, 12 of us went on to either teach, coach, or have some direct involvement in sports in our careers or in addition to our regular jobs. And all of us remain competitive.

"People accuse me of being competitive sometimes, like it's a bad thing," said Holly Andersen Blanchette, now a highly successful real estate broker, laughing when she spoke of how being an athlete has affected her. "But it doesn't mean I'm a sore loser; it means that sports has empowered me. It gives you self-confidence and makes you more determined. Like running a few more suicides than you think you can."

Holly played basketball at the University of Iowa and coached junior high and high school basketball and volleyball, as well as her son's youth soccer team. She also coached a soccer program for kids with special needs for 10 years, and for more than 30, she has been a ski pro at resorts near her home in northern Illinois.

Judy Becker coached the freshman girls' basketball team at Niles West for a short time. After a Hall of Fame career at Division III Elmhurst College, Tina Conti Grusecki did basketball promotions for an athletic apparel company, and her daughter Jacqui was a standout for the DePaul women's basketball team.

Barb Atsaves Pabst, a self-proclaimed "5-6 slowish guard" graduated as DePaul's all-time leader in scoring, assists, and steals and later was named to the university's Hall of Fame. In her first few years out of college, she was a grad assistant for the DePaul women's basketball and softball teams, did color commentary on women's college basketball for a local sports cable network, and coached and coordinated the Niles West basketball feeder program.

The Atsaves family has been a feeder program of its own with Barb and siblings Toni, Cindy, and Louis producing 14 children who went on to star at Niles West in a variety of sports and activities, several advancing to the collegiate level.

When Barb's dad, Pete, passed away in the fall of 2017, Barb said the family was offered the option of holding the wake on a Friday night, which would have interfered with a critical football game and kept the team's three standouts—the quarterback (Barb's son) and star receivers (her sisters' boys)—out of action. The family, including the boys' grandmother Pat, wouldn't hear of it, and the wake was delayed.

"My dad went to all the games," Barb laughed. "He would have insisted they played."

Professionally, Barb followed her stints coaching and commentating with a sales assistant position at WGN Radio in Chicago, and she rose through the ranks to manager of network operations.

Karen Wikstrom, who coached and officiated middle school volleyball, worked in clinical research for a major pharmaceutical lab in the Chicago area, conducting trials for the prostate cancer diagnostics test that is today considered the mammogram for men, and helped develop drugs that suppress HIV. Nancy Eck coached park district softball and became an emergency room nurse in the Chicago area.

Pam Hintz Duda earned a doctorate in special education and has devoted 30-plus years to working with deaf and blind children as a clinical assistant professor at Illinois State University. And Lynn Carlsen Nichols became a physical therapist assistant working with severely disabled children in Camas, Washington.

Debbie Durso, who coached basketball, softball, and volleyball at three separate high schools, was dean at Plainfield (Illinois) Central High School from 1999 until October 22, 2018, when, to the shock of her teammates and heartbreak of all who knew her, Deb died of unknown causes. We cherish the memory of her wonderful giggle and sweet, unselfish nature.

Diane Defrancesco (DD)

FOR DIANE DEFRANCESCO'S 20th high school reunion in 2000, she went into her attic, got her varsity letter *N*, and sewed it on a cotton letterman-style jacket she bought for the occasion.

"I saw Barb there, and someone was taking a panoramic picture and told me, 'Go get in the middle.' But I didn't feel like I belonged in the middle," she said.

They never entirely leave us, the regrets of high school. Those things we should have done or should have said and those we shouldn't have. Diane—it turns out she hated the nickname "DD"—had enough of those to fill her attic, but as she looked back, she did not make excuses or cast blame.

"When you guys won [state]," she told me, "I felt left out, and I remember telling my daughter Hailey, 'You don't want to ever feel like that. I should've been a part of that and I messed it up.' As soon as you try to tell your kids something, they'll say, 'But you did it.' But I don't deny it. I'm upfront. I let them know I regret certain things."

At age 20, Diane survived a near-fatal car accident. She married young, had two daughters, divorced, and went back to school to finish her bachelor's degree and to take graduate courses in special education, ultimately going on to work with kids with learning disabilities and behavioral problems.

"I wanted to get into counseling because you want to go back and fix some aspects of your life, and my way of doing it was helping kids like me who nobody could reach," she explained. "I had plenty of people trying to help me, but you think you know it all. I couldn't physically go back to high school, nor would I ever want to, but if you want to fix something, helping others is the best way to do it."

Diane lived in Florida when we talked the first time for the book in 2005, not far from her sister and her parents, who were celebrating their 51st wedding anniversary, and she still sounded exactly as I remembered her. I told Peggy we had spoken, and she said, "God, I can still picture her coming into the gym . . ."

I finished her sentence, ". . . sliding in on her socks, no sign of her shoes."

We laughed.

"But God she was great," Peg said.

Peggy Japely

AFTER HIGH SCHOOL GRADUATION, Peggy Japely met Al King at a pub in downtown Chicago, the first time she had seen her biological father since junior high. She wanted to tell him that she had made it, that she had earned a full ride to DePaul University, that she was a success. Maybe, she allowed herself to dream, they would even make amends.

Peggy had begun drinking several months before, when a few drinks at parties had escalated quickly into a dependency. She told her father she played basketball, that she was a state champion, and that she had accepted a major college basketball scholarship. "Where will that get you?" she remembered him railing at her. "There's no girls' pro teams.

"Did your mom ever tell you that you were nothing but a mistake?"

Peggy assumed she had inherited a predisposition to alcoholism from her father. It was no great mystery where her self-esteem had begun to unravel. And from there, the girl with the steady jump shot, tenacious defense, and heart of a champion unraveled as well.

Things started promisingly enough. Peg played well at DePaul for two seasons until it became obvious she could not flourish under the brash, aggressive style of her coach Ron Feiereisel, the father of JoAnn, our nemesis at St. Scholastica. She transferred to Fresno State, but there, she blamed an emphasis on maintaining a certain weight, and a coach's badgering on the subject, for the start of a battle with anorexia that continued for years.

After college, a friend introduced her to a modeling agency, which would put her to work at trade shows until another prospective modeling job led her to quit the business altogether when the photographer asked her to pose topless. But the heavy drinking continued, and soon, her mother told her she could not live at home any longer.

She kept in touch with Jerry Sloan, her hero and then head coach of the Utah Jazz, and he would write her back telling her that he was proud of her, to hang in there, that she should come visit him and his family on his farm in downstate Illinois. But she was too embarrassed. She and I drifted apart, mostly because I lived out of state, and when I did see her, she was careful to be sober or at least act like it, and she always appeared as if everything were normal.

But the alcohol caught up with her.

In her late 20s, Peggy barely survived a long stay in intensive care with pancreatitis due to her drinking. Doctors told her she would certainly die if she continued.

There were two broken engagements and one abusive marriage. She had already been taking Dilantin for withdrawal-induced seizures after the pancreatitis, and the doctor from the clinic told her to stop immediately after it was learned she was pregnant. She stopped the medication cold turkey, and in her fifth month of pregnancy, she had a grand mal seizure. She was given Dilantin again to save her life, and it went straight to the baby.

Clint was five pounds, 11 ounces, at birth, and doctors told Peggy that he would probably be autistic and that he might never walk or talk. One day when Clint was still an infant, Peggy's husband didn't come home. After some digging, Peg found out that "Tom" had lost his job the day he had left, that he had seven DUIs, and that he was married to another woman. By the time he called months later, Clint had begun to take his first steps. "Screw the doctors," thought Peggy, "he's going to be fine."

A one-time reunion with Tom ended with him breaking her nose and ribs, and with Peg escaping with the baby into the night. Determined not to keep running from her husband as she had from her father, Peggy opted to prosecute. She and Clint went to a women's shelter in Michigan, and Tom went to jail for 90 days.

Two months later, Peg's mother brought her daughter and grandson home to Morton Grove. Eventually, Tom called Peg again, sobbing into the phone that he couldn't go on living without her and Clint. "I told him, 'You had your chance. I can't trust you. You almost killed us, and I'm not going to put me and my child's life in jeopardy just because you wouldn't go to therapy,'" Peggy recalled.

They hung up. And early the next morning, in a small port city in Michigan's Upper Peninsula, Tom died of a self-inflicted gunshot wound. A suicide note told Peggy that he would be watching over her and Clint, and that he was sorry.

Peggy harbored suicidal thoughts of her own and begged God to let her get through each day. She stopped eating for two weeks, subsisting on screwdrivers until her mother once again intervened. Not knowing where else to turn, her mother wrote to Jerry Sloan, who responded immediately with a long letter of encouragement, a two-hour phone call, and offers to put Peggy into treatment.

Two weeks later, Peggy was put on a plane, and when she got off, an ambulance was waiting to take her to a rehab facility, paid for by her mother with help from friends and relatives.

After rehab, Peggy stayed sober for two years. She held a job as a receptionist and got her own apartment in suburban Glenview. But eventually, she began drinking again. She called herself a "functional drinker," like that uncle whom her grandmother referred to as "the finest drunk around."

"I thought, 'I'm not an alcoholic,' then slowly but surely it catches up with you," she said.

Trying to regain her sobriety on her own, Peg decided she needed to start her life anew. So she packed some basics, what little savings she had, and drove with Clint to California where she didn't know a soul. She changed her first name to Maggie. "I honestly didn't know where I was going," she said. "I don't know if I had a lot of strength or a lot of stupidity."

Though developmentally delayed, Clint was progressing at a quicker pace than predicted. But at four years old, he began the habit of hitting his head with his hand as if his head hurt. Mary Japely flew to California and took her daughter and grandson to a specialist she had read about in San Francisco. There they found a tumor roughly the size of an egg in Clint's brain. The 12-hour surgery that followed was termed "experimental," and doctors told Peggy the risks. He could be a football running back or he could end up paralyzed.

Clint recovered, but the surgery set him back more. He would have limitations, but not to Peggy. She continued working, controlled her drinking, and moved north to Dana Point, California, where she had heard about a special education program reputed to be among the best in the country. She enrolled Clint in swimming and horseback riding lessons, where he flourished, and she looked for a Catholic church to join. A priest she trusted and who ultimately deceived her was another major setback. Resisting alcohol as an old familiar crutch but still desperately needing control over her life, Peggy found herself retreating to anorexia, a problem she had been fighting most of her adult life.

Our 25th state championship reunion was scheduled for

February of 2004 and for months, no one could track Peggy down, and no one could remember having heard from her in several years. Gene Earl sent out an email telling us who was coming to the reunion and concluded, in his own inimitable way, that he was very sorry to say, "We've lost Peg."

Our team manager wrote back a group email saying how sorry she was to hear that Peggy had passed away and asking if any of us knew the circumstances.

Peg cracked up at that one. "Great investigative reporting there," she tore into me shortly after answering the phone at her home in California, where I "found" her months later. "Half the creditors in the world can find me and you can't? Did you think of, I don't know, calling my mother?"

Same old Peg. Except that when she came home the next Christmas and attended a party at my house where she saw many of our teammates for the first time in nearly 20 years, she weighed barely over 100 pounds. She was not the same Peg at all.

She had had about 150 grand mal seizures in her life, usually after she tried to stop drinking cold turkey, she told me. She said she was chronically anemic, requiring regular blood transfusions and looking so weak I could not imagine how she was going to get back on the plane with Clint by herself for the trip home.

But she did. And every time we talked, she sounded a little stronger, a little more determined to beat the demons back down. We talked mostly about the adults in our lives, especially her mother, Mary, who, despite her circumstances, was a brilliant example of strength and resilience and love, sending all three of her children to college on full or partial scholarships.

We also recalled the laughs we had had, the lessons we had learned, and the strength we had gained that she still possessed. "I remember all that stuff they told us about setting goals and not letting each other down," she told me. "I remember the nurturing of Mrs. Mulder and her telling us, 'Who cares if you're a girl? You can do it.' I still have the book she gave us, *The Prophet*, and

I remember her telling us that we'd understand it more when we got older.

"That experience has allowed me to handle what I handle today. If I wasn't an athlete, I'd be in the gutter drinking or dead. I'm sure of it."

Instead, she searched for strength and found it in her faith. Nearly every morning while Clint was growing up, they went to church. And every night, she and her son knelt on the wooden floor of their kitchen, beneath the crucifix on the wall, and prayed. They'd give thanks to all the important people in their life, and then they'd pray for all those who had no one to pray for them—the poor, the lonely, the depressed, the homeless. Then they'd ask, "Who can help Mommy stay sober?" and pray to Matt Talbot, considered by some in the Catholic Church to be the saint of addictions, and conclude by reciting the Lord's Prayer.

In 2018, at age 27, Clint was diagnosed with advanced testicular cancer, and with a strength he clearly inherited from his mother, he endured two major surgeries and debilitating chemotherapy treatments, Peggy nursing him through it all and, as always, staying tough.

If she is nothing else after all she has experienced, she is, remarkably, thankful. And she is, in her heart and in her soul, a survivor. A warrior. A jock. There is a voice that still speaks to her and motivates her, she said. A voice that will never leave her.

"Basketball made us better, stronger people," she told me. "All those wind sprints, all those times up and down the stairs in the gym hallway. We never stopped. It empowered us to push beyond our limits. It gave us a sense of belonging and confidence. I know it gave that to me. I thank God it gave that to me."

Me

WHEN OUR DAUGHTER, Amanda, was five years old and playing park district soccer, her team wore deep-purple satin shorts and an emerald-green-and-purple striped satin jersey with her number on the back.

I loved that uniform.

Amanda was more concerned with accessorizing and could not possibly appreciate how lucky she was. Or how jealous it made me. The uniform, to me, was always the most tangible barrier to sports equality. And like this project, it was a process.

Although the telling of our story has evolved over the course of five decades, it has been more than a dozen years since the conception of this book. First there was my *Chicago Tribune* column on our 25th reunion. And after that, a column following the death of our principal Nicholas Mannos in 2008, the story of an ordinary man who did extraordinary things and the best friend we girls never knew we had—an obit that wound up on the front page of a newspaper that did not typically do such things.

That same year, I wrote a *Chicago Tribune* magazine story on my parents' parallel experience with, and 25-year decline from, Alzheimer's. It was a rare departure from sports for me and a foray, as well, into writing about myself.

We are taught, or at least my generation of journalists was taught, that we are not the story. And so I questioned myself, mostly about what my parents would think of me writing about their final years in such a public way. But it also made me remember just how important my high school years were in one of the last cogent phases of their lives.

Those memories helped revive and reshape this project while helping ease my flagging confidence after being laid off from the *Tribune* in 2009 after 19 years with the paper. It kept me going through nine years with ESPN, and it continued to be a part of my life as I entered my new career, teaching journalism at Northwestern University.

The book has experienced much tweaking and outright revisions, going from a basketball story to a people story, from a young adult focus to a tale, in many ways, of my own mortality and the frightening realization that my brothers and sister and I could well fall victim to the same disease that our parents did.

We joke about it because that is what we do, our memory lapses mocked and laughed about so that, I guess, we do not become obsessed with the possibilities. But as a writer and the daughter of one of the best storytellers I have ever known in my mother, Francine, I have been acutely aware that I needed to get this story down on paper before it fades away completely.

In that respect, I am so glad I began this research a dozen years ago, when my memories and those of my teammates and, remarkably, our coaches, some older than us by 20 years or more, were that much sharper.

In 2016, I sent my teammates a group email both apologizing for hanging on to their scrapbooks for so long and assuring them that the book really was still happening and not an imaginary hobby. Many of them responded by telling me it was OK, that they trusted me to tell our story, however long it took, and that it was a worthwhile story to tell.

As more time passes, I am that much more certain of this, not that it's any more worthy of being told than any other story, but simply that it is important and valuable and that I want it to be shared.

I am struck by and feel bad about some of the characterizations in these pages—our irrational fear of traveling to Waukegan East; our narrow-mindedness about the perceived connection among girls, sports, and homosexuality; our impatience with woman officials. But that's how it was, and so that's how it is in the book, and I can only hope we are not judged now for some of those feelings.

When I entered that state championship game against East St. Louis with less than a minute to play, it was admittedly a weird feeling. I remember the thrill of just running onto the Assembly Hall court (without tripping), of being in the title game even though the celebration had already begun on the bench and in the stands. I remember trying to affect a swagger as if it wasn't the first time I had entered the game and the outcome hadn't already been decided. The alternative—not playing at all—would have been far worse.

And it was with unadulterated and genuine joy that when that final buzzer sounded, I jumped into Peggy's waiting arms and sobbed with my teammates. At that moment, there were no starters or benchwarmers, seniors or freshmen, only the collective feeling of satisfaction and gratitude and love for each other.

I looked up in the stands and saw my parents waving down at me, and I can still see them now, so happy and present, a look I know I detected, however briefly, in my mother's eyes 25 years later.

I have two children now with my husband, Rick. Amanda never did become a jock but has always been a great team player who attacks every goal she sets—becoming a nationally recognized public speaker in high school and a gifted writer—and is now pursuing her master's degree in nursing. After ruining baseball for our son, Alec, by over-coaching his throw, I watched with Rick from the sideline as he played soccer and became the editor of his high school newspaper. But he found his true passion in music, and with a self-discipline I envy, he is studying tuba performance at Northwestern, dreaming of a professional career with a symphony orchestra.

My kids laugh at me when I talk about our glory days. I tell them if they visited Niles West now, there would surely be a shrine to our state championship trophy and maybe even a velvet rope around my old locker, to which they respond with some predictable eye-rolling and restrained acknowledgment of my flickering displays of athleticism.

In the back of a basement closet, my red satin state championship jacket hangs inside the vinyl bag that my father once begged off the dry cleaner. I still have our championship medal, of course, stowed away in a box with the flannel varsity *N*. And on a prized shelf in my office bookcase, there sits a 27-inch strip of warped and faded black cardboard with yellowed lettering that says 10 ISAACSON.

Every once in a while, I'll pull it out and smile like a goof, never without a sense of wonder and a feeling of pride. I can still close my eyes and go back there, back to the big gym and to the day when we saw our names shining down from the scoreboard like a Broadway marquee.

As I told Birch Bayh, the former US senator and author of Title IX, when I interviewed him the first time, he did more than give us the opportunity to play competitive sports. At the end of our conversation, I hesitated, not wanting to waste his time, but ultimately, I spilled my guts as I usually do.

"Thank you," I told him. "What you did changed our lives. It changed who we are. It made me choose the career that I did, the man whom I married, how we raised our children. It gave me and my teammates an identity and self-esteem that girls just a few years older didn't have the same chance of having."

He thanked me graciously, and I hung up wondering if I had made a fool of myself or if I hadn't gushed enough. I didn't tell him, as Becky told me, that it saved us. But I know that it did.

ACKNOWLEDGMENTS

WHEN A BOOK TAKES A DOZEN YEARS TO COMPLETE, it is clear the author needed considerable help, guidance, and above all, support. Fortunately for me, there was a steady supply of all those things, and the only difficulty now is not leaving anyone out in my gratitude.

The bond I had with my high school teammates over the course of my four years at Niles West I will hold in my heart forever. They inspired me then and they inspire me now, however far the years and distance may have separated us. Every one of them, and in some cases, their parents and siblings, too, generously allowed me to probe their memories, ransack their scrapbooks, and extract emotions so necessary in reconstructing our story with the clarity I think we did.

Specifically, I want to thank Becky Schnell Tuecke, who gave me constant encouragement and help over the years; Karen Wikstrom, who read an early version of the manuscript and gave honest feedback; Connie Erickson Brown for, as always, her unselfish and giving nature; Peggy Japely for her memory of all things funny; and Shirley Cohen Katz for a friendship that will endure forever.

While on the subject of amazing friends, Holly Bland Katz and fellow Niles West alum Karyn Kogen Hurwich endured more discussion about this book than I care to admit but never, ever wavered in their patience, support, and faith in me. Ditto for Wooder Kathy Lisco, and Bari and Alan Harlam.

My "old" friend Marjorie Lewis, throughout the labor of her own book, provided the kind of necessary coddling, blunt input, and unwavering support only a true buddy and fellow writer can give.

Lauren Levy, who didn't even go to this school, also read the manuscript—aloud, no less—to her dear husband, Bill, both lending their unconditional backing.

I simply cannot adequately thank Scott Price, who was dragged into the undertow of my blurry vision from the very beginning and, even if it was once every couple of years, somehow managed with his sage advice and gentle prodding to keep me focused and on course.

Bob Levy was the one who saw the bigger story in 2004, and if it wasn't for him, there probably wouldn't be a book. His continued guidance and friendship is priceless.

Others who read, listened, talked, and lent much-appreciated help and counsel include Chris Hunt, Lissa Muscatine, Marion Miehl, Aishwarya Kumar, Marla Alexander, Debby Shulman, Rick Kogan, Renee Gandolfo, Patrick Stiegman, John Walsh, Chris Ballard, Kent McDill, John Mullin, Todd Musburger, Steve Mandell, and Herb Rudoy.

As always, the "adults" in our story were there for me, from Jerry Turry to Leanne Heeren to Judi Sloan to Billy Schnurr, as eloquent and humble as always. But there is absolutely no way I could have done this without the unending kindness and generosity of Arlene and Al Mulder and Gene Earl.

The bulk of my interviews with Mrs. Mulder came during her years as the mayor of Arlington Heights, a job even more exhausting when you have the unparalleled work ethic that she did, but she always—always—had time for me, and I will remember her lessons forever. And thank God for the encyclopedic memory of Coach Earl, as my teammates, women in our 50s, still call him. His recall of not just specific games but specific moments was incredible and invaluable.

A note here about our opponents: While this book is about Niles West, it could have been about virtually any group of girls who came of age in the immediate post–Title IX era. I have also had the great privilege of interviewing Jackie Joyner-Kersee, most recently in September of 2018, when she said that Niles West was the motivation she and her East St. Louis team needed to go undefeated and win the state title in 1980. I will never forget Floyd Brown telling her in a halftime interview in '79 that he heard she was a good athlete. In fact, our most famous opponent would win six Olympic medals in four Olympic Games and be widely recognized as the greatest woman athlete of all time, overcoming childhood poverty to also become a powerful and generous activist for children, women's rights, and racial equality. A more gracious superstar I have never met.

I have never had a book editor before, and I cannot imagine what I did to deserve Jessica Easto, a woman who saw the story within our story, whose patience with me was extraordinary, and who probably taught me more about writing in one year than I have learned in the last 30. I am so grateful to Jessica, Doug Seibold, and everyone at Agate Publishing for their faith and backing.

As is the case with any long-term project like this one, an understanding family is essential, and in my case, my family has lived this reality with me for far too long. From my sister, Susie, and brothers, Barry and Richard, whom I counted on for filling in some much-needed family history; to my in-laws Art and Sandie

Mawrence, who read an early manuscript and insisted they loved it as they love everything I do; to my daughter, Amanda, who actually dug in and helped with her clear eyes and open heart, editing when no one else would; to my son, Alec, who was, as always, a valued sounding board, my moral compass, and my cliché meter, I love and thank them all.

And finally to my husband, Rick: he obviously was not around during the period I chronicled, and yet I feel like, somehow, he experienced it, too. As I worked on the book, he inhaled it, endured my every dry period and self-doubt, and stoked every spark of energy and enthusiasm, and ultimately, like everything else in my life, he shares this with me.

READING GROUP GUIDE

1. *State* explores themes of individuality and community. How does being part of a team help the girls shape authentic identities? What factors stifle self-expression for Missy and her teammates?

2. Although Missy and her teammates didn't realize it at the time, the passage of Title IX had a profound effect on their lives. Do you think the presence of Title IX has affected your life? How? Do you see its effects today in competitive sports?

3. The opportunity to participate in competitive athletics helps shape the Niles West girls' sense of identity and community. Did you participate in sports or extracurriculars in high school? What kind of effect did it have on you?

4. Isaacson writes, "The closest most of us had come to being athletes was being labeled 'tomboys' for most of our childhoods. And that never had a positive connotation" (page 9). Isaacson views "tomboy" and "athlete" as two distinct identities that were often conflated. How do you see these two identities as being different? How do these labels play into the girls' sense of identity?

5. Reflect on the presence of sexism and prejudice in the book, particularly in the ways in which girls and women are treated when participating in sports. What has changed for women's sports since the 1970s? What hasn't?

6. Missy's excitement over her basketball uniform is mentioned several times in *State*. Why is the uniform so important to Missy and her teammates?

7. Missy's teammates frequently deal with complex concerns over their self-image. As Mrs. Mulder tells her team, "You are always young ladies, and I never want you to give up your femininity. . . . But on the court, you are also athletes" (page 47). How do you think this binary of femininity and athleticism shapes the girls' self-image? Do you think society's definition of femininity has evolved since the 1970s? In what ways has it changed or stayed the same?

8. Compare and contrast Mrs. Mulder and Gene Earl. Discuss their coaching styles. How are they alike? How are they dissimilar?

9. Do class and social standing play a role in the team's ability to bond with each other? Examine how Missy talks about the "rich" suburban students in contrast to the way she talks about her own teammates. Why is family background so important for the story?

10. While writing the book, the author made a conscious choice to interview her coaches and teammates in order to weave their perspectives and backstories in with her own. What effect does this have on the overall narrative? Why do you think the author chose this over a more traditional first-person narrative?

11. Billy Schnurr helps Mrs. Mulder learn how to coach basketball, but he makes a conscious choice not to overshadow her on the court. What does this tell you about his character?

12. Compare the treatment of Niles West's girls' basketball team to that of the boys' team. Do female athletes still face different barriers than their male counterparts? At what level or age group do you start to see a difference in the way the girls' team is treated versus the boys' team?

13. What are the particular challenges that Missy faces at home, in school, and on the court?

14. Did *State* change your perspective on sports, particularly your perspective on women in sports?

15. The epilogue includes insight into the lives of Missy's teammates after the 1979 state championship game. How did basketball "save" the lives of Missy's teammates?

ABOUT THE AUTHOR

MELISSA ISAACSON is an award-winning sportswriter, author, lecturer, and public speaker. Over her 36-year career, she has had long tenures with the *Orlando Sentinel*, the *Chicago Tribune*, and ESPN.com, covering every major US sports championship and the Summer and Winter Olympic Games. She was the *Tribune's* first woman general sports columnist as well as its first woman beat writer on the Bulls and Bears, covering the Michael Jordan–led Bulls over their six NBA titles. She is the author of *Transition Game: An Inside Look at Life with the Chicago Bulls* and *Sweet Lou—Lou Piniella: A Life in Baseball*. She is currently on the faculty of Northwestern University's Medill School of Journalism, and she blogs at MelissaIsaacson.com. She and her husband, Rick Mawrence, live in the Chicago area and have two children, Amanda and Alec.